Nursing Today

Stress and Self-awareness: a Guide for Nurses

Meg Bond

Cartoons by Cath Jackson

BUTTERWORTH
HEINEMANN

Butterworth-Heinemann Ltd
Halley Court, Jordan Hill, Oxford OX2 8EJ

 PART OF REED INTERNATIONAL BOOKS

OXFORD   LONDON   GUILDFORD   BOSTON
MUNICH   NEW DELHI   SINGAPORE   SYDNEY
TOKYO   TORONTO   WELLINGTON

First published 1986
Reprinted 1986, 1987 (twice), 1988, 1990 (twice)

ISBN 0 7506 0125 6

Typeset by D. P. Media Ltd, Hitchin, Hertfordshire
Printed and bound in Great Britain by
Biddles Ltd, Guildford and King's Lynn

Contents

Introduction   vii

1 Nurses and stress   1

2 Understanding emotions   14

3 Relaxation   33

4 Meditation   67

5 Assertiveness   96

6 Receiving and giving support   134

7 Creative problem-solving   178

8 Exercise, diet and physical health   196

9 Transforming stress   219

Index   223

Introduction

Nurses are under stress, at all levels and in all branches of nursing. In the midst of organisational changes and financial cut-backs, nurses continue to care for patients, teach, manage and do research, often at great personal cost. Many have to work under the threat of losing their jobs. In addition, developments in the way patients are nursed and in methods of teaching, management and research mean that we have to get more emotionally involved with the people we work with and have less opportunity to hide behind roles. So, we are more stressed with less of the traditional protections against stress. Yet there is little being offered to nurses to help us find new ways of coping. Courses in stress management are offered in comparative abundance to people in industry, yet nurses who seek secondment to go on such courses are often told it is 'not relevant' or cannot get funding. Nurses go on caring but there is little care for us as carers.

This self-help book is intended to give nurses a much needed opportunity to learn more about self-care and mutual support.

It provides a framework within which to gently explore stress as it relates to you as an individual nurse. In particular, I hope it will enable you to discover or remind yourself of your strengths and resources for coping with stress and to use these as the foundation upon which to move forward in your personal development. It will not provide instant solutions or 'the answer' to stress, but it will provide ideas, shared experiences and exercises which may be useful in helping you to find your own answers.

I have attempted to make this book easy to read, personally

relevant to you as a nurse, encouraging in terms of personal expectations and offering plenty of choice. There are many other books about stress available but most suffer from one major limitation or another. Those written in the accepted academic style are interesting to those nurses who are familiar with academic use of language. But they leave the majority of people puzzled and feeling left out and they encourage intellectual discussion at the expense of personal relevance. Many books on stress and personal development written in the humanistic style also have their own jargon which is incomprehensible to people who do not move in those circles. They also tend to dangle the image of the perfect 'self-actualised' person in front of the reader which is an unrealistic and unattainable goal. Some books attempt to promote only one method of coping with stress and fail to mention the pitfalls involved in overdoing it. Others give questionnaires to affix a number to your stress levels or a label for your personality but give little in the way of suggestions about building your personal coping skills.

So in writing this book I have taken note of the shortcomings of the existing books on stress and tried to do something different. I have made the content, style and language reflect the interests and ways of expression of the thousands of nurses who have attended the many workshops on stress that I have facilitated. These nurses have come from all branches and levels of the profession.

How to use the book

I suggest that you read Chapter 1 to see which aspects of coping would be most usefully explored for you. Then read Chapter 2 for the explanation of the purpose behind the skills-building exercises in this book and for my emphasis on accepting emotions. Each of the other chapters stands on its own so that you can read them in the order you like.

The ideas and examples are based on what nurses have told me during workshops and on my own experiences in nursing and self-exploration. I make some generalisations, which I acknowledge as my own personal impressions: you are invited to assess how much you think they apply to you personally, if at all, and whether or not you agree with them as generalisations. The examples and quotations are composites of experiences which have been commonly described by nurses and only relate to specific individuals when their permission has been given.

The exercises have been adapted from structured workshop activities which have been tried by many nurses and found to be useful. They are distinguished in the text by a vertical line running beside them in the margin. You can carry out most of them on your own. The advantage of trying them on your own (especially if you have had little opportunity to take part in self-exploration exercises in a safe supportive group) is that you do not have to worry about being criticised or pressured into doing something against your will. On the other hand, if you get together with some colleagues and compare notes, you are likely to be reassured that you are not alone in many of your feelings and experiences. Furthermore, you will notice that when others share things about themselves, they often express something which also applies to you but is difficult for you to put into words. If you agree beforehand to use the ground rules listed in the trust section of the chapter on receiving and giving support, then doing the exercises together may feel much safer.

The exercises can be subtly powerful. Often they will be pleasant and reassuring, but sometimes they will be emotionally or intellectually uncomfortable. Personal learning always has its inevitable downs, but provided that you are doing what is right for you at your own pace, the ups will more than compensate for the downs. Each chapter has a 'pitfalls' section which tries to outline realistically the risks involved. As in any other form of learning, you will make mistakes and these will provide half of the many opportunities for further learning. The other half come from your successes: it is important to acknowledge and consolidate these successes, however small they seem to be. There is no magic solution to stress, or a single key to personal and professional development, just a lot of very small steps forward in the directions which are right for you in each particular phase of your life.

If anyone tries to push you into doing any of the exercises or indeed into reading the book against your will, then I strongly suggest you refuse to comply. (I only hope the book stays long enough in print to be still available if and when you change your mind!) All the exercises and suggestions have been formulated on the assumption that you have free choice about reading, trying out or following them.

I have some points to make to tutors who wish to convert the exercises back to structured experiential learning activities for use in the classroom. First, I strongly urge you to offer only those exercises which you have tried out for yourself and are willing to join in with. Second, I urge you to respect the power of such activities, particularly in a group setting. While they can often be pleasant and fun, they can equally be uncomfortable. When they are uncomfortable, neither you nor the group members have failed — discomfort is an inevitable part of learning. Try not to lead an exercise in such a way as to force the group to enjoy it or as to create discomfort. Instead allow the individuals to discover their own reactions to it.

It is essential to stick to the ground rules outlined in Chapter 6 in your actions as well as your words. The choice clause can be particularly difficult for a teacher to genuinely implement. It is vital to be aware of your own need to influence and control things and to keep this in check (it is not enough to deny that you have this urge). In order that participants can make real choices about whether or not to join in, they need to know the purpose and the structure of each activity before it begins. There are many group facilitators and research psychologists who use manipulation and trickery, claiming would-be 'objectivity' as their excuse for giving free rein to their urges for power. If you become tarred with the same brush, you will find it impossible to build the climate of trust which is essential in this kind of work.

Participants also need the opportunity to reflect on what they learn from each exercise. By learning, I mean noticing their own personal reactions and insights. They need the freedom to express their own unique insights without having to fit anyone else's expectations of the 'right answers'. Finally, to avoid dangerous tinkering with other peoples' psyches, I believe that tutors interested in promoting self-awareness in course members need to have a strong commitment to their own personal exploration and to be willing and able to delve deeper into themselves than they would expect group members to do. There are now many opportunities for tutors to attend courses on personal development. For instance, co-counselling courses feature on the English National Board's refresher course list. However, I know only too well that many tutors are having great difficulties getting the training and support to expand their skills in facilitating the development of self-awareness. They often have to do the necessary training in their own time and at their own expense (that was certainly the case when I first became involved, but I admit I could have been more assertive). Colleagues and seniors often denounce this field as being 'too dangerous', in spite of it featuring on every nurse training curriculum in some way. It is probably only human to be afraid of something when you are unclear of the risks and the safeguards that are necessary. Perhaps this book will help to reduce this anxiety. The ground rules referred to earlier provide the safeguards, and the 'pitfalls' sections will show that the risks are not so terrible. The dangers of not expanding this kind of work in nursing can be seen in the high rate of stress-related sickness among nurses.

Content and style

This book assumes that stress is a serious problem in nursing, but it does not set out to argue or prove the point. There is plenty of research to suggest strongly that this is so. The book's content has been chosen for its relevance to the day-to-day lives of nurses, using the principle of 'try-it-yourself-first': all the exercises have been applied for my own personal use as well as (mostly) with other nurses in workshops. In most aspects I have explored the self-awareness elements at a greater depth for myself than I would expect anyone to go in using this book. This partly explains why there are many omissions in the range of approaches presented: I may not have had the opportunity to try others myself, have found them unhelpful so far or feel that they are inappropriate for such a book.

The 'pitfalls' sections of each of the practical chapters are based on the mistakes commonly made by people who explore the methods (including myself).

In common with every other author who writes in the English language, I have been faced with the dilemma of deciding what to do about expressing neutral gender. Since a higher percentage of nurses and patients are female than are male, I have adopted 'she' across the board, rather than the conventional 'he'. I hope men do not feel ignored: that is not my intention.

The referencing system I have used is also a little uncon- ventional. It is designed for practicality rather than literary acceptability.

Acknowledgements

I would like to thank the following people for their direct help with this book: Gunna Dietrich, Gordon Evans, Shirley Goodwin, James Kilty, Lin Lamdin, Diana Lomax, Helen Marshall, Cathy Watson, Lorna Wells and Diana Wright. I wish to acknowledge that a lot of my inspiration was originally derived from the work of Anne Dickson, John Heron and James Kilty. Many thanks also to the friends (particularly the members of the women's group), family and colleagues without whose support I would have found writing this book much too stressful a challenge. They all deserved a lot more attention than they got from me while I was preoccupied with writing it. I am grateful also to the many nurses and others who have shared something of themselves with me and from whom I learned a lot about myself.

Haslemere 1986   Meg Bond

Nurses and stress

What is stress?

Most nurses, when asked about their use of the word stress, describe combinations of unpleasant situations and unpleasant inner personal experiences. We seem to take a more integrated view of the concept of stress than many scientific researchers and writers who tend to define it in terms of either a stimulus or a response. To nurses, the concept of stress usually covers both. For instance, shortage of staff is stress, and anxiety is stress. Although our use of the word implies a negative experience, the next point most often raised when nurses discuss stress is that some degree of stress is desirable and necessary. The concept of stimulation seems to take over here, representing one of the positive facets of stress.

Figure 1.1 attempts to summarise common concepts linked to stress and includes the words frequently used by nurses to explain their experiences of stress and stimulation. Note that words that describe emotional experience are featured highly.

The human function curve, beloved by many writers on stress, can be used to highlight the insidious progression from stimulation to stress and the effect on health (it does not take into account the resting state). (See Fig. 1.2.) It is a symbolic graph and not one based on anything that you can measure. The graph represents the negative effects of under and overstimulation. The downward curve conjures up the concept of a slippery slope towards ill health when there is increasingly too little or too much pressure. The

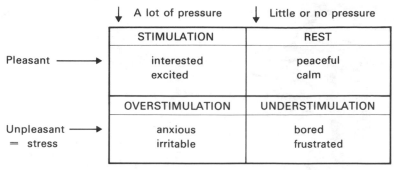

Fig. 1.1   *Distinguishing between stress, stimulation and rest.*

transition may be gradual and difficult to notice. Therefore, the main reasons that it is good to explore one's own stress are:

1. To develop skills of noticing the negative signs of stress.
2. To build the skills for getting oneself into an improved positive state of health.
3. To achieve the right balance between amount of pressure and our own individual resources for dealing with it.

This must be an individualised process; there can be no 'right' answers applicable to everyone.

What is experienced as a lot of pressure, little pressure or no pressure, and pleasant or unpleasant, can vary considerably between individuals. For instance, the pressures of the frequent crises involved in the work in an intensive therapy unit may be experienced as stimulation by one nurse and overstimulation by another. Likewise the slow process of health education involved in health visiting may feel like stimulation to one nurse and boredom to another. Not only do the experiences differ between nurses, but between different days and phases in one nurse's life: the ITU nurse having an 'off day' may pray for an undramatic shift, while the HV in a quiet commuter area may pray for something unusual to happen. Indeed, the ITU nurse and the HV may eventually tire of their respective types of pressure and swop jobs.

So, we can define stress as: the experience of unpleasant over or understimulation, as defined by the individual in question, that actually or potentially leads to ill health. There are many other definitions and perspectives: Tom Cox (1) and Sharol Jacobson and Marie McGrath (2) give some interesting overviews of these perspectives in the literature on stress.

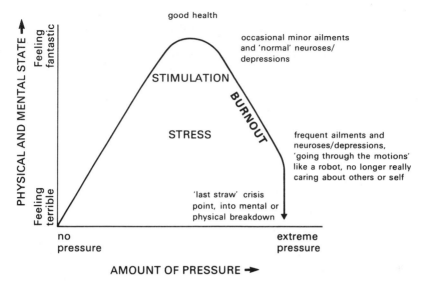

Fig. 1.2 *Adaptation of the human function curve.*

Changing beliefs about stress in nursing

In the past nurses were thought to be impervious to stress. But now there is increasing acknowledgement that nurses, along with other human beings, do have stress. Indeed we are seen to have more stress than most people due to the nature of the job and the system within which we work. Beliefs about stress in nursing seem to be related to how people see the nurse's role in relation to involvement with patients' emotional problems. The quotations in Table 1.1 summarise the evolution of these beliefs.

Which of the opinions in Table 1.1 is closest to your own? Which have you come across during the course of your nursing career and when?

Effects and causes of stress

Although acknowledgement of stress is growing at an intellectual level, nurses are often still wary of admitting to stress within themselves. This results in considerable emotional isolation: when the majority of nurses are showing a brave face to the world,

Table 1.1   *Evolution of beliefs about stress and nurses.*

Beliefs about stress in nursing	Corresponding interpretations of the nurse's role
A 'Nurses are not the type to feel stress. If they do they shouldn't have come into nursing in the first place.'	'It is not part of the nurse's role to get involved with the patient's emotional problems.'
B 'Nurses can have stress but they shouldn't think or talk about it. If they do, it will only create more problems than they can cope with.'	'Nurses shouldn't get involved with a patient's emotional problems otherwise they'd never be able to switch off when they get off duty.'
C 'Nurses are human too — of course they experience stress. They can learn more about coping with stress if they are given the chance.'	'Nurses who are willing to admit they are human, that they too have stress, can be more sensitive to patients' emotional needs and be more helpful in preventing and alleviating patients' stress.'

the individual nurse can feel that she is the only one to feel stressed inside. To resolve this isolation, I have suggested some structured discussions during stress workshops for nurses (3). First a contract is established based on ground rules of confidentiality, free choice about opting in or out, no put-downs, an equal opportunity to talk, and each person speaking for herself only. (See 'trust' section of Chapter 6.) Then in small groups the nurses list examples of the ways in which they themselves have experienced stress, considering physical effects, effects on emotions, on thinking and on behaviour. Some of the effects they list are shown in Table 1.2. But before reading the table do the following exercise.

List the ways you have noticed that you yourself have been affected by stress. Consider the four headings: physical effects, effects on emotions, effects on thinking, effects on behaviour. Avoid listing things you have noticed about other people. Merely list those you have experienced yourself. Then compare your list to the list of examples. What other effects listed in the examples have also applied to you at some time?

Table 1.2 *Examples of effects of stress experienced by nurses.*

Physical effects

Menstrual problems. Nausea. Palpitations. Tight throat. Fast respiration. Breathlessness. Sweating. Wanting to pass water. Stomach ache. Restlessness. Flushing. Headache. Tense muscles. Tightness in jaw. Repeated swallowing. Dry mouth. Visual disturbances. Sleeplessness. Raised blood pressure. Butterflies in stomach. Exhaustion. Trembling. Feeling cold. Feeling faint. Heavy, lethargic feeling. Migraine. Indigestion. Tingling in arms and back of neck. Tightness in shoulders. Feeling tired. Sniff a lot. General aches and pains. Constipation. Wind. Diarrhoea. Sweaty palms. Squeaky voice. Wobbly knees. Shallow breathing. Holding my breath. Pallor. Acne. Shivering. Cold hands and feet. Blushing. Frequency. Perpetually hungry. Jumpy.

Effects on emotions

Anxiety. Fear. Anger. Depression. Crying. Hysterical. Bewildered. Sorry for myself. Emotionally cold. Helplessness. Upset. Apathetic. Frustrated. Withdrawn. Feelings of hopelessness. Feeling unworthy. Despair. Feeling stupid. Vulnerability. Feeling inadequate. Guilt. Euphoria. Lonely, even when with other people. Feeling I'm losing my mind. Sorry for myself and others. Feel hurt. Deflated. Defeated. Sad. Full of hate. Feel insecure and negative. Feel rejected. Immobilised. Unwilling to do anything. Worry about what people think of me. Premenstrual tension. Bored. Pretending to myself I'm happy. Worrying about stupid little things.

Effects on thinking

Thought blocks. Lack of concentration. Suppression of feelings. Putting myself down e.g. 'Oh God, I've done it again', 'I should have known (done) better . . .', 'I'm stupid', 'I'll never be able to . . . I'll never make it', 'Why the hell did I let myself get into this situation', 'Why can't I cope? What's the matter with me, everyone else copes', 'I give up', 'I'm hopeless'. Procrastination. Difficulties in decision-making. Doubting myself. Preoccupation with cause of stress. I imagine the worst. Sluggish thinking. Amnesia. Forgetfulness. Shutting out thoughts. Lack of objectivity. Make mistakes. Over-intellectualising. Not being able to see another's point of view, missing the point. Not being able to see the wood for the trees. Trying to get other people to make my decisions for me. Stick to usual way of doing things, frightened to think for myself.

Changing my mind every five minutes. Overestimate my abilities. Don't plan enough. Confused and muddled. Easily distracted. Misjudge situations and people. Irrational. Escapist thoughts. Hypochondria. Getting hypercritical, bitchy. 'Indispensable' syndrome: can't delegate. Being more objective about others' problems than my own. Dreaming a lot, nightmares. Don't allow enough time to do things. Missing the obvious. Tunnel vision. Over-reacting to minor mistakes, my own and other people's. Obsessional about minor details. Avoiding problems, pretending they don't exist. Inflexible, not willing to change plans.

Effects on behaviour
Stuttering. Saying provocative things. Silent. Outbursts. Critical of others. Involved in arguments. Unreasonable. Shout at people. Non-verbal aggression. Gripping something tightly. Clumsiness. Rushing around. Hyperactive. Inertia. Insensitivity to others/glowering/grousing/hurting people through thoughtless action/words. Slow reactions to danger. Loss of interest in things I usually like. Last minute effort. Seeking affection for personal gain. Impulsive. Late. Early. Competitive. Procrastinate. Talk excessively. Withdraw. Reject people. Isolate myself. Exaggerate movements. Swear. Drinking. Smoking. Over-eating. Aggressive drinking. Yawning a lot. Running away. Can't say no. Take on too much. Talk too much. Hysterical laughter. Over or under-affection. Destructiveness. Manic behaviour. Look for a scapegoat. Take pills. Wakefulness. Compulsive sex. Take sick leave when not really ill. Continue working when I'm ill. Handwriting deteriorates. Letting myself go, less care about health, diet, hygiene. Poor timekeeping. Illogical behaviour — gambling, dependence on others, useless activity. Taking ages getting started. Become a wimp. Take unnecessary risks. Become clingy.

Collected together in this way, the results in Table 1.2 might lead some readers into thinking that the nurses who have reported these signs of stress must have been the failures of the profession or just the young learners. The contrary is the case. The examples are taken from groups of mature, successful nurses: people who were merely willing to admit to being human. Very similar results have been obtained with many other groups such as doctors, teachers, top executives and the general public.

Other readers might feel relieved on seeing these signs listed by people who are coping very well by conventional standards. This has often been the case for workshop participants. The feeling of isolation can be dissipated by knowing that other people have similar experiences. It can also be useful to be reminded of the many signs which one can easily ignore, or even get used to, allowing a gradual increase in negative effects of stress without noticing. Of course, most of the signs can be innocuous in the short term and when there are only a few at a time. But in the long term, with a multiplicity of coexisting signs of stress, ill health becomes increasingly likely. The task for the nurse seeking to expand her self-awareness and ability to cope with stress is to become more adept at noticing the onset of stress as opposed to stimulation or rest. This is the first step towards being able to deal with it appropriately.

How do you feel after comparing your own reactions to stress with the examples given in Table 1.2? What did you notice or learn about yourself by doing this exercise?

Examples of causes of stress in nurses' lives have been compiled in the same way using a model which suggests that causes of stress include not only environmental and interpersonal stresses, but causes from within oneself.

Before reading Table 1.3, list examples of causes of stress which you have experienced in your life, inside and outside work, using the following headings: causes of stress from other people, causes from within myself and causes from the world at large. Then compare your list to the list of examples. What other causes listed in the examples have also applied to you at some time?

Table 1.3   *Examples of causes of stress experienced by nurses.*

From other people

Inefficient organisation by others. Having to deal with other people's problems. Husband stresses. Uninterested students. Other people's expectations. Demands of children and partners. Family expecting me to be the strong one all the time. People who put me down. Not being liked or accepted by others. Crises in the family. Unsympathetic people. People who do not recognise my needs. Family not helping with the housework. Lack of cooperation, being taken for granted. When someone else is nasty or hostile to me. People seeing my role and not me as a person. When my contributions are ignored or rejected. When others cannot see my point of view. Conflict between needs of family and work.

Anomalies in hierarchies. Identifying with someone making a 'pig's ear'. When what I'm saying is not 'getting through'. Being shut out of a group, personality clashes. Wishy washy people who dither. Disloyalty. Manipulative people. Dependent people. Bad atmosphere, people arguing or sulking. When someone in the team lets the rest of us down. Not letting me have time to myself. Being 'piggy in the middle': when people further up and lower down the hierarchy all take out their frustrations on me. Over-reactions to minor mistakes. Being unsupportive. Breaking agreements. Not being allowed to make decisions about things I'm responsible for. Non-nurses on management teams who want to be seen as implementing government policies to get on the honours list and don't care a damn about patient care.

From within myself
Perfectionism — expecting too much of self and others. Comparing myself to other people. Needing to compete. Trying to keep up with others. Need to be best. Feeling inferior and inadequate. Internalised parental expectations. Not delegating. Accepting too much responsibility. Unable to say 'No'. Wanting to impress. Wanting to be liked at all costs. When I think people don't like me (even when untrue). Guilt, e.g. about loss of interest or drive. Putting things off. Taking on new unfamiliar tasks. Doing something I know is wrong and feeling guilty. Burning the candle at both ends. Bad time allocation, leaving things to the last minute, being late. Thinking I'm a failure. Not saying what I want. Wanting to be in control all the time. Feeling responsible for other people's problems and for their actions. Imagination. Fear of failure. Ambition. Needing to get things done. Watching the clock. Feeling I lack in knowledge. Taking on too much work. Setting impossible targets. Not taking myself into account. Owing money. Fear of not getting organised properly. Fear of the unknown. Getting stressed about myself and the person I am. Stress at not being able to achieve all the things I want to do. Discontentment.

From the world at large
Death and illness. Pain. Loss. Gain. Some groups. Being in a lift. Going to the dentist. Hospitals. Taking a driving test. Exams. Political violence. Talk of wars. The nuclear threat. Heavy workload. Racism. Injustice. Poor housing. Weddings. Lack of suitable alternatives to problems. Dealing with child abuse. Inadequate resources, shortage of staff and equipment. Frustration from other people being in control. Having to tell people off, give bad news. General lack of support, guidance, knowledge. Menopause. General everyday survival pressures. Lack of space. Seeing or being involved in accidents or near misses. Having to wait. Emergencies. Barrage of disasters in the papers and on TV. The state of the world. Initiating a phone call. Uncertainty of job. Trains late.

Having to play roles. Aircraft noise. Crowds. Motorway driving. Buying and selling a house. Living in a new area. Divorce. Marriage. Childbirth. Retirement. Affairs. Unknown situations. Claustrophobic situations. When unprepared and the 'unexpected' happens. Anticipation of a teaching session. Being ill and dependent. Others being ill. Disorder in excess. Frustrating situations, e.g. inability to make progress. If I don't know what is happening, Lots of decisions and no feedback. Talking to a group. Need to make money, cost of living, owing money. Lack of pleasant excitement. Telephone interruptions. Heights. Deep water. Smells. Traffic jams. Finding a place to park. Encounters with the police. Travelling. Environmental pollution.

You may notice that many of the examples of causes of stress under the categories 'from other people' and 'from the world at large' have links with those under 'from within myself'. For instance, it might be the case that a few instances of short-term shortage of staff are inconspicuously dealt with by a nurse taking on too much work. The people responsible for managing staffing levels may not realise the nurse is overloaded and make no attempt at increasing staff numbers so the shortage becomes permanent.

There are also similarities between some of the examples of effects of stress and those of causes. Some of the effects of stress are also quoted in the 'causes from within myself' category. For instance, under the 'effects on thinking' situation, we have 'put-

Fig. 1.3 *The causes of stress can be the effects and vice versa.*

ting myself down': this seems to equate to 'getting stressed about myself and the person I am' and 'feeling inferior and inadequate'.

Indeed, when doing the exercises, most people find difficulties in deciding whether many experiences are causes or effects of stress. Many effects can also be causes and vice versa. This would seem to disprove the simplistic stimulus/response theories of stress which give the impression of stress as being 'out there' and the nurse being the helpless victim of it.

So the nurse is inextricably involved in the process of stress in her life: her very existence influences these processes. While she is not to blame, she has some responsibility for them. The nurse who is motivated to improve her ability to deal with stress needs to become more aware of the ways in which she influences the stress process and of how she can change those ways for the better.

Methods of dealing with stress

Most people have immense personal resources for coping with stress, and have developed their own individual set of coping strategies. However, the speed at which technological, economic, organisational and social changes occur is increasing. Well-established coping mechanisms can become less effective. Indeed, over-reliance and over-use of some methods of coping can in turn cause further problems. An obvious example is the use of drugs: hypnotics to help you sleep, or alcohol to help you relax, can be valuable on an occasional basis, but regular use can lead to addiction. Methods to achieve a healthier life, such as physical exercise, can also be overdone: for instance, too much vigorous exercise can cause damage to the heart or joints. We need to have a large repertoire of coping mechanisms to draw on, in order to be able to cope appropriately with each stressful situation.

When setting out to increase the number of methods we can use to deal with stress, it is important to aim to achieve a balance between the various types of coping methods.

Make a list of the ways in which you have dealt with stress to date, including the many ordinary, everyday methods. Then delete those which you would consider are negative such as those causing damage, e.g. getting drunk, kicking the cat. Then look at the examples which follow and add to your list any which have applied to you.

The following examples are positive methods of dealing with stress which nurses have quoted. I have categorised them under four headings: active mental or physical distraction, self-nurturance, emotional expression and confronting the problem.

Table 1.4 *Methods of dealing with stress.*

Active mental or physical distraction

Hobbies: gardening, sewing, woodwork, reading, listening to music, crosswords, houseplants, chess, cooking, writing letters, do-it-yourself house renovation, upholstery, watching TV, listening to radio, going to cinema, theatre.

Physical exercise: walking, jogging, squash, tennis, cycling, digging, golf, swimming, hatha yoga.

Chores: housework, laundry, ironing, mending, washing and polishing car, chopping wood, shopping.

People: ordinary chit-chat with friends, thinking about or helping someone worse off than me.

Self-nurturance

Rest: taking proper breaks, ensuring enough sleep, taking catnaps, relaxation exercises, breathing exercises, meditation, yoga, just putting feet up, doing nothing, long hot bath or shower, sauna, steam bath, jacuzzi, sunbathing, massage (giving one or having one), getting away from stressful situation, having proper holiday.

Diet: having proper breakfast and lunch, more wholefoods, less refined foods, not a lot of any one kind of food (e.g. meat, wheat, coffee, dairy produce), finding out if I have any allergies.

Treats: buying something special, new clothes, hairdo, making special meal, sex, having a drink, having a cuddle, stroking the dog/cat.

Emotional expression

Talking and writing about the stress: unburdening to a friend/colleague/pet, having a moan session, telephoning someone, writing down feelings, e.g. in a letter to a friend, scribbling down feelings in a gush then tearing it up, joining/starting a support group, e.g. co-counselling.

Catharsis: having a good cry, bashing, knocking or throwing cushions, punching punchbag, shaking, yelling at the dog/cat, stamping feet, screaming or shouting into a pillow, swearing loudly, smashing or ripping up something not valuable (e.g. cardboard box, cracked crockery, old clothes).

Creative emotional expression: poetry, painting and drawing, writing short stories, sculpture, singing, making music, amateur dramatics, dancing.

Confronting the problem

Thinking: working it through step by step; pinpointing and analysing the problem; clarifying the causes of the stress; brainstorming solutions; deciding what I really want/need, deciding priorities, making a plan; getting the information I need for dealing with it.

Other people: asking for help/advice; asserting wants and needs; challenging someone if they are causing the stress.

The organisation/system: telling people in power (e.g. managers, MP) my opinions; giving them any information they need to help make a case for change; starting/joining a joint action group; joining a pressure group (e.g. peace group, union).

Categorise the methods on your list under the four headings. Notice which categories are stronger and which are weaker, and pinpoint the methods you use often and those used seldom. Identify the methods of dealing with stress you would most like to develop or use more often in order to achieve a more balanced repertoire of coping mechanisms.

I suggest that when one or more of the categories are less well represented or less often used than the others, there is an imbalance in the individual's use of coping mechanisms. This may lead to further stresses. For instance, if little attention is paid to self-nurturance or distraction, the individual may exhaust herself. If emotional expression is lacking, there can be problems arising from emotional repression (see Chapter 2). If problems are seldom confronted, then avoidance can lead to an escalation of pressure.

Nurses often seem to be strong in the 'mental and physical distraction' categories, particularly on hobbies and chores, and weaker in the others.

It is for this reason that the rest of the book sets out to offer readers ways of exploring methods of dealing with stress which are predominantly to do with self-nurturance, confronting the problem, and emotional expression.

References and further reading

1. Cox T. (1978). *Stress*. London: MacMillan.
2. Jacobson S. F., McGrath M. H. (1983). *Nurses Under Stress*. Chichester: John Wiley & Sons.
3. Bond M., Kilty J. (1982). *Practical Methods of Dealing with Stress*. Guildford: Human Potential Research Project, University of Surrey.

Understanding emotions

Negative attitudes to emotions

Emotions have a bad name in nursing. The dangers of emotional involvement are often pointed out, but not the dangers of emotional shallowness. Emotional maturity is considered as the absence of emotions rather than skill in being aware of them and expressing them appropriately. We speak of controlling emotions rather than encouraging them. 'Getting emotional' is seen as failure, whereas being rational is over-valued. Emotions are 'subjective' and so written off as worthless, whereas reason is 'objective' and therefore 'right'. We aim to make emotions socially acceptable, not personally effective. Emotions are listed in the signs and symptoms of mental illness but seldom acknowledged as signs of mental health.

With such a negative billing, it is no wonder that the average nurse learns to keep quiet about her own emotions. Follow the progress of the learner nurse and note the progressive emotional coldness which is imposed on her by the climate of the nursing culture. Listen to experienced nurses deriding the 'interest in people' and 'desire to care' which often brings young people into the profession. However in spite of her conditioning, the nurse, like every other human being, does actually feel emotional at times. But who wants to be labelled as 'immature', 'hysterical', 'neurotic' or 'not cut out for the job'? So she bustles around looking efficient, doing things by the book and when she notices that she feels an emotion, tries to ignore it and hopes that it will go away. But often it will not, so she doubles her effort to hide it in order to avoid being found out. Her colleagues are doing the same. Thus we have a profession of human beings daily confronted by the most emotional of life's events, all striving to hide the one thing that we all have in common, our humanity. Pretending not to be the one thing which is inescapable, i.e. human, puts a severe strain on nurses. It is such a negative way of dealing with not only our emotions, but ourselves and other people. We are trying to kill off one of the greatest resources we have for coping with stress and for helping others to do so.

A more positive approach is to regard emotions as resources which with understanding and skill we can use to advantage. Very little is offered in nursing textbooks to explain emotions as natural phenomena, probably because of an over-reliance on medical and behavioural sources of reference. Yet it is vital that such universal and intangible experiences be explained in order to begin to reduce the fear of the unknown and to see them as potentially positive. This chapter attempts to offer a explanation of emotions derived from humanistic psychology. Given a framework for understanding, we can then go on to pinpoint the skills of dealing with emotions, and consider ways of building these skills.

What are emotions?

Emotions are often confused with thoughts, intuitions and sensations. The word 'feelings' is usually used to include thoughts (beliefs, opinions, ideas and values), intuitions (hunches and insights), physical sensations and emotions. Nurses who are adept at emotional denial and repression may think that they are identifying or expressing their emotions when in fact they are talking about something else. This results in some confusion in awareness of self and in communication with others. Sometimes this muddle is a form of defence against emotions, particularly in the climate of non-acceptance of natural human emotion.

An emotion is an integrated body/mind experience, sometimes called a 'gut reaction' (because some emotions are felt in the abdomen). Thoughts are mental constructs which may or may not be accompanied by emotions.

The following statements may appear at first glance to express emotions, but they are actually describing something else:

1. *I feel we should get on and do something about this instead of just sitting round analysing it.*

This is an opinion, not an emotion, which is being experienced. Behind it there may be an emotion. For instance:

I'm getting anxious about our spending so much time analysing it and I want to get on and do something about it instead.

Here the emotion expressed is anxiety.

2. *I have a feeling she's the right one for this job but I can't tell you why.*

This may be an intuition or hunch. There may not be any apparent logical reason for the viewpoint yet it can sometimes prove to be right.

3. *You're so nice to work with.*

This is expressing a thought about the other person. A statement of emotion would be: *I really enjoy working with you* — enjoyment being the emotion expressed.

4. *I'm feeling so hot in here. Can we have the window open?*

This expresses a physical sensation.

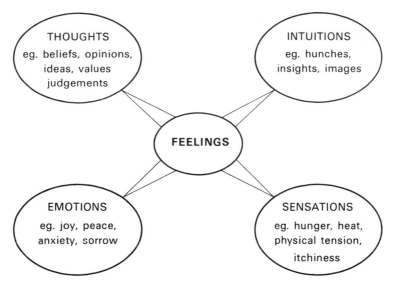

Fig. 2.1   *Four types of feelings (based on Jung's four functions).*

5. *I feel there's something going on.*

If there were identifiable signs that 'something was going on', this would be classified as an opinion. If there were no such signs, it would be termed a hunch or intuition.

6. *I'm so tired, I've walked miles today, though the scenery was lovely in that valley.*

This probably expressed a physical sensation of tiredness, rather than emotional tiredness.

7. *I feel really picked on, you're just victimising me because my face doesn't fit.*

This is an opinion or belief. An expression of the emotional feeling might go something like this:

I feel so upset and angry because you seem to be picking on me more than anyone else just because I'm different.

Categorise the following into either thought, intuition or sensation.

• I feel we ought to discuss this with the patient first.

- I'm feeling hungry, I haven't had any lunch today.
- I've got a feeling he'll come back though I know he said he wouldn't.
- You're a cold fish, nothing seems to bother you.
- I feel it's time to finish this and get the report written.

Many nurses are so used to expressing themselves in thoughts, intuitions and sensations that they find it hard to put emotions into words.

Think back over some emotional situations you found yourself in recently: consider both pleasant and stressful examples. Look through Table 2.1 and note which words describe the various emotions you experienced during the course of that situation.

What causes emotions?

John Heron's explanation is particularly useful (2). He suggests that each human being has three main groups of basic emotional needs:

1. *Love needs:* the need to love and be loved: to give and receive caring, affection, warmth, appreciation, support.
2. *Understanding needs:* the need to understand and to be understood: to grasp the reasons behind what is going on around us and within us and feel that other people can comprehend what we are trying to express to them.
3. *Choice needs:* to choose and to be chosen: to be able to take part in the decisions which affect our lives, and to be chosen as someone special because of our own particular qualities and abilities.

When these needs are met, the emotional reaction is positive and pleasant: we can feel warm, loving, confident, excited, energetic, content, calm, happy, joyful, interested, motivated and so on.

Think back to a situation recently when you felt happy in some way. Which of the emotional needs identified in this chapter were being met at that time? One nurse's example: 'I was cycling home the other day through the park, with the sun setting behind the trees. There were people of all colours playing and walking and lots of laughing going on. I felt fantastic. I suppose the emotional needs that were met were the 'choice' need: I had the freedom to

Table 2.1 *Some words which express emotions.*

Pleasant		Unpleasant	
absorbed	loved	afraid	hurt
affectionate	loving	angry	impatient
alert	moved	anxious	insecure
amazed	optimistic	bad	irritated
amused	overjoyed	bitter	jealous
appreciation	peaceful	blue	lazy
astonished	pleasant	bored	lonely
breathless	proud	brokenhearted	mean
calm	quiet	cold	miserable
carefree	relieved	confused	numb
comfortable	satisfied	cross	puzzled
confident	secure	depressed	rage
contented	sensitive	desperate	resentful
cool	splendid	devastated	sad
curious	stimulated	disappointed	shocked
delighted	strong	discouraged	small
eager	surprised	disgusted	sorry
elated	tender	dislike	surprised
encouraged	thankful	dismay	tense
energetic	touched	distressed	terrified
enjoyment	trust	disturbed	tired
enthusiastic	warm	embarrassed	trapped
erotic		exhausted	troubled
excited		fearful	uncomfortable
exuberant		fed-up	uneasy
fascinated		frightened	unhappy
free		frustrated	upset
friendly		furious	weak
grateful		gloomy	weary
happy		grief	worried
helpful		grumpy	wretched
hopeful		guilty	vulnerable
inquisitive		hate	
interested		helpless	
involved		horrified	
joyful		hostile	
keyed-up		humiliated	

Adapted from *The Good Health Guide* (1)

Fig. 2.2   *A nurse's positive emotional reactions to her emotional needs being met.*

1. Able and allowed to show caring, affection, support, appreciation, to patients and colleagues.
   Given and able to accept appreciation, support, caring, affection etc.

2. Is listened to, with sincere attempts made (and demonstrated) to understand her point of view, feelings; works with likeminded people who are on her wavelength.
   Has mental framework to help understand what's happening to and around her. Gets explanations given for things that happen in a language she understands, and detailed information about impending changes/events.

3. Asked to make her special contributions to the work of the health care team because of her own individual talents, abilities, not just because of role or qualifications.
   Able and allowed to take part in and influence decisions which affect her work. Her viewpoint taken into account. Allowed to make decisions for herself, in her own way, within own capabilities.

Feelings of job satisfaction, excitement and energy for work, interest in the people and tasks involved, motivation for work, realistic confidence in self and others, calmness, peace, genuine caring and warmth towards others.

---

get on my bike and pedal at my own rate — which is more than my patients have. There were so many beautiful things to look at and hear and smell that I couldn't help but love life, so that's the 'love' need, though it feels a bit funny putting it that way.'

But these needs cannot be met all the time. We get hurt. Heron describes primary hurts and secondary hurts. The primary hurts arise from the basic limitations of being human and are inevitable, such as separation from people we love, the inability to understand much of what happens in life, the vulnerability of the human body to trauma and illness.

Fig. 2.3 *Examples of primary hurts and natural emotional responses.*

1. Patient or colleague she's fond
   of, and who was fond of her, goes
   away or dies.
   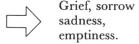
   Grief, sorrow
   sadness,
   emptiness.

2. Witnesses or is involved in
   suffering for which no human being
   can fully understand the reason.
   Cannot make herself understood by
   someone with a different background
   culture, values or language.
   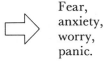
   Fear,
   anxiety,
   worry,
   panic.

3. Things happen over which she has
   no control, such as her own or
   other people's physical injury
   or ill health. She is not chosen
   in situations where not everyone
   can be chosen, e.g. job interview.
   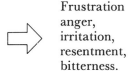
   Frustration
   anger,
   irritation,
   resentment,
   bitterness.

Secondary hurts are those in which the meeting of the basic emotional needs is blocked by other people (who themselves have been hurt). Although some of these hurts may be malicious and intentional, many are unintentional and may even be well meaning. Many of the hurtful practices inherent in the nursing hierarchy and structure are carried out because the people involved are well meaning — they think they are doing it for the best.

These hurts, the frustration of basic emotional needs, look very much like many of the causes of stress in nursing reported in Chapter 1.

The emotional reactions to these hurts is natural and only human: we feel distressed. The type of distress we feel can sometimes be related to the frustration of particular emotional needs. The grief, sadness, emptiness, sorrow type of feeling can be loosely linked to the frustration of the love need. Fear, worry, anxiety, panic type of feelings could originate in the frustration of the understanding need. Feelings of anger, resentment, irritation, bitterness (or depression and guilt if turned inwards) are linked to the frustration of the choice need. Emotions are much more complicated than these categories and links suggest, but this

Fig. 2.4   *Examples of secondary hurts and natural emotional responses.*

1. Taken away from the care of a particular patient, or put on opposite shifts to a colleague because she's getting too involved/matey. Never given any thanks or praise, because she's expected to work to a high standard, and that's taken for granted. Kept at a detached distance by the people around her, no show of warmth or human support.

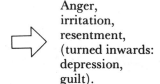 Grief, sorrow, sadness, emptiness, loneliness.

2. Expected to carry out tasks and instructions without questioning the reasons. Only given a few of the facts about impending changes. Not listened to or opinion not sought, expected to be 'seen but not heard'. Expected to fit into others' values, use of language, routines etc.

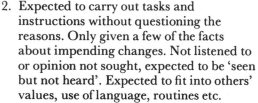 Fear, anxiety, worry, panic.

3. Not consulted about decisions affecting her work. Expected to follow set procedures and usual traditions of practice rather than make own decisions. Treated as a cog in a wheel, stereotyped according to her role, expected to have identical qualities and abilities to everyone else playing that role.

Anger, irritation, resentment, (turned inwards: depression, guilt).

explanation can help us to understand some of our reactions to some stressful situations.

So, distress is a natural reaction to emotional needs being blocked. Unfortunately, in the British culture and particularly in the nursing culture, this distress is unacceptable. We are taught, whether covertly perhaps by example and hints, or overtly, by direct instruction, how to attempt to avoid experiencing and expressing these feelings. We learn the mental defence mechanisms which psychologists describe (3). These are listed here:

Rationalisation: assigning logical reasons or plausible excuses for what we do impulsively, e.g. liking/disliking as an excuse ('I didn't really want the job anyway'); blaming — when something goes wrong, finding someone to attack and pin all the blame on; necessity — citing necessity as an excuse, e.g. the Sister not taking a break from the ward due to her extreme anxiety.

Projection: e.g. attributing one's own faults to other people, e.g. malevolent gossip, criticising behind others' backs; attributing one's own true feelings to others.

Reaction formation: overdoing the opposite of the emotion, e.g. a nurse over-protecting and smothering a patient who irritates her; playing the 'mother hen' role when the nurse herself needs a lot of caring.

Disassociation: distancing from feelings by excessive theorising, categorising or compulsive routines.

Substitution: carrying out activities guaranteed to succeed rather than those which might risk failure, e.g. busying oneself with the minutiae rather than tackling the larger issue of poor resources.

Repression and denial of own emotions: this is an intrinsic part of each of the above defence mechanisms, e.g. 'It doesn't bother me at all, water off a duck's back.'

Observers have noticed that in nursing we have developed our own particular versions of these defence mechanisms; they are part of the social fabric of our profession. Over 25 years ago, Isobel Menzies identified ten social systems used in nursing as defences against anxiety (4). I write them in the past tense, but you are invited to notice which still seem to apply in your experience.

- Splitting up a nurse/patient relationship: task allocation on wards and pooling caseloads on the district were ways of effecting this split.
- Depersonalisation, categorisation and denial of the significance of the individual: this was applied to both patient and nurse. The patient was referred to as 'the hernia in bed 4'. He was labelled 'difficult' and 'neurotic' if he displayed distress. The nurse was referred to by her status title, such as 'sister', 'staff' and 'charge nurse', rather than by her name; the uniform clearly categorised and reduced individuality.
- The attempt to eliminate decisions by ritual task performance: over-standardising procedures and routines.
- Reducing the weight of responsibility in decision-making by checks and counter checks: over-supervising and over-dependence on the hierarchy.

- Collusive social redistribution of responsibility and irresponsibility: using particular groups of people as scapegoats, e.g. blaming the youngest generation of nurses for poor standards, the 'student nurses aren't as responsible as they used to be in my day' syndrome, blaming all nurse managers and all nurse tutors.
- Purposeful obscurity in the formal distribution of responsibility: fudging the issue of who's responsible for what.
- The reduction of the impact of responsibility by delegation to superiors: passing the buck upwards.
- Idealisation and underestimation of personal development possibilities: labelling oneself or others as being either a 'born nurse' or 'not cut out for the job'.
- Avoidance of change.

Effects of emotional repression

All these defences result in our bottling up emotions. Over time we build up a backlog of unexpressed emotions. Triggers in everyday life can stir up these repressed feelings and result in a number of responses which are over-reactions or under-reactions to the real-life situation, are unhelpful for our health and relationships and cause further stress.

Physical effects

We often react with physical tension and illness. The anger hormone noradrenalin, prepares the body for the fight response which when not expressed results in physical tension, particularly in the shoulders, arms and jaw. We even talk of irritating people being a 'pain in the neck'. The fear hormone, adrenalin, leaves residual tension in the legs and chest, and unexpressed grief leaves tension in the chest and abdomen. In addition, many illnesses are now being associated with repressed emotions. For instance, repressed anger is considered a significant factor in the development of cancer in women.

Mental effects

These can include mental blocks; impaired concentration, decision-making and logical thinking; forgetfulness.

Effects on beliefs

We can develop rigid and irrational beliefs, opinions, values and prejudices about ourselves and the world at large, particularly internalised negative beliefs about our own worth and what we imagine other people think of us. These beliefs may be conscious, but are usually largely unconscious. They influence the way we see ourselves and others. Some examples: 'I'm stupid', 'People in authority think I'm hopeless', 'Never trust a woman boss'. As a tutor, I found that many intelligent, experienced nurses, when returning to the classroom for further training, resurrected very negative beliefs about their own intelligence. Often the origins lay in humiliating experiences in previous nurse and general education and the legacy of repressed emotional reactions to those experiences.

Effects on behaviour

Rigid, distorted patterns of behaviour may be triggered off. These are habitual ways of attempting to cope which are inappropriate to the real-life situation, ineffective and out of date. Some examples: placating and avoiding any hint of conflict; setting oneself up to fail (by setting impossible targets) or to be put down or taken advantage of; unconsciously choosing the wrong type of person as a friend or partner; not allowing someone who is suffering to express their feelings.

Emotional effects

The defence mechanisms not only have the effect of bottling up uncomfortable emotions, but positive feelings too. If we become so adept at holding back negative feelings all the time, then we are likely to become numb in situations where positive emotions would naturally come through. Nurses are often accused of being cold or hard. We lose the ability to show genuine love, caring, delight, pleasure and so on. This numbness will tend to alternate with emotional outbursts. For instance, there is the 'last straw' syndrome, when we hit out verbally or physically at ourselves or other people in an over-reaction to real or imagined misdeeds. It is as if the pressure builds up so much in the emotional 'bottle' that the cork flies and too much comes rushing out at once.

It is because of this phenomenon that emotions have got a bad name, a sort of 'all-or-nothing' expectation. This theory for understanding emotion indicates that we must build into our culture, and this can apply particularly to the nursing culture, more acceptance and more opportunities for developing and using emotional skills.

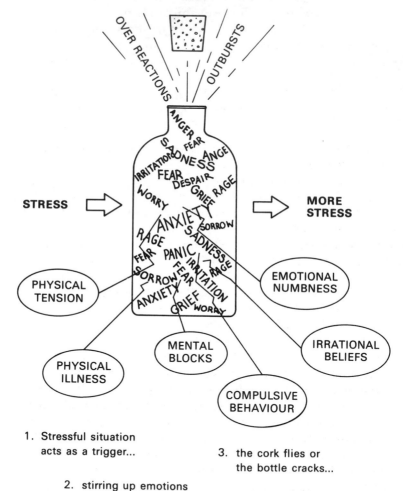

1. Stressful situation acts as a trigger...

2. stirring up emotions which have been bottled up from previous stressful situations...

3. the cork flies or the bottle cracks...

4. resulting in even more stress...

Fig. 2.5 *Effects of emotional repression.*

Emotional skills

Our system of nursing education tends to place the emphasis, with respect to skills, on technical skills, and to some extent, thinking skills. Communication skills are starting to come onto the scene, but very little attention is paid to emotional skills. Perhaps the concept of 'skill' in using emotions is a difficult one for nurses to grasp, beyond 'keeping them under control': John Heron's model can be useful here. He says there are four main aspects to emotional skills:

1. *Awareness* of own emotions and the extent to which they can influence behaviour. This is a difficult starting point for nurses who have become adept at repressing their emotions. But other skills cannot be developed without this first step.

2. *Choice* between control and spontaneity involves choosing when to control and hold back emotions or choosing to let them out spontaneously as appropriate. Choosing to be spontaneous may sound like a contradiction in terms, but choices are made in a split second, often unconsciously. After all, there is an unconscious choice when someone shouts abuse at their children (safe for them though not for their children) rather than shouting at their manager (unsafe for them; they would lose their job if they bullied the manager the way children are often bullied).

Again, awareness is important: becoming aware of the unconscious choices we already make about the use of emotions can help us to make better decisions. We can decide to take the risk of expressing emotions or to hold them back.

Some spontaneity is vital in nursing. For instance, when one feels genuinely tender and caring towards a patient or colleague, it might be worth taking the risk of rejection and reaching out spontaneously to express that emotion. The potential power of anger in galvanising people to action is often underestimated; many of the most effective reformers act out of passionate concern for the injustices of the system. Indeed the UKCC code of professional conduct exhorts us to express our concern and to initiate reforms where necessary (5). Peer support is vital in this respect. (See Chapter 6.) Sheila Hillier has observed that because of the inhibiting effect of the nursing culture on the development of both personal and supportive ties, the prevailing emotions among nurses about collective activity are apathy and fear (6). We must question our values in this respect and acknowledge and use our anger positively and set out to challenge our own culture as well as the injustices of the system.

However, the control element of emotional skills is not undervalued here. There are occasions when we need to hold back rather than hurt someone. There are many times in nursing practice when patients are depending on us to act efficiently for their care and safety. For instance, it would be totally inappropriate for a nurse to stand and shake and sob out of the anxiety produced by her patient having a cardiac arrest; she needs to act quickly, calmly and efficiently. But she also needs to be allowed and to allow herself some time later to express her anxiety. Emotional control is essential in nursing, but it is not the only important emotional skill. It is regrettable that it is the only skill which tends to be taught in nurse education.

3. *Sharing* emotions with other people as appropriate. Self-disclosure helps to reduce superficiality in relationships. It includes taking the risk of sharing positive feelings, such as telling or showing a patient or colleague you care about them or are fond of them, or showing appreciation. It also involves telling or showing uncomfortable feelings, perhaps unburdening an upset, or telling someone how they affect you emotionally. Allowing others to share their emotions with you is an essential part of sharing.

Most of these examples are part of an assertive approach (see Chapter 5 on assertiveness). So developing assertiveness in nursing might help to build the trust needed for emotional sharing. The ground rules outlined in the chapter on peer support, Chapter 6, are useful if not essential for trust in this area.

Talking about emotions often helps, particularly in reducing emotional isolation and in increasing self-acceptance, but it does not actually release them or get rid of them. Feelings are physically and emotionally released through catharsis.

4. *Releasing emotions cathartically:* it is important to clarify what is meant by catharsis as an emotional skill. It is made up of four elements.

i.   *Controlled letting-go:* the person is aware of the process and chooses to do it — in other words, the person is 'in control of letting go'. This idea may be rather peculiar to many people who find it hard to understand that catharsis is *not* letting it all hang out through physical or verbal violence, or disintegrating when other people are relying on you. It involves creating and choosing an appropriate time and place to let go.

ii. *Letting-go:* the second element is allowing oneself to let go physically and emotionally. Physical letting-go involves releasing physical tension by making sounds such as deep sobs, wailing, shouting or screaming. (Noises can be made into a pillow or cushion to muffle the sound — feather pillows absorb the noise better than others!) Physical release also involves ridding the relevant muscles of tension by pounding, kicking, stamping or throwing, using strong pillows or cushions (not people or property). Emotional letting-go is allowing the emotional pain to happen along with any painful memories. Naturally this feels very uncomfortable while it is actually going on.

When reading about this form of release, a common reaction is for readers to feel stirred up emotionally and for all kinds of judgements to come into play — such as 'nurses don't do that kind of thing'. Nurses do. It is a natural and human response to the suffering experienced in our jobs. The problem is that most of this release is done secretly and with shame. The shame is unnecessary and the secretiveness is an indication of our inability to care for each other. Many nurses have described how they have hidden in linen cupboards, the linen absorbing the sound of their sobs, or created noise by banging bed pans or running bath taps to hide the sound of their crying or furious foot stamping. Some have been discovered and have been humiliated and pilloried for this lonely expression of their emotional skill. Many nurses have described crying with patients and the shame which they have felt at doing something which they saw as a weakness. However, patients appreciate this spontaneous demonstration of empathy and caring and subsequently are able to give themselves permission to heal some of their own emotional pain in this way. As a student nurse who herself was dying once wrote: 'Would you really lose so much of your precious professionalism if you just cried with me sometimes and I could feel that I was dying amongst friends?' (7). It has been suggested by Elizabeth Kübler-Ross that each ward should have a 'screaming room' — a soundproofed place where staff, patients and relatives could go to let off steam. She has also said that anger, if expressed, lasts only about 15 seconds, but may last 15 years or more if not expressed (8).

iii. *Insights:* the third element of catharsis is that of catching the intuitive and spontaneous insights which are the normal results of emotional release. You may remember times when you have allowed yourself to let go, and discovered some thought, whether as a word, phrase or as an image, a picture in your mind's eye, which has given you comfort, peace or a sense of emotional healing. Noticing and listening to these insights is part of the skilled use of catharsis.

iv. *Decision-making:* lastly, having moved through emotion, then intuition, the last stage of catharsis when used as a skill is to use your intellect to consolidate the learning and to make an action plan which identifies appropriate changes which you can make for yourself. The period of letting-go clears the mind so that better decisions can be made.

Think back to a recent situation when you felt upset. Which of the basic emotional needs identified in this chapter were not being met at that time? Which defence mechanisms did you use and which emotional skills did you use? One nurse's example: 'I got a letter in the post the other day telling me I hadn't been accepted for the health visitor course I'd applied for (that's the not being chosen bit). My first reaction was to swear like mad and tear the letter into little pieces. Perhaps that was what you'd call an emotional skill — it let off some steam and didn't do anyone any harm. I didn't look at it that way at the time, I felt a bit ashamed of myself. Maybe I needn't have done? Anyway, I sat down and had a cup of tea and calmed myself and went to work and put it out of my mind for the rest of the day. That's the control skill. Oh except for a moan session I had with a colleague at lunchtime; I suppose I bitched a lot about the tutors who interviewed me. Was that rationalisation? Then that night I had a bit of a weep on my husband's shoulder — that's the catharsis skill again. Perhaps I was sad because in the back of my mind I thought they'd turned me down because they didn't like me? I reckon we all want to be liked, really. Looking back on it, maybe I didn't handle it too badly after all.'

Developing emotional skills

Contrary to popular belief, emotional skills can be learned and developed. Misconceptions about a person's potential for change may originate in lack of clarity about the nature of emotional skills. These skills are not commonly identified, discussed and systematically practised. Instead there is an expectation that a person reaches a state of 'maturity', having somehow learned all she can about emotions by picking it up in a haphazard way as she goes along. Many nurses believe that once a person's personality comes to maturity (and of course no adult would consider themselves immature), then it is fixed and nothing can be done to change and develop it. However, given appropriate opportunities to gain the necessary knowledge and practice, we can become more able to be self-aware, to act from choice, to share with others and to release emotions appropriately. This book sets out in a small way to provide such opportunities.

Because of the limitations of the written word, the exercises in this book focus on the self-awareness, choice and sharing skills rather than the skill of catharsis, though details of training opportunities are given for all four groups of skills. Some of the exercises may seem a little odd or artificial but this is inevitable in human skills training. To explain this we could use 'keep fit' exercises as an analogy. When you do bending and stretching exercises to keep fit, you are behaving in an 'artificial way' in that you would not normally go around touching your toes or waving your limbs about. But the act of practising each of the exercises strengthens and stretches particular muscles so that you are stronger, have more stamina and are more flexible in your response to physical pressures. For instance, if a heavy patient falls on you, you will have quicker reflexes for getting into a safe position and more strength to protect yourself and the patient from getting hurt. Likewise, practising emotional skills will give you greater emotional strength, stamina and flexibility to respond appropriately to each emotional pressure.

The various chapters in the book attempt to provide the opportunity to develop a range of skills so you can achieve balance in your ways of coping with stress. For instance, in the same way that concentrating only on press-ups can give you magnificent shoulders but leave the rest flabby, so concentrating only on passive methods like meditation can leave you 'flabby' in your communications with other people.

Skim through the rest of the book. Then start reading properly at the chapter which most relates to the methods you have identified for expanding your repertoire of coping skills. Skip over the sections which are of least immediate relevance to you and concentrate on those which are. You can always go back another time and pick up the points which did not attract your attention immediately.

References and further reading

1. Open University/Health Education Council/Scottish Health Education Unit (1980). Chapters on 'Expressing your Feelings' and 'Thoughts and Feelings' in *The Good Health Guide*. London: Harper & Row.
2. Heron J. (1977). *Catharsis in Human Development*. Guildford: Human Potential Research Project, University of Surrey.
3. Hilgard E., Hilgard R., Atkinson R. C. (1979). *Introduction to Psychology*. New York: Harcourt Brace Jovanovich.
4. Menzies I. (1960). *A Case Study in the Functioning of Social Systems as a Defence against Anxiety*. London: Tavistock Institute of Human Relations.
5. UKCC (1983). *Code of Professional Conduct for Nurses, Midwives and Health Visitors*. United Kingdom Central Council for Nursing, Midwifery and Health Visiting.
6. Hillier S. (1981). 'Stresses, Strains and Smoking'. *Nursing Mirror*, February 12, pp. 26–30.
7. Anonymous Student Nurse. 'Thoughts on Dying'.
8. Kübler-Ross E. (1984) Lecture, Wembley Conference Centre. September 9.

3

Relaxation

Nurses and the busy syndrome

Relaxation is not about doing, but about *not doing*. The concepts and skills of relaxation are not easy for nurses who are caught in the 'busy syndrome' to grasp.

Nurses often work in conditions where there are swings between periods of intense activity and lulls, and between periods when tasks of vital importance need to be carried out and when mundane tasks are done. Yet even in the lulls we seem to rush about looking busy and important. There seems to be a sort of work ethic that we must be on the go all the time to be considered to be really working. Nurses talk about 'getting the work done', meaning the practical aspects of the nurse's role. Those aspects which more obviously demand a relaxed approach, such as explaining things, teaching, counselling, planning, evaluating, discussions with colleagues and liaison with other departments are rarely included in the term 'the work'. Thinking and communicating are often not considered real work.

Tasks need to be done so we adopt a 'busy' attitude, moving quickly from task to task, in a state of physical tension. This 'busy-ness' can range from bustling to frantic hyperactivity. Some tasks get done, which is satisfying to the nurse, but something which may also be satisfying is the image of the 'hard worker' which is conveyed. She may even receive praise for giving this impression. It seems that praise is most often given in nursing for the amount of work done, rather than for the quality of the work,

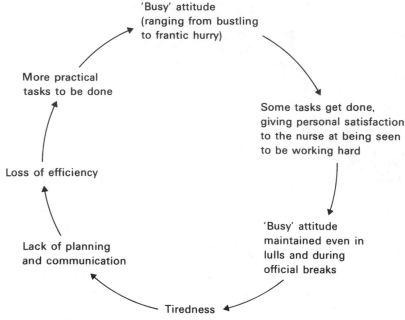

Fig. 3.1   *The busy syndrome.*

encouraging quantity and not quality values. In the lulls when the pressure is off, or even during official breaks, the nurse cannot switch off the 'busy' attitude since it becomes part of her self-image and she continues to find tasks to do. Even when official breaks are taken, she is likely to remain tense. Inevitably this leads to tiredness with difficulty in thinking and communicating clearly. The resulting loss of efficiency leads to more tasks needing to be done and the cycle goes on.

Becoming more aware of physical tension

Physical tension is a waste of effort and energy. You would think it a ridiculous waste of energy to carry around a weightlifter's dumb-bell all day, but you may be wasting just as much muscular effort with unnecessary physical tension (1).

Table 3.1   *Common examples of physical tension.*

Fixed frown or raised eyebrows. Fixed smile. Squinting eyes. Screwed up nose (e.g. to hold up spectacles). Clenched teeth, chewing inside of cheek and using chewing gum. Thrust out or held in chin. Raised, hunched forward or pushed back shoulders. Chest thrust out or sunken. Pulled in elbows. Clenched fist, gripping something unnecessarily. Holding breath. Twisted or abnormally curved spine from poor posture. Hips thrust forward or back. Abdominal muscles held in. Legs crossed tightly; ankle bending. Knees held together. Feet held together. Foot tapping. Generally putting more physical energy into doing things than is necessary (e.g. holding telephone too tightly).

Note which of the above apply to you right now as you are reading this.

Often these tensions become habitual and we remain tense even in relaxing circumstances. Some of the tensions are the result of sex-role conditioning: boys may copy 'manly' postures, thrusting out chest, pushing shoulders back and swaggering. Girls may develop 'dainty' habits: elbows in, knees together and tummy pulled in tight. Women's fashion shoes and would-be elegant gait can play havoc with muscular alignment and cause bodily tension and sometimes facial tension because of the pain! Habitual tensions become so accepted that it is difficult to notice them in ourselves. The sense of what feels relaxed becomes distorted.

The following exercises are useful in building awareness of the extent of your ability to 'switch off' muscles. With repetition you can develop increased skill in deliberately letting-go physical tension.

Spend some time in front of a large mirror sitting or standing in the positions you often adopt in daily life. Note the areas of tension.

Ask a friend to help you with some tension spotting exercises as follows:

Lie on your back on the floor. Your friend kneels or sits at your head and gently takes your head in their hands, slowly and gently turning from it from side to side. Allow your head to be supported as much as you can. Note how much or how little you can let your head go, and ask for feedback about how heavy your head feels, and how much you seem to help her move or support it.

Stand and let your partner lift each arm in turn, moving it gently without your assistance. Note the extent to which you can let go and allow the arm to be heavy, or the extent to which you help her to lift and move it.

Enhancing everyday methods of relaxation

Physical relaxation is a natural skill everyone possesses to some degree. We achieve it using a number of natural methods, all of which can be enhanced by conscious choice.

While you are reading this book, notice if any of your normal wriggles, fidgets or daydreams come under any of the following categories:

- Pausing: looking away from the page, or idly focussing on one part of the book, while doing nothing in particular.
- Stretching: shrugging shoulders, twisting body and head, yawning, extending arms and fingers, pressing fingers of one hand against those of the other hand or against a firm surface, pointing toes.
- Adjusting posture: such as forehead or chin in hands, hands on lap or table, body forward or back. Changing posture can give certain groups of muscles a rest while others do the work of holding you up.
- Switching off or turning down certain muscles: this often happens after stretching or a change in posture.
- Deep breathing: sighing, yawning.
- Self-massage: rubbing tense muscles, such as in forehead, neck or back.

Mini-relaxations can be integrated into daily life and involve consciously using some of these natural methods to enhance their effectiveness.

Pausing

Many nurses berate themselves for being unable to concentrate non-stop for long periods. In fact, non-stop concentration is impossible — the mind and body frequently automatically switch off. For instance, some studies have shown that students switch off

This is my head.  These are my hands. and these are my legs.

Together they do a million wonderful tricks.

 They make decisions. They get things done. They whizz around between patients and departments.

They are always busy.

 This is my body.

It's the wrong shape. It gets full of aches and pains.

 It contains my heart which gets broken when I see people suffering and there's not enough resources to really help.

I have as little to do with it as possible.

 Lucky for my body that i need it to join up my head, hands and legs.

 Otherwise OUT it would go!

MB/CJ
Adapted from an original cartoon by Jules Feiffer.

at least every three minutes, which is why teachers are encouraged to use visual aids so students can catch up with the lesson. One way to help yourself to relax is to stop fighting the natural pauses, and to deliberately give yourself time to pause.

For instance, when you see an asterisk at the end of this sentence, focus gently on it or look away from the page, while staying absolutely still, except for your normal breathing, and just notice the breathing for the duration of a breath or two.*

Pauses can only take a few seconds — there is no need to make them like petit mal epileptic episodes! Overworked nurses get into 'jumpy' habits of over-reacting to stimuli. If you find yourself jumping to telephones or your name or title being called or waffling when asked a question, try practising pausing first (unless it's an emergency of course). You could tell yourself 'stop' and just be still for a few seconds. Finding the energy or collecting your thoughts will be easier.

Stretching, adjusting posture, 'turning down' muscles and deep breathing

These tend to go together. It is difficult to take a deep breath in a hunched position, and the breath itself stretches the spine. As you breathe out, make sure your spine stays elongated rather than letting it collapse. Try this mini-relaxation now while reading this book.

Take a slow deep breath in, expanding abdomen as well as chest. Hold your breath and uncross your legs and move back in your chair until the base of the spine is as far back in the chair as possible. As you slowly breathe out (perhaps with a yawn), stretch your toes outwards then let your legs flop so both feet are on the ground, while imagining that your spine is stretching upwards. At the end of the breath, imagine that the tension is draining out of you from top to toe, while maintaining an upright spine to stop your spinal column crumpling when you breathe out. Imagine you are being suspended from the top of your head (like that skeleton in the school of nursing lecture room!). Take one or two more deep breaths if you want, then breathe normally and keep that relaxed position while reading on. Resist the temptation to cross your legs again and slouch down in the chair.

These routines can be applied to almost any situation through-out the day. If you make the deep breaths and the stretching unobtrusive, no one need be aware that you are giving yourself a mini-break.

Adjusting posture and conserving energy

Relaxation breaks are useful in themselves, but habitual tensions easily reassert themselves when you begin to move around. Moving with poise and balance results in minimising effort and in greater efficiency and calmness in carrying out the task.

Think of someone you know who has poise, perhaps a colleague who seems to get things done without bustling. Try to remember, or even better, go and observe what exactly she does *not* do that helps her to be poised.

One way of considering posture is in relation to how much muscular effort is put into holding you up. Often nurses look as though gravity is defeating them into slouched, rounded postures. Alternatively, some look determined to fight gravity, using too much effort against it. Either way, poise and balance are lost, with resulting waste of effort and the possibility of long-term damage, such as back problems. You can train yourself to improve your posture by focussing on one aspect at a time until you can create new habits.

Set yourself a time limit, such as one day. During that time, make a contract with yourself to notice each time you do one of the following and adjust to the preferred posture:

Notice:	**Adjust to:**
1. Standing with weight mostly on one leg.	Both feet carrying equal weight.
2. Crossed legs while sitting.	Both feet flat on floor, legs relaxed.
3. Shoulders high.	Shoulders dropped.
4. Body leaning forward or back.	Upright though relaxed. Again imagine you are suspended, like the skeleton in the school of nursing.

Training in the Alexander Technique can make dramatic changes in your poise, posture and energy levels. It involves one-to-one lessons with a teacher trained in the Alexander Technique, and it is not possible to distill sample exercises for the purpose of this book. Although the technique begins with a form of posture training, it encompasses training in total use of self in daily life (2). However, the basic posture-correcting exercise given above might begin to build awareness and improve posture.

So to be relaxed at work you do not have to do yoga asanas in the office, lie flat on your back in the middle of the ward or snooze in the back of the car between visiting patients. You can give yourself frequent relaxation mini-breaks from a few seconds to a few minutes throughout the day and adjust your posture, and so feel more relaxed and energetic.

Deep relaxation

The body needs regular doses of deep relaxation (3). Flopping in front of the television or going to sleep cannot be guaranteed to give the level of physical relaxation needed. Tense habits continue unconsciously. Films of slumbering research subjects have shown that people give frequent signs of tension even while deeply asleep.

In the same way that instruction impulses from the brain make muscles tense up so that you can move and do things, you need to consciously instruct your muscles to relax. As with skilled movements, practice improves performance and often the skill becomes automatic without much conscious effort. You need to put aside a regular time to practise, such as 20–30 minutes every day or every other day. Deep relaxation practice helps you to:

1. Give yourself definite times for a proper rest and to break the 'busy syndrome' cycle. As the saying goes, the time to relax is when you have no time to relax.
2. Enhance the rest value of whatever periods of rest you take, whether mini-relaxation, breaks, watching TV or sleeping.
3. Establish the habit of taking time for yourself and it also gives a reason for your time alone which most family members or colleagues will accept. If you have always made yourself available to people around you all the time, suddenly asserting a need for time alone might make them feel rejected at first. Relaxation practice

sometimes gives you an acceptable reason for this change in your lifestyle.

Deep relaxation routines are best practised lying flat on your back on a firm surface. A lot of people find this difficult at first, and may need to start by sitting in an arm chair or reclining chair with head and feet supported (chairs are more socially acceptable too), or lying down with a small cushion under head, neck, back, knees or feet. Alternatively, lying with knees bent and leaning against each other can prevent discomfort in the back.

There are a number of structures used for relaxation. They all help you to focus your attention on various parts of the body to instruct the muscles in that area to relax. People often develop preferences and dislikes for particular routines, therefore it is important to bear in mind that one structure may help you to relax whereas others do not.

You can learn deep relaxation by attending classes, doing a correspondence course, using commercial tapes, making your own tapes, buying or borrowing a biofeedback machine, getting someone to talk you through relaxation routines, or doing it totally on your own.

Using relaxation tapes

Commercially produced tapes are advertised in health magazines and are on sale in some health food shops. Before buying one, try to find out what relaxation routines are used and listen to the sound of the voice and any extra music or noises to check that you find them relaxing. Try also to find out what sort of mental pictures are used to aid relaxation.

The intonation and accent of one voice may be very relaxing to some people but exceedingly irritating to others. Some tapes have music or sounds, and again individual reactions may differ. Repetitive orchestral, choral, guitar, flute or electronic music may be triggers which relax some people, but irritate others. Ocean sounds, running water, whales singing, intrauterine sounds or Tibetan bells put some people into a state of relaxed bliss, while they make others climb the walls or rush to the bathroom! Tapes of the sounds of an English hay field in summer have even been known to make people sneeze!

Some commercial firms claim that their relaxation tapes are hypnotic in the sense that they will put you into a state of deep relaxation and implant auto-suggestion messages into your mind. If you have a lot of money to spare, you can buy tapes which are claimed to be specifically designed to help you sleep, feel more confident, improve concentration, solve problems, lose weight, stop smoking, enjoy sex more or become richer. One way of saving money (though becoming a millionaire or even getting an inflation-linked pay rise is definitely not guaranteed!) is by finding one tape which helps you relax, and then as a result, all the other things like sleep, sex and confidence are likely to improve.

There are some tapes available incorporating visualisation therapy for sufferers of particular conditions such as cancer or arthritis. The visualisation techniques are said to mobilise their physical and mental resources to combat the condition. Some people find them helpful, but the overall effectiveness of visualisation therapy, as with hypnosis, probably depends largely on the person-to-person relationship between the therapist and patient. Specific tapes of this type are likely to have more benefit than an ordinary relaxation tape only if they are used as an adjunct to one-to-one therapy and feature the voice of the therapist herself.

Commercial tapes are not usually cheap and it may cost you a lot of money to find a tape which suits you if you do not investigate first. As an alternative to buying a relaxation tape, you could make your own. Ideally, the tape should feature your own voice, then it will be easier to internalise the relaxation routine and to do without the tape. In practice, most people are appalled when they first hear the sound of their own voices on tape. This is because a recording does not give the resonance in the skull which we feel when we speak. If you have not become used to the sound of your voice recorded on tape, you could ask someone with a relaxing voice to record the scripts for you.

If you are attending a class, the teacher may agree to your recording the 'talk down' sessions, provided it does not interrupt the session. The tape needs to be long enough to include the whole relaxation session. Alternatively, a friend or colleague may be willing to read a script into a recorder. Ask them to speak slowly but in a matter of fact manner: hypnotic tones are only required for sleep tapes.

Scripts for relaxation routines

These scripts illustrate a number of different structures for relaxa-

tion. They can be adapted or combined to suit individual preferences. Note that each full stop in the script denotes a pause of
about 5 seconds; 2 full stops represents 10 seconds and so on. Each
comma represents a short pause of about 2 seconds.

Relaxation script no. 1 is a short relaxation (about 5 to 8 minutes)
using the countdown method.

'Find a comfortable position, sitting with feet flat on the floor,
hands by sides . I'm going to count down from 10 to 0 and you'll be
as relaxed as possible when I reach 0 . TEN . feeling the body
becoming heavy . sinking into the floor or chair . NINE . legs
relaxed . . EIGHT . . trunk relaxing . . SEVEN . . chest relaxed . .
breathing relaxed . . and regular . . SIX . . arms feeling heavy . .
hands warming . . . FIVE . . shoulders and neck relaxed . . .
FOUR . . . head relaxed . . . THREE . . . jaw relaxed . . . TWO
. . . more and more relaxed . . . . deeper and deeper . . . . ONE
. . . . the whole body is relaxed . . . . deeper and deeper . . . . more
and more relaxed . . . . ZERO . . . . deeply relaxed . . . . more and
more relaxed . . . . peaceful . . . . relaxed but alert . . . . relaxed
. . . . I'll count back up to 10 again, when I reach 10, open your
eyes, move your fingers and toes, stretch and take a couple of deep
breaths. 0, 1, 2, 3, 4, 5, 6, 7, 8, 9, 10 . . now treat yourself gently,
and maintain as much as you can of this feeling of relaxation as
you move about and carry out your activities.'

Relaxation script no. 2 is a relaxation routine that concentrates on
the muscles of the face and hands. It is based on the idea that since
the major part of the motor cortex of the brain is concerned with
these areas, then developing the skill of relaxing these will make
total body relaxation relatively easy. Each full stop represents a
five second pause.

'Find a place to lie flat on the floor on your back, or in a chair with
your head supported . have your feet about a foot apart and your
hands a few inches away from your side, palms upwards . take a
couple of deep breaths, slowly breathing in and exhaling gently . .
then let your breathing become gentle and relaxed . notice the
points where your body touches the floor or the chair . let those
points relax and let yourself sink into the floor or chair . let the
back of your head relax . let your scalp relax . behind your ears .

the top of your head . put your attention into your forehead . imagine the space between your hairline and eyebrows widening . let your forehead relax and become smooth . imagine the space between your eyebrows is widening . let this become relaxed and smooth . let your eyes rest gently in their sockets, not looking in any direction . floating . relaxing . let the skin on your cheeks relax . more and more relaxed . allow your jaw to relax and feel your temples relaxing at the same time . let your mouth be open with the lips slightly apart or only just touching . allow your tongue to rest gently behind your lower teeth, so it is not touching the top of your mouth . let your throat relax . you may want to swallow or yawn . feel your neck and shoulders relaxing . . now put your attention into your right arm . let the upper arm relax . the lower arm . and imagine that the skin on the palm of your right hand is warming and relaxing . imagine the capillaries opening and the blood warming the skin . the back of your right hand is warming and relaxing . the thumb . index finger . middle finger . ring finger . little finger . the whole of your right hand is warm and relaxed . . now put your attention into your left arm . let the upper left arm relax . the lower arm . and imagine the skin on the palm of your left hand is warming and relaxing . the back of your left hand . the thumb . the index finger . middle finger . ring finger . little finger . the whole of your left hand is warm and relaxed . . feel your chest and upper back relaxing . your breathing shallow and rhythmic . heart rate slowing down . it's quite safe . more and more relaxed . your lower back and abdomen are relaxed . deeper and deeper . more and more relaxed . the pelvis and buttocks are relaxed . the right leg is relaxed . the left leg is relaxed . . the whole of your body is relaxed . . the whole of your body is as relaxed as you want it to be . . more and more relaxed . . deeper and deeper . . staying alert, but relaxed . . . more and more relaxed . . relaxed . . peaceful . . relaxed . . now your whole body is totally relaxed . . no tension . . . . just relaxed . . . peaceful . . . you can use this method of relaxation whenever you choose . to relax . rest . unwind . recharge your batteries . regain your energy . and alertness . when you're ready . move your fingers and toes gently . sit up slowly, treating yourself gently . stretch your limbs and take a deep breath or two.'

Relaxation script no. 3: this incorporates some of the standard phrases used in autogenic training (3). There are four main

stages: allowing the limbs to become heavy then warm, calming
the heart rate and breathing, and enhancing alertness.

'Begin the exercise in a sitting or reclining position with your eyes
closed . . if external sounds distract you, repeat the phrase "external sounds do not matter" silently to yourself three times . . . put
your attention into your right arm and repeat silently to yourself
three times "my right arm is heavy" . . . with your attention in
your left arm, repeat silently "my left arm is heavy" three times
. . . right leg, "my right leg is heavy" . . . left leg . . . neck . . .
shoulders . . . then with your attention back into your right arm,
imagine the capillaries relaxing and allowing more blood into
your arm as you repeat silently to yourself three times "my right
arm is warm" . . . left arm . . . . right leg . . . left leg . . . neck . . .
shoulders . . . then with your attention on your heartbeat, repeat
the phrase "my heartbeat is calm and regular" three times, but if
there is any discomfort about this go on to the next stage . . . then
with attention on breathing, repeat the phrase "my breathing is
calm and regular" three times silently to yourself . . . with your
attention on your forehead, "my forehead is cool" . . . . then take
some quiet time, perhaps repeating the phrase "I am at peace
with myself and fully relaxed" . . . .
begin to return by repeating the phrase "I am refreshed and alert"
three times . . . now take a deep breath and stretch.'

Relaxation script no. 4: this routine uses an approach which
features tensing muscles in the opposing groups to those normally
held tense. This makes the habitually tense muscles relax (4).
This particular script illustrates the use of this approach by
contradicting the most common tensions: your own tense habits
may not exactly correspond, therefore you may need to adapt the
routine. For instance, it assumes that you tend to hunch your
shoulders up: if instead your habit is to push them back and down,
military style, then you need to adapt the exercise to contradict
the habit, by pushing up and forward.

There are three steps to each exercise: (1) contradictory tension, (2) holding the position and noticing the relaxation in the
normally tense muscles, (3) relaxing by allowing the deliberately
tense muscles to let go while retaining the relaxation effect in the
other muscles. Each exercise is then repeated three times. Each
full stop represents a five second pause.

'Find a space to lie flat on your back on the floor, or in an armless chair with your head and feet supported . . check that your feet are apart and hands by your sides . . push your head back into the floor or chair . . STOP and hold the position . . let go and release the tension . . . push the head back and STOP . . let go and release the tension . . . push the head back and STOP . . let go and release . . . . open the jaw wide and STOP . . let go and release so your jaw is relaxed, mouth slightly open . . open jaw wide and STOP . . let go and release . . open jaw and STOP . . let go and release . . . press your tongue downwards in your mouth, curling upwards and pressing against lower teeth, feel the position and STOP . . let go and release so your tongue rests gently behind the lower teeth without touching the roof of your mouth . . press tongue down and forward and STOP . . let go and release . . press tongue down and forward and STOP . . let go and release . . . pull your shoulders down towards your feet and back into the floor or chair and STOP . . let go and release . . shoulders down and back and STOP . . let go and release . . . push your elbows out wide away from your body and STOP . . let go and release and feel the relaxation . . elbows pushed out and STOP . . let go and release . . elbows out and away and STOP . . let go and release and feel the relaxation . . . push your fingers and thumbs as far away from you and from each other as possible, STOP . . let go and release, letting your fingers, arms and shoulders relax . . fingers and thumbs pushed away and apart and STOP . . let go and release . . fingers and thumbs pushed away and apart and STOP . . let go and release . . . push your body into the floor or chair and STOP . . let go and release allowing the floor or chair to support you . . push into the floor or chair and STOP . . let go and release . . . push your legs apart and hold the position and STOP . . let go and release to a more comfortable position, maintaining relaxation . . push legs apart and STOP . . let go and release . . . push your feet away from you with your toes pointed and STOP . . let go and release and feel your legs maintaining the relaxation of the muscles at the front of the legs . . push feet and toes away and STOP . . let go and release . . push feet and toes away and STOP . . let go and release . . . now let your whole body relax . . . let go . . . release tensions . . . . relaxed . . . . letting go, more and more relaxed (one minute silence) more and more relaxed (two minutes silence) relaxed . . . . move your fingers and toes, stretch and when you are ready gently and slowly get up, maintaining the relaxation.'

Heat

A lot of nurses quote common methods of relaxation which involve heat: sunbathing and having a hot bath are most commonly mentioned, although saunas, Turkish baths and jacuzzis are gaining popularity.

Saunas are becoming widely available in Britain and many local authority sports centres now offer them as part of their range of facilities. A sauna is a wood-lined room with a heater which creates a hot, dry atmosphere. Sitting or lying in the room for short periods (up to ten minutes) alternating with cool showers or immersion in a cool swimming pool, seems to have a relaxing effect. There is physiological stress involved in coping with atmospheric temperatures of 75 to 100 degrees centigrade, even for short periods, therefore saunas are only suitable for people with a clean bill of health. Although in some people there is a slight reduction in blood pressure following a sauna, in a few cases there is some increase.

Turkish or steam baths have a similar effect, but involve a high level of humidity as well as heat. Jacuzzi or whirlpool baths normally have water at approximately blood heat, and have underwater jets which have a massaging effect on the body. They are common in health clubs and gymnasiums though not many nurses frequent these because membership is expensive.

If the more exotic heat methods of relaxation are out of your reach financially or time-wise, the relaxing effect of hot baths can be enhanced. You need to allow yourself time to relax, rather than just treating the bath as a functional event. Make sure no one else will disturb you for half an hour to one hour. Use something to rest the back of the head, a rolled towel or a bath pillow, and take the time to do nothing. You could use some relaxation or meditation techniques if your mind continues to race. After the bath, take your time, dry yourself carefully, and treat yourself to some body lotion or 'splash-on' cologne.

Self-massage

Massaging oneself is a common and natural relaxation method: rubbing a tense forehead, neck or back, washing yourself without a flannel, putting on sun oil, face cream, body lotion or body cologne are common methods of self-massage (5). You can learn specific techniques of self-massage, such as the Chinese method 'Do-In' (6), but just paying attention to how you already touch yourself is a good starting point.

If you find yourself treating your body just as a machine that needs cleaning and oiling, this might tell you something about how little you value yourself or how cut off you are from your physical self. If your washing, drying and oiling is automatic with your mind on something else, or on getting the task over and done with, you are denying yourself an important method of relaxation. You need to be aware of your body and how you treat it in order to have any control over its tensions and relaxations. If all this discussion about touching yourself makes you recoil, or reject it as self-indulgent or even a bit 'kinky', then look at it in another way.

Consider how nurses touch their patients, perhaps even ask your patients — 'What do you notice about the way different nurses touch you when they're caring for you?' If you have been a patient yourself, think back and compare the types of touch you experienced. Patients who can put their feelings into words about this issue can teach nurses a lot. For instance: 'I was feeling pretty groggy after my op, and I needed help with washing. There were two nurses who helped me during those few days and they were as different as chalk and cheese. The first one just touched me as if I was a lump of meat. I felt kind of, well, dirty, as if she was saying "you're dirty and I'm jolly well going to get you clean". She was trying to be nice though, kept chattering away and asking me lots of questions. Though it smacked a bit of "talk to patient" on her list of things to do. I felt exhausted when she'd finished. The second day the other nurse didn't say much, which was fine because I didn't feel like talking, but when she moved me or washed or dried me, I just got this feeling that she cared. I can't say exactly how, it's as though she was saying "I know you're feeling rotten, I care about you and want to make you feel more comfortable". It's not as though she was any slower, in fact it was all done quite quickly, but she didn't seem to rush. I felt much more relaxed afterwards and even got some sleep, even though it was daytime.'

If a nurse cannot touch herself with care, attention and respect then how can she touch her patients this way? Learning self-massage is one way of becoming more aware of touch and being able to use it more positively in communicating with patients.

The most important feature to remember is similar to the

meditation technique of 'noticing'. While you are washing or oiling your skin, pay attention to or notice:

- How your hands feel, the sensation they are picking up from touching the skin.
- How the part of the body being touched feels, the sensation received from the touch of your hands.
- How your hands and the part being massaged look — the shapes, colours, textures, without judging or criticising (notice and put aside negative thoughts about the lumps and blotches).

Receiving a massage

Friends or colleagues may be willing to give you a massage if you ask. Professional massages are sometimes available at sports centres. Freelance bona fide professional masseuses will sometimes visit your home but usually only on personal recommendation.

Whether the massage is professional or informal, it is important to try to overcome barriers to allowing oneself to enjoy receiving a massage, such as embarrassment or difficulty in changing from being a habitual 'giver'. Perhaps run through a physical relaxation routine. Trust your body to the other person, allowing them to lift your head or limbs without your help at all. Just accept the massage. There is no need to give verbal feedback to make the giver feel good. The masseuse will be able to tell from your state of relaxation that you are appreciating what she is doing. However, do say what you want, e.g. more pressure, or less oil or movements in a different direction etc.

Massaging someone else

It can be very relaxing for you to give someone else a massage if you approach it in the right way (7).

Who to massage?

When you are putting sun oil on a friend or cream on a patient, or rubbing a colleague's sore shoulders, you are massaging, so you might as well make it a relaxing rather than a clinical experience for both of you. You need to feel comfortable about touching that particular person, that for instance she or he is not going to interpret the touch as a sexual come-on (unless that is what you want). Sadly, quite a lot of Western people can only allow touch in a sexual context, which causes problems when the need to touch and be touched leads to unwelcome or inappropriate sexual activity.

Positioning and relaxing yourself

Both of you need to be in a comfortable position. If you are uncomfortable, you will be tense and neither of you will get the benefit of the massage. For instance, you might be massaging a colleague's shoulders and neck (excellent for headaches) with the colleague sitting upright on a chair. You need to stand directly and closely behind, with your feet comfortably apart, each of them taking equal weight. A mini-relaxation exercise may help you to prepare yourself, in addition to shaking tension out of your hands. When you are ready to start, touch the person gradually and gently when you first make contact. Being grabbed suddenly is anything but relaxing. Find out about which spots to avoid and which the receiver particularly wants massaged.

Massage movements

There are many techniques which can be learned from various schools of massage, but sticking to some basic points will make you proficient at relaxation massage without having to do extensive training or study.
1. You are aiming to massage skin, muscle and tendons and not bone, therefore avoid putting pressure on bony points of the body. It will cause pain. For instance, when massaging shoulders and neck avoid pressing on the cervical spine, but press rather on the muscles on either side of the bony prominences.
2. You can use stroking movements along the muscles, circular movements or chopping percussion of the muscles. Whatever the movements, try to ensure that any effort which you put into using the fingers and thumbs comes from leaning your body forward. Digging in your fingers and thumbs with only the pressure of your arms behind them will be tiring for you and will feel tense to the person receiving the massage. For instance, if you are massaging shoulders, rock forward from your feet when putting pressure through your hands.

3. Pay attention to your own hands, the place you are massaging and the total level of relaxation or tension of the person you are massaging. You will notice from their body language if they are uncomfortable with what you are doing.

4. Keep quiet if possible, apart from checking verbally about amount of pressure if you are not sure what she wants. Not talking helps you both to pay attention to the relaxing effect on both of you.

5. Give some warning when you are about to stop, perhaps by holding your hand still on the area massaged for a while. Don't just suddenly stop and take your hands away, this can be off-putting and a bit of a shock to someone who is well relaxed after your efforts.

Face massage

The receiver lies flat on her back on the floor; the giver sits or kneels at the head end. Face cream could be used but this is not usually necessary. The direction of movement is as in the diagram, using thumbs and/or balls of fingers. In addition, you could define circles on the cheeks (gently) and on the temples (firmly). Do not press on eye balls, but go gently around the sockets. You could go on to massage the scalp using the same kneading movements a hairdresser uses when washing your hair.

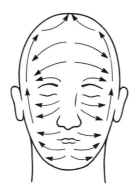

Fig. 3.2   *Directions of strokes in facial massage.*

Foot massage

The massage strokes need to be firm to avoid ticklishness, and often oil or cream is necessary. One specialist therapeutic massage, reflexology, is devoted to foot massage and claims to influence the health of other parts of the body by the massage of particular pressure points on the foot. Whether it fulfils all the specific therapeutic claims is a moot point, but it is certainly pleasant and very relaxing both to give and receive.

Body massage

It is socially acceptable to rub suntan oil on a friend's body or to massage a patient's pressure points. You can make this into a relaxation massage session or even do the body massage for its own sake.

Supporting surface: it is preferable for the receiver to be on a hard surface; an ordinary mattress has too much 'give' for firm body

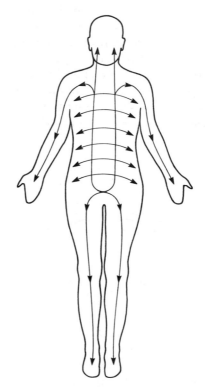

Fig. 3.3   *Directions of strokes for body massage.*

massage strokes to be comfortable. A massage table is the ideal, but the floor is satisfactory.

Clothes: the receiver should decide how much clothing she wants to discard. Obviously, this depends on which part of the body is being massaged: the head and neck and the feet do not require extensive stripping. A back or trunk massage is more effective without clothes but can be done when the receiver is fully clothed.

Oil: the massage can be given with or without oil. Almost any oil will do: the cheapest is odourless vegetable oil; alternatively use baby oil, to which perfumes can be added. Talcum powder or cream could be used. Oil or cream your hands first — never pour it directly on to the body as this can be disconcerting to the receiver. Remember that oil on the skin will reduce the temperature of the skin so make extra sure that your receiver is warm. Keep a sheet or towel near at hand.

Direction of stroke: you can use either the whole hand or just the thumbs or just the fingers to stroke mainly in a direction which radiates out from the centre of the body (the umbilicus at the front and the sacrum at the back), avoiding the genitals. Alternatively, the receiver may want strokes down the spine sometimes.

Use your body to apply pressure via your hands. Move from your pelvis for some of the larger movements so that you do not strain yourself. If you breathe and move correctly, there is no reason why you should ever be exhausted after giving body massage.

Yoga

Yoga is a system of physical, mental and spiritual exercises which originated in India and was intended to enable the person who practises it to move towards spiritual enlightenment (8). Many people in the West also practise yoga to that end, but the most common emphasis is on the physical exercise it provides. Committed adherents of the full system of yoga criticise this Western selectivity, maintaining it is indicative of a seriously unhealthy split between soul and body and can lead to psychological problems. Whether people brought up in a Western culture, with their unhealthy psychological and spiritual values, are better or worse off using yoga in their own way is difficult to ascertain from the standpoint of the purist.

Nevertheless, many nurses (and their patients) have success-fully taken up the physical exercises of yoga as a means towards physical well-being. They find this result satisfying and are con-tent with it. Some have gone on to discover that taking care of their bodies in this way gave them a desire to progress in a spiritual direction.

If you are interested in taking up yoga, you need to be very clear about your intentions and find a teacher whose approach corres-ponds or is compatible with yours. Otherwise you may be put off yoga: a pragmatist might find the spiritual exercises so much mumbo-jumbo, whereas a more spiritually-minded person might find that a purely physical approach is too limited.

As far as physical relaxation is concerned, hatha yoga exercises seem to be organised extensions of the natural desire to stretch to relieve physical tension. In learning a system of exercises, the emphasis is not on achievement of postures, but on gentle, slow movement towards certain positions, allowing time for the muscles and ligaments to stretch, and with regulated breathing. The physical control you can gain through practising hatha yoga helps you to relax your muscles, regain balance and poise and be more economical in your movements in daily life.

The Sun Salutations are an example of a sequence of yoga exercises, traditionally carried out in the morning as the sun rises, by the banks of the Ganges. Even if your facilities offer nothing more exotic than your bedroom floor, and there is nothing to salute but mist and clouds, they can be a relaxing way to start the day by gently stretching your spine. Figure 3.4 shows the positions: ignore the breathing sequence until you have practised each position and can remember their order.

Start by standing upright with the palms of your hands together, feet a little apart. Pay attention to your posture: balance yourself, with your spine correctly aligned, using the minimum amount of tension to keep yourself upright. Lift your arms slowly over your head, palms forward, and stretch gently backwards as far as you can comfortably manage, keeping your legs straight. Gently and slowly stretch forward and down until your fingers are as near to your toes as you can manage. Bending your knees, put your hands on the floor on either side of your feet. Then stretch your left leg out behind you, and your head up and back as far as you can without it hurting. Bring your right leg back and straighten your body as though you are about to do press-ups.

Fig. 3.4 *Sun Salutations: a sequence of yoga exercises.*

Move back into a foetal position with your hands still in front of you. Move your head in a curve forward, upwards and back, supporting yourself on your hands again. Bring your bottom up and your head down so your body makes an inverted V shape. Move your head in a curve forward, upwards and back, while bringing your left foot up between your hands. Bring your right foot up to your hands and your head down so that you are back in the touching-your-toes position. Stretch your arms up and back into the second position of the series, then to the first position, standing with palms together. Make the exercises a gentle, slow, continuously flowing movement with the breathing synchronised. Repeat the routine three or more times.

Biofeedback

Many aspects of bodily functions which are normally considered to be involuntary can be brought under voluntary control (9). Some of these skills can be learned with the help of the relevant type of biofeedback machine. One type of biofeedback machine can help you to learn to relax. Galvanised skin response varies according to the state of arousal of the autonomic system and is monitored via electrodes strapped to the tips of two fingers. If tension increases, the pitch of the noise emitted by the machine rises; as you relax the pitch lowers. This gives quick feedback about the level of tension and can help you to learn to relax by

giving encouragement when the success of the relaxation techniques can be heard.

The machines are fairly expensive but many clinical psychology departments use them and may be willing to lend you one or to allow you to try it on the premises. Other biofeedback machines monitor skin temperatures, alpha and theta brain waves, myoelectric activity of specific muscles, blood pressure and pulse rate, all of which can come under some degree of conscious control.

Relaxation and driving

Reducing unnecessary tension while driving will make journeys less tiring. The following suggestions, adapted from a 'Relaxation for Living' pamphlet, might be useful in this respect (10).

Try to break habits of rushing: allow plenty of time for the journey, and look at maps or street plans before you start out. Develop a slow ritual when getting into the car; sit well back in the seat, put on the safety belt, check mirrors, check that the gear stick is in neutral. Start and move off gently. While driving, minimise the effort by holding the steering wheel lightly, checking your head is balanced and face relaxed with loose jaw. When you are stuck in a traffic jam or at lights, treat it as a 'gift of time'. Let your hands drop and do a mini-relaxation exercise. Make getting out of your car a slow ritual. Never use a relaxation tape in a car as it can be dangerous; it might have a hypnotic effect and send you to sleep.

Pets

Pets can provide the relaxing emotional and physical contact which is often lacking in relationships between human beings in the British culture. It is socially acceptable to stroke and cuddle pets to your heart's content and most people find this relaxing. Studies of physiological reactions to stroking a pet show a similar relaxation effect to massage between human beings. Dogs and cats seem to tune in to the emotional state of humans remarkably accurately and can be a great comfort at times of distress since they often have the courage to take the initiative to make contact. They are excellent listeners, they do not interrupt and will forgive humans for outbursts of abuse since they seem to understand the need for emotional release. Dogs play wonderful games with owners to provide socially acceptable ways of having a good yell: they can be gloriously disobedient until they realise the owner has had a sufficiently therapeutic dose of shouting. Cats can create a peaceful atmosphere by their very presence: their relaxed elegant movements give them powerful charisma.

So pets can not only provide useful ways of dealing with stress, but can teach human beings a lot about relaxation and emotional support.

Sleep and relaxation

During the relaxation exercises suggested so far in this chapter, the intention is not that you should go to sleep but that you remain awake and alert. Some of the scripts included instructions to remind you in case you became drowsy. The purpose behind this is to help you build the skills of conscious relaxation, so that you can easily relax whenever you want while you are awake. If, however, you have a sleep deficit then it will probably do you good to have a few minutes of sleep during the exercises sometimes, but you lose the skills-building effect.

People who regularly use deep relaxation and meditation often find that they need less sleep. They become less tense during the day and find they are less wound up at night. The quality of their sleep is improved so they need less of it. So nurses who think they cannot find the time to do relaxation exercises may be missing a golden opportunity to make *more* time available for themselves. Twenty minutes a day of deep relaxation is likely after a while to mean you need forty minutes less sleep at night: twenty minutes a day, that is over two hours per week — more time to fit in something else which will help you cope with stress, such as more exercise or a new hobby.

Insomnia

The key to insomnia may lie in lack of skill in relaxation during the day. You cannot expect the body/mind to switch from high to low revs like a machine. So learning relaxation or meditation and applying it during the day will enable you to sleep better at night. Some other ways of dealing with insomnia which nurses have found helpful include the following:

1. Taking more exercise during the day makes the body need the sleep more and helps the mind to calm down. Leaving the exercise until last thing at night can, however, have the opposite effect.

2. Gradually winding down before the time to go to sleep: sometimes nurses work themselves up rather than down before bedtime, whizzing around finishing last-minute tasks, such as washing or ironing clothes to wear the next day. Instead, try to plan your evening (or morning if you are on night duty) so that essential things get done well before you go to bed and you have time to do something quiet like reading a book, listening to relaxing music or doing relaxation exercises. Late night television helps some people to relax but has the opposite effect on others (quite a lot of late night programmes include the violence or suspense which cannot be portrayed earlier in the evening when children may be viewing). If you are in the latter category and are a TV addict, you need to find a way of keeping away from it for an hour or two before you go to sleep.

3. Getting into a routine which deals with all the practical aspects such as the heating, lights, ventilation, bed-clothes, prevents your suddenly realising, just on the point of sleep, that you have left the heating on, etc.

4. A late night drink such as milk, herb tea or a small nightcap helps some. The calcium in milk is said to be a muscle relaxant, but the traditional milky cocoa actually contains caffeine and can be counterproductive for some people. Other caffeinated drinks such as coffee, tea or cola can keep some people awake and so must be avoided for at least four hours before bedtime. Some health food shops sell specially blended herb teas to aid sleep. They contain combinations of such herbs as lavender, chamomile, fennel, valerian, aniseed, thyme, woodruff, lime and others. Alcohol in small quantities is a muscle relaxant but too much can make you dehydrated and have frequency of micturition, so disturbing your sleep.

5. Occasionally hypnotics or tranquillisers can help to break wakeful patterns but, as you will be aware, there are risks of addiction even with the benzodiazepines which were formerly thought to be physically non-addictive.

6. Using relaxation or meditation during wakeful periods in the night can be helpful.

Making a night tape

The main aim of such a tape is to help you make good use of your time when you have insomnia. A secondary aim is to help you to go to sleep but you have not failed if it does not always work. Deep relaxation and meditation are much better for you than fitful sleep.

Use the same preparations for making a relaxation tape. This script adds up to about three-quarters of an hour (depending on how quickly it is read) so you need at least a 90-minute tape in order to get it all on to one side. It incorporates sections of some of the relaxation and meditation tapes; copy these sections and have them laid out in the correct order so that there is no distracting paper rustling on the recording. Each comma represents a pause of about two seconds and each full stop five seconds.

In contrast to an ordinary relaxation tape, the tone of voice can progress towards a deep, slow, hypnotic tone. Start off with a relaxed, fairly matter-of-fact tone which is slower than normal speech, then allow the voice to become gradually deeper and slower throughout the script. Make sure you are sitting upright; otherwise you may talk yourself to sleep and only your snores will be recorded!

Use a player which does not make a noisy click at the end of the tape because it could disturb your state of relaxation or wake you if you have fallen asleep.

Relaxation script no. 5. (some sections are adapted from a tape by Matthew Manning (11):

'The main aim of this tape is to help you to make the best use of your time while you are awake, it might help you to get to sleep but don't worry if it doesn't, deep relaxation and meditation are much better for you than fitful sleep, make sure everything is right for you before you settle down, the light, window, amount of bedclothes and so on . when you are ready, settle into a comfortable position . keep your eyes open now for a moment, pick out a spot on the wall or on the ceiling or anywere in the room and gently focus on it . I'm going to count backwards from number 10 to number 1 . slowly blink your eyes on each number, simply close and then open your eyes as you hear me say each number, 10, 9, 8, 7,,6,,5,, 4 . 3 . 2 . 1 . close your eyes now, just leave them closed . that was to relax your eyelids . there is probably a feeling of relaxation in your eyelids now, perhaps a comfortable tired feeling or just a pleasantly heavy sensation . whatever the feeling is in your eyelids just allow it to multiply, magnify and become greater . allow your eyelids to become completely and pleasantly relaxed . just take your time to completely and pleasantly relax your eyelids . relax the muscles of your eyelids to the point where they just will not work, where they feel so heavy and so tired that you don't even want to open them . . . . . and now just let the relaxation that is in your eyelids flow right through your entire body . starting to do the same thing with your whole body, the same thing that you did with your eyelids, completely and pleasantly relaxing your entire body . just imagine yourself slowing down a little bit, imagine yourself slowing down a little bit more and a little bit more . imagine all the muscles in your face, your neck, your shoulders and chest, the muscles of your arms and hands, your stomach, your thighs, your legs and your feet all just letting go and relaxing, your whole body slowing right down, your breathing slowing down and becoming deeper . allow your breathing to happen slowly . imagine that as you breathe in you are breathing in peace and tranquility . each time you breathe in let your lungs fill with a sense of calmness and peace, and let that feeling flow to every part of your body . and each time you breathe out imagine that you are breathing out all tension . releasing it from your body . let go of any stress and anxiety . each time you breathe in you can breathe in the feeling of quietness and let it fill your lungs with a sense of peace, and let that feeling flow throughout your entire body . . your body is becoming calm and quiet, calm and quiet and still, so still, so peaceful . and very soon you are going to find a pleasant, comfortable, heavy sensation sweeping over your body . just welcome this feeling and enjoy it as it comes . (excerpt from Relaxation script no. 1 here, from "I'm going to count down" to "more and more relaxed . . . . peaceful" N.B. substitute "bed" for "floor or chair") . now you're going to concentrate on your face and hands . (excerpt from Relaxation script no. 2 here, from "let the back of your head relax" to "now your whole body is totally relaxed") . you are now relaxed in mind and body, and to help you enter an even deeper and healthier level of mind I'd like you to imagine yourself in a place which to you represents an ideal place of relaxation, perhaps a mountain top, perhaps the seashore or a woodland, just enjoy it mentally for a couple of minutes and I will stop talking to you so that you may just enjoy it, and when I begin

speaking to you again my voice will not disturb you . going deeper
and deeper . . . . relax now, take a deep breath and go
deeper, deeper and more relaxed with every breath you take, more
at ease, more in perfect harmony with every breath that you take
. . . imagine now a gentle, healing light within you, feel it as it
spreads softly through your entire being, bathing every muscle,
every cell in soft, glowing, healing, energy . this healing light is
alive within you, feel its warmth . its shining radiance, quiet,
gentle and timeless, and let it flow in gently spreading waves to
every part of your body . . let it grow deeper, stronger and
warmer, bringing deep relaxation, recuperation and peace, and
very soon you will probably find yourself drifting off into sleep .
into sleep . imagine yourself now free of anxiety, totally relaxed,
asleep, drifting into sleep, no longer bothered by anything . . even
now healing energy is spreading through your body, this healing
glow is growing warmer and stronger, and your body is growing
healthier, more energetic, stronger and stronger . . and as you
sleep or relax be at peace . . . .'

Possible pitfalls in using relaxation to prevent or cope with stress

Mistakes will be made in developing any skill. Indeed, part of the
process of learning that skill involves noticing mistakes and learning from them. Possible mistakes outlined here are related to lack
of practice, taking certain aspects to the extreme, and negative
attitudes to emotions. They are mentioned to help you notice and
correct them as they happen.

1. *Lack of commitment:* building any skill needs practice and you
need to commit yourself to regular times to practise relaxation.
You will not develop your skills very much by doing each of the
exercises in this chapter once, then congratulating yourself that
you have 'done' relaxation and rushing on to something else.
Alternatively, trying a few exercises, finding they do not 'work'
and rejecting relaxation techniques out of hand is taking an
unrealistic approach.

2. *Over-dependence:* it is possible to become over-dependent on
something or someone who has become strongly linked in your
mind with your ability to relax or sleep. For instance, if you attend
classes without doing the relaxation practice between sessions,

you may become dependent on the teacher or the group atmosphere and find that at the end of the course you are back to square one. Likewise you could become so dependent on a relaxation tape that when the tape or the tape player breaks, or you forget to take it with you when you go away from home, you are unable to relax or sleep without it. Sometimes people can also become dependent on biofeedback machines, especially if the belief that the machine is making you relax takes hold. You can avoid dependence by practising relaxation without any aids at all, on your own.

3. *Passivity:* over-reliance on passive methods such as relaxation may lead you to increasing passivity in your life as a whole. You may allow people to pile on the stress without setting limits. You may make no effort to contribute towards the changes you would like to see in the organisation, community or society in which you live. You may become too 'laid back' or *laissez-faire*. However, you can prevent or correct this by consciously becoming more assertive and playing a part, however small, in democratic processes open to you.

4. *Going to sleep in the car:* relaxation tapes should never be used in a moving car because the driver may become dangerously drowsy.

5. *Hyperventilation:* people who breathe rapidly and shallowly from the chest may learn to breathe more deeply using the diaphragm, but may make the mistake of continuing to breathe quickly. You can avoid this by ensuring that all deep breathing exercises are carried out very slowly, and that your breathing returns to normal after only a few deep breaths. If you have made the mistake of over-oxygenating your blood, with symptoms such as tingling hands and feet, and light headedness, you can deal with it by physical exercise such as shaking the limbs, or by breathing in and out of a bag until the symptoms go.

6. *Making an inflexible ritual out of relaxation practice:* while regular practice sessions are desirable and necessary to learn deep relaxation skills, forcing yourself to do it when something else would be more appropriate, or building your whole life around the practice schedule, can be counterproductive. You need to strike a balance between making time for yourself to develop the skills, and meeting the other needs you have in your life.

7. *Trying too hard to succeed or win:* you might find yourself trying to achieve some hypothetical state of total relaxation and berate yourself for falling short of it. You need to remember that relaxation training is about becoming more relaxed than you were, and that total relaxation is probably impossible except in a deep coma. When trying to retrain yourself out of poor posture habits, you might find yourself overcompensating and becoming tense in the opposite way. You may find yourself competing to become, or to appear to become, more relaxed than other people. To correct this you need to remind yourself that relaxation is about *not doing*, about allowing natural relaxation to occur, at your own pace.

8. *Ammunition for put-downs:* awareness of tension in yourself or others can be used as ammunition for put-downs. You may feed your own negative self-image by judging your tensions negatively and blaming yourself for not being the perfect person who can deal with anything in a totally relaxed manner. Alternatively, you could undermine other people's confidence, hitting below the belt, by pointing out their tensions to them. These pitfalls may be avoided by accepting the existence of tension in a matter-of-fact way, and by not giving feedback to other people about their tensions unless it is requested. You might also be too self-critical of yourself or others with regard to the pitfalls mentioned in this section. It is very likely that someone learning relaxation will make mistakes; it is better to accept and learn from the mistakes than to agonise about having made them.

9. *Imposing your idiosyncratic methods on other people:* it is possible that excitement and delight at discovering something that works for you can bring on an attack of messianic zeal. You may find yourself trying to bulldoze friends, family and patients into learning relaxation, or forgetting that people may find different relaxation methods relaxing. You may need to remember that your particular relaxation methods may not be appropriate for everyone else. For instance, avoid playing 'relaxing' music or sounds unless you know that the people listening definitely find them relaxing.

10. *Emotional repression:* it is possible to become so adept at concentrating your mind on physical relaxation routines that they become repeatedly over-used as a means of hiding and escaping from emotions. You may become adept not only at hiding emo-

tions from yourself, but at hiding them from other people by presenting a blank, unresponsive, permanently relaxed appearance. Other people will find it difficult to relate to you as a human being, feeling as distant from you as if they were talking with a robot, a china doll or a wall of cotton wool. This can be dealt with by allowing ways of releasing emotions, and by allowing yourself to feel whatever emotions are happening for you and to react to them to some extent when relating to other people.

11. *Negative attitudes about one's own emotions:* physical tension can have the effect of repressing emotions, so when you physically relax you might sometimes find yourself crying or shaking. The catharsis in itself is not harmful, in fact you will feel better for it if you can accept it as natural. The pitfalls lie, first in worrying about or being ashamed of this natural phenomenon and, second, in going it alone — if you have a lot of bottled-up emotions rushing to the surface at once this can feel frightening. Do not allow embarrassment or shame to make you hesitate to seek and accept some help from someone who is used to dealing with emotions, perhaps a counsellor or a co-counselling teacher.

References and further reading

1. Laban. R., Lawrence F.C. (1974). *Effort*. London: Mac-Donald and Evans.
2. Gelb M. (1981). *Body Learning*. London: Aurum Press.
3. Rosa K. (1976). *You and A.T. – Autogenic Training*. Dutton.
4. Mitchell L. (1977). *Simple Relaxation*. London: John Murray.
5. Struna M., Church C. (1984). *Self Massage*. London: Hutchinson.
6. Delangre J. (1980). *Do-In (Books 1 and 2)*. Happiness Press. (Book 2 is the more practical.)
7. Downing G. (1974). *The Massage Book*. Harmondsworth: Penguin.
8. Devi I. (1972). *Yoga for You*. Wellingborough: Thorsons.
9. Karlins M., Andrews L. M. (1973). *Biofeedback*. Garnstone Press.
10. Lloyd A. (1979). *Drive and Survive*. Relaxation for Living (see below). See also: Madders J. (1979). *Stress and Relaxation*. London: Martin Dunitz.
11. Manning M. *Fighting Insomnia* (tape). Matthew Manning Centre, Bury St. Edmunds, Suffolk.

Where to learn more about relaxation

Health centres: some health centres have community nurses who run relaxation classes for patients registered there.

Adult education institutes: some offer classes in relaxation, yoga, stress management, or the Health Education Council sponsored 'Look After Yourself' classes, which include relaxation.

Extra-mural departments of universities and polytechnics sometimes offer classes as part of their programmes of short courses open to the public.

Getting something started yourself: if your local health centre, adult education institute, university or polytechnic do not have courses, you could try putting in a request. They may not realise that the demand is there. Alternatively, you could get a group of people together and bring in a relaxation teacher privately.

Relaxation for Living is a registered charity which trains relaxation teachers and provides information on relaxation. Write, sending a stamped addressed envelope to Dunesk, 29 Burwood Park Road, Walton-on-Thames, Surrey KT12 5LH for a list of their teachers. You can then contact the one nearest to you for details of local classes. Relaxation for Living also sells correspondence courses in relaxation.

The Centre for Autogenic Training provides in-depth relaxation training. It is not cheap. Write for details to Dr. Malcolm Carruthers, Centre for Autogenic Training, 101 Harley Street, London W1.

The Yoga for Health Foundation offers residential courses in hatha yoga, including special courses for the handicapped. Its address is Ickwell Bury, Northill, Nr. Biggleswade, Bedfordshire.

The Wheel of Yoga co-ordinates the training of many yoga teachers and can give information about courses. Its address is Acacia House, Centre Avenue, Acton Vale, London W3 7JX.

4

Meditation

Mental 'chatter' and meditation as a natural skill

Nurses are responsive to the needs and demands of other people. Often these demands come together or in quick succession, causing interruptions in whatever task or train of thought is in progress at the time. Many nurses report that they seldom have the chance to complete a task or a period of concentration without being interrupted. This results in the mind being in a constant state of agitation, 'grasshopping' between searching through memories of the recent past to assess what has not been completed, and planning and replanning what needs to be done in the near future. This mental preoccupation with the past and future makes it increasingly difficult to concentrate on the present: the mind races in both directions, like a tape recorder with the 'fast forward' and 'fast rewind' buttons fighting to take control, while the 'play' button is disconnected.

This state of mind may be necessary during busy periods but, as in the physical busy-ness of the 'busy syndrome', it becomes a habit. Nurses often find they cannot switch off and the mind continues to race during quieter periods at work and when they are supposed to be resting. Concentration on a book, a conversation or a TV programme becomes difficult, and although we may appear to be reading, listening or watching, little or nothing has been taken in. People close to us may complain about our mental preoccupations, that we are just not fully present with them; they may go elsewhere for companionship. The mind is in over-drive and we have forgotten how to change down into a lower gear.

Forgotten is the operative word here; every human being has had the skill of meditation but in the Western culture, particularly in the nursing culture, it is easily forgotten. Children meditate naturally, until they are conditioned out of it by being overstimulated with objects jangling in front of them each time they stare into space, or by being told off for doing nothing or daydreaming. In nursing, the old work ethic still holds strong, and sitting or standing still, even for a few moments, is likely to lead to an accusation of laziness. However, in spite of that conditioning, the chances are that you do still meditate naturally to some degree.

Which of the following have you found yourself pausing to notice and savour recently?

Looking: watching clouds, a candle flame, flames in a fireplace, children playing or asleep, a cat, a favourite picture, someone you care about, flowers, plants.

Hearing: listening to music, the sounds of children playing happily, birdsong, sea breaking on the shore, a cat purring.

Smelling and tasting: the smell of fresh air after leaving a stuffy building, sea or country air, flowers, new-mown grass, a favourite perfume or after-shave, the skin smell of someone you love, food cooking, fresh fruit, the taste of favourite foods, a relaxing drink.

Touching: the texture of a pet's fur, a velvet garment or cushion, a piece of fruit, someone's skin or hair, grass under bare feet.

Mental rhythms: repetitive thoughts, such as prayers, positive statements, comforting words, tunes, poems.

Mentally picturing: daydreams about pleasant places, such as your own special bolt-hole, where you go on holiday, an imaginary peaceful scene, memories of pleasant experiences, fantasies about good things which you'd like to happen to you.

All these are natural methods of meditation and your skill in using them at will can be enhanced by training and practice in meditation.

It may be possible that you have the ability to switch off at will and put yourself into a state of deep peace without consciously focussing your mind on anything in particular. If this is the case you probably do not need to read the sections on meditation methods; you have retained the ultimate meditation skill which other people may take years of practice to relearn.

Definition

Meditation is a process of contemplation which results in an altered state of consciousness, a state of mind and body higher than that experienced most of the time in our ordinary state. Joseph Chilton Pearce describes meditation as 'a fixed goal and highly flexible plan for getting to that goal. The goal is realisation of one's inner self, which means one's own unique unity with the creative process' (1).

This journey to the centre of the self can be particularly useful for nurses as a means of resting and calming the mind, improving concentration and attention spans, gaining stronger acceptance of yourself, increasing creative thinking, and possibly opening the doors to levels of human potential which have been closed by cultural conditioning, such as healing abilities and psychic and spiritual awareness. We often speak of feeling 'frayed at the edges' as though we have lost a sense of our own boundaries. Meditation is a way of drawing in to yourself and finding your true centre.

You can learn some basic techniques of meditation by using some of the exercises in this chapter. They are described as scripts, which can be used to make tape recordings, to have read to you, or just to give you the general idea of how to do the exercise on your own. Alternatively, meditation can be learned at special classes, which may be secular or linked with religious groups such as branches of Hinduism, Buddhism, Islam, Judaism or Christianity. It may also be included in yoga and relaxation courses. If you want to take your meditation beyond basic mind-calming, self-awareness and creative thinking skills, it is advisable to have the regular guidance of someone who is experienced in meditation and skilled at teaching it. Some of the deeper meditation experiences may seem rather peculiar and possibly frightening without the support of someone you can trust.

Using biofeedback

There are some biofeedback machines on the market which are selective electroencephalograph machines; via electrodes placed on the head, they pick up certain brain waves which are known to increase in frequency during meditation, and they translate the reading into a sound. Alpha waves increase as the mind calms, and theta waves as the meditator uses creative fantasy. The tone of the sound produced indicates the relative number of either alpha or theta waves, according to the type of machine. The aim of the meditator is to make the tone of the sound become lower and lower as more meditative brain waves are produced.

The machines are very expensive, but you may be able to borrow one if you attend meditation classes at a centre which uses them in training.

on upright chair

on upholstered
chair or sofa

legs crossed

legs akimbo, not
actually crossed

on a 'back' chair

sitting on heels

on a meditation
stool

lying down (beware
of going to sleep)

Fig. 4.1   *Positions for meditation.*

Positions for meditation

If possible it is important to be upright for meditation, so as to be neither uncomfortable nor so comfortable that sleep takes over. You can sit in a chair, preferably one without arms so that your hands do not rest on the arms of the chair pushing your shoulders up. You need to have the base of your spine as far back in the chair as possible, with both feet on the ground and hands in your lap or on your thighs. Try not to sink back into a soft chair, but stay upright. You may prefer to sit cross-legged or on your heels, on the floor or on a bed or sofa. Experiment with cushions to find a comfortable angle at which to sit. You can buy meditation stools, which are solid wooden pods; you kneel and sit backwards as though to sit on your heels, with the seat of the stool supporting your bottom and the leg of the stool between your calves. 'Back' chairs give a good position for meditation. Ensure that you are going to be warm enough while sitting still for the duration of the practice session, yet not so warm that you become sleepy. Avoid meditating just after a meal; this too will send you to sleep.

Some basic meditation techniques

Techniques of meditation are taught as ways of unlocking the mind's blocks towards self-realisation, but some experts in meditation abandon the techniques as they outlive their usefulness. There are some basic methods which are common to most of the schools of meditation. (See Table 4.1.)

Table 4.1 *Some basic meditation techniques.*

Focussed meditation:	internally focussed
	externally focussed
Noticing:	internal noticing
	external noticing
Fantasy:	structured fantasy
	free fantasy

Focussed meditation

This involves holding the attention of the mind on something specific and as the attention wanders, gently taking it back to the object of the focus, without forcing yourself to concentrate.

Externally focussed meditation is using something outside yourself to focus on, such as the sight, sounds, smells and textures mentioned in the list of natural meditation methods given earlier in the chapter. Formal meditation practice may include using: a candle flame, a flower, a picture, a treasured object, a religious symbol such as a Star of David or a cross, or a special circular picture of complex and intricate design called a mandala.

Internally focussed meditation involves using a mental image as the object of focus. This could be a static picture or scene (those involving water are commonly used, lakes seem to be associated in many people's minds with peace), or a word, a phrase or tune. A mantra is such a phrase. Commonly used mantras are 'love', 'peace' and, in the Hindu tradition, 'Om' and 'Om namah shivaya' (2). (These Hindu words mean approximately 'I honour my own spirituality', although the literal translation is a statement of reverence towards the god Shiva, the god of consciousness; Hindus know that this named god is merely a symbol of the inner spirituality of each one of us, rather than any external deity.) Sometimes a mantra has a tune and is sung or chanted. In some schools of meditation, such as Transcendental Meditation (3), each student is given their own mantra.

Religious traditions other than Hinduism also have their mantras, although that term may not be specifically used: for instance, the phrase 'God is Love' is used by meditators in a number of religions. Short repetitive prayers serve the same function.

If your aim in meditation is to relax and slow down the mind then almost any word or phrase will do as a mantra. Leon Chaitow quotes 'bananas' and 'coca-cola' as being as good as any! (4) It is the rhythm of repetition and having a point of focus which gives the mind a chance to slow down. Those with loftier aims for meditation might be affronted by such prosaic suggestions, but it could be argued that there is no reason why bananas and cokes cannot also open the door to cosmic consciousness!

The following are two scripts which can be used to practise externally and internally focussed meditation. They can be adapted and added to one of the relaxation scripts, or can be used on their own. As in the relaxation scripts, each full stop represents a pause of about five seconds, and each comma a pause of about two seconds.

Externally focussed meditation: arrange to have something beautiful or symbolically important to look at, such as a flame of a candle or a fire, a flower, an ornament, a picture or a religious symbol.

Meditation script no. 1:

'Find a comfortable position, sitting with your spine upright . imagine a golden thread is running through your spine from the tip of the coccyx up through the top of your head and you are suspended . your spine is lengthening without effort . your head is balanced on your neck with minimum effort . take a couple of slow deep breaths using your abdomen . . . . now let your eyes focus on your special object . notice the shape, contours, colours of the object . . gently focus your mind on the object . . . when your thoughts begin to stray, gently bring your attention back to the object . be gentle with yourself, forgive yourself for straying, just gently focus . . . gently focussing on the object . . . . focus . . . . . gently focussing (one minute silence) gently focussing (two minutes silence) gently focussing . . . the exercise is over; so take some time to reflect on what you noticed and experienced during those few minutes.'

Internally focussed meditation: meditation script no. 2:

'Find a comfortable position with your spine and head upright . . relax your body . . take a couple of slow deep breaths using your abdomen . . . . breathe normally . close your eyes gently and allow your mind to conjure up a scene or a word or a phrase or an object or a sound which is linked in your mind with peace . choose your mental image . when you have it, hold it gently still in your mind's eye . . gently focus on the image . . . when your mind wanders, gently bring your attention back to the image . forgive yourself for straying, just focus gently on the image . . . . gently focussing . . . . . gently focussing on the image (one minute silence) gently focussing (two minutes silence) gently focussing . . . the exercise is over, now take some time to reflect on what you noticed and experienced during that time.'

Noticing

Rather than narrowing the focus of the mind on to one thing, noticing is about expanding your awareness either outside or

inside yourself. External noticing involves allowing yourself to take in all the sights, sounds, smells, sensations and tastes that can pierce your consciousness. The skill lies in noticing these things as they happen, allowing them to happen without judging any of them. For instance, if you are noticing the view out of a window, rather than judging it as a dreary scene, you notice the shape and colour of the clouds, the way the rain drips off the building, the changing sound of the wind, the shape of the trees and the way they move with the wind and so on. When the nurse becomes skilled enough to turn this technique on at will, it can greatly enhance her powers of relaxed, perceptive observation and the ability to pick up what is important to attend to.

To use internal noticing you imagine yourself standing back from your mind and observing what it is doing. You allow whatever thoughts, feelings or images which come into your mind to happen without trying to get rid of them, judging them, doing anything with them or getting caught up in them. For instance, if you notice you are thinking about tonight's supper, rather than getting caught up in planning what to buy and prepare, you tell yourself 'I'm noticing I'm thinking about supper' and allow another thought to come into the mind, rather like clouds floating across the sky. You might forget about the meditation technique and get caught up in planning supper, then suddenly notice what you've done; just tell yourself 'I notice I forgot to use the technique, it's OK to forget'. If you notice that you are feeling agitated, rather than berating yourself for not being in some ideal state of peace, just tell yourself 'I notice I'm agitated; that's fine, it's alright to be agitated' and allow the next thought to come in.

Inner noticing as a meditation technique is a disciplined exercise in self-acceptance. It helps to undo the mental habits of straining to get it 'right' and helps you to learn to forgive yourself for not being perfect. Nurses have been observed to be hypercritical of themselves and each other, expecting superhuman standards of perfection which are impossible to reach. This meditation technique may therefore be of particular relevance to us.

The following scripts for practising noticing as a meditation technique include two exercises each for external and internal noticing. They can be read out to you or into a tape recorder, or can just give you the general idea of how to do the exercise. Each full stop represents a pause of about five seconds, two stops for ten seconds and so on. Each comma represents a short pause of about two seconds.

External noticing: meditation script no. 3:

'Find a comfortable position with your spine upright, using the minimum of effort to remain so . relax your body . . take a couple of slow, deep breaths using the abdomen . . . . breathe normally . look around you and notice the shapes, colours, stillness or movement of the things around you . describe without judging what you see, silently or out loud, by completing the sentence beginning "I notice ———" . . "I notice" . . . "I notice" . . . . "I notice" . . . . . keeping your eyes open, listen to the sounds and the silence around you, notice repetitions and changes in types of sound, volume, tone . . describe without judging, what you hear, silently or out loud, by completing sentences beginning with "I notice ———" . . "I notice" . . . "I notice" . . . . "I notice" . . . . . put your attention into what you are touching and notice the way the floor and chair feel, the way your thighs feel against your hands, the way your clothes and jewellery feel on your skin, the loose parts, the tight parts, notice the way the air feels against your skin, breezy or still, and describe without judging, what touch sensations you feel, by completing sentences beginning "I notice ———" . . "I notice" . . . "I notice" . . . . "I notice" . . . . . notice now any tastes and smells you experience and describe them, without judging, out loud or silently, completing sentences beginning "I notice ———" . . "I notice" . . . "I notice" . . . . "I notice" . . . . . now notice simultaneously sights and sounds, no need to use the sentences, just notice sights and sounds together . . . notice tastes/smells and touch simultaneously . . . sights and touch together . . . sights and tastes/smells simultaneously . . . sounds and touch together . . . sounds and tastes/smells . . . notice all at once, sights, sounds, touch, tastes, smells . . . notice . . . notice . . . . . notice . the exercise is over, take some time to reflect on your experience of this meditation practice session.'

Meditation script no. 4:

'In a comfortable sitting position, relax your body . with your spine upright and head balanced . relax . take a couple of slow, deep breaths, expanding your abdomen as you breathe in . . . . let your breathing become relaxed . with your eyes open, begin to notice what you experience, through your senses, from the environment . just accept what you notice as it is . avoid judging what you notice as good or bad, as whether you like it or not, just accept it as it is . . . notice and accept . . . . notice what's around you and accept . . . . . notice and accept (one minute silence) notice and accept (two minutes silence) notice and accept . the exercise is over, so now take time to reflect on the experience.'

Internal noticing: meditation script no. 5:

'Sitting with a comfortable, open, upright posture, let your body relax . imagine your spine effortlessly elongating upwards . your head balanced . take a couple of slow, deep breaths using your abdomen . . . . let your breathing become normal, relaxed and rhythmic . with your eyes closed, imagine your mind is like a large, airy room with doors at both ends of the room . and that you are looking in on the room . just accept the image, don't judge it as good or bad, just accept . imagine that the thoughts, emotions and sensations coming into and out of your mind are like a wind blowing through one door and out of the other . picture the room with the wind blowing through it . are your thoughts, emotions and sensations rushing through like a gale or gently like a summer breeze . do they go in, straight through and out or do they eddy around inside the room and then go out . . is there one wind or a number of winds going in the same or different directions . . whatever you notice about your thoughts, emotions and sensations, just accept that's the way it is, don't judge good or bad, should or shouldn't, just accept and allow them to happen . . if you find yourself forgetting about the room and about observing its contents but getting carried along and involved with some of the thoughts, emotions or sensations, then gently draw yourself back to observing the room . and imagine yourself opening a door to let the thoughts, emotions and sensations blow away, while noticing what comes in at the other door . . whatever they are just notice and accept . . . notice and accept . . . . notice what's going on in your mind and accept . . . . . notice and accept . . . . . . notice . the exercise is over, now take some time to reflect on the experience.'

Meditation script no. 6:

'In a comfortable, open, upright sitting position, relax, let go your tensions . allow your spine effortlessly to elongate . balance your head . take a couple of slow deep breaths using the abdomen . . . . then let your breathing become relaxed, rhythmic, gentle . with your eyes closed, imagine yourself standing back from your mind . allowing and observing what is going through your mind . notice thoughts, emotions, sensations, images, whatever is happening . allow, notice and accept, no judging good/bad, should/shouldn't, just allow and accept whatever comes into your mind . . allow, notice and accept . . . allow each thing to come in and then out of your mind, allowing the next thing to take its place . without censorship . allow, notice and accept . . . if you get caught up in the thoughts, just notice and accept, then observe and allow them to pass . . allowing in new thoughts . . . . notice and accept . . . . allow, notice and accept . . . . . allow, notice and accept (one minute silence) allow, notice and accept (two minutes silence) allow, notice and accept . the exercise is over now, so take time to reflect on the experience.'

The focussed meditation and noticing methods are useful ways of training the mind to be able to concentrate on the present rather than racing about between the past and the future. Using the tape player analogy, you are reconnecting the 'play' button and being able to switch it on and switch off the 'fast forward' and 'rewind' buttons at will. Peace of mind seems to be largely connected to being able to stay in the present. This does not mean that reviewing the past and planning for the future is not important, but that life is more peaceful if they can be done at will and put aside when appropriate.

Fantasy

Fantasy, or day dreaming, can be deliberately and positively used for five main purposes: (1) to escape temporarily from or defuse an emotionally difficult situation; (2) to enhance a pleasant experience or give yourself a mental 'treat'; (3) to increase self-awareness; (4) to release the creative potential of the right brain to give you ideas, insights and to use your intuition; (5) to release your healing potential with regard to yourself and others.

Fantasies can be free or structured. Free fantasy is allowing any image to come into your mind, then imagining it changing and developing with minimum control and censorship. Structured fantasy involves using particular frameworks within which to allow images to arise.

Defusing a tense situation: one common example of this use of fantasy which nurses report using in situations where they feel frightened or intimidated by someone in authority is to imagine that person in some undignified situation, such as naked or on the toilet. Evidently quite a few difficult interviews with managers and tutors have been coped with by using this technique! Another fantasy technique commonly used for temporarily dealing with fury is to imagine all the nasty things you could do or say to the person who is the object of your fury, which you would of course never consider doing in real life.

Meditation script no. 7.

The 'TV dot' fantasy may be useful for helping to defuse a tense situation, as is illustrated by the following script:

'Find a comfortable, upright, open position . take a couple of slow, deep breaths using the abdomen . . . . allow your breathing to become relaxed and rhythmic . imagine your mind is like an enormous TV screen . conjure up a picture on the TV screen which represents the problem or difficulty you are facing at present . . let the picture remain static on the screen . . imagine the picture very gradually getting smaller . slowly smaller and smaller . and eventually disappearing like the dot in the centre of a switched-off TV screen . finally the pinpoint of light goes out and the screen is blank . . imagine now that another pinpoint of light comes to the centre of the screen but it is a different colour, a beautiful colour, a positive pleasant light . as the spot slowly becomes larger on the screen, you can see in miniature, a scene which represents the opposite of the previous scene . in this picture, the problem does not exist or is solved . . the picture very gradually gets larger . . slowly larger . . . gradually becoming larger to fill the screen . . . notice how you feel in response to the positive picture . . the exercise is over, take some time to reflect on the experience.'

This fantasy has been used more than a few times in writing this book, the first scene depicting a woman at a desk with a pad of blank paper in front of her, chewing a pen. The second scene was the same character writing furiously with an enormous pile of paper covered in writing next to her! No prizes for guessing what the problem was!

Temporary escape: when preoccupied with a problem so much that the mind is going round in circles, or when you want to be able to concentrate on something else for a while, you can create structured fantasies to help you to put the problem aside temporarily. The following is one example.

Meditation script no. 8:

'Sit in a relaxed, upright, open position, with your eyes closed . take a couple of slow breaths using the abdomen, then breathe normally . . . . . let your mind focus for a while on the problem which is preoccupying you . . . . now allow your mind to conjure up an inanimate object which represents the problem, it can be a known object you have seen, or you can create one . . . . picture the size, shape, colour, texture of this object . . imagine yourself standing back from it and viewing the object from various angles . . imagine that next to the object is a box similar in shape to the object but larger . next to the box are a pair of scissors, a roll of sticky tape, a ball of string, some wrapping paper: picture each of these in turn, their size and shape and colour . . . . now picture yourself putting the object into the box and wrapping it up into a parcel, go through every step of wrapping up a parcel in your mind . . . . . . imagine yourself putting the parcel somewhere safe where you cannot see it as you go about your life, but where you will have easy access to it . . . whenever the problem preoccupies you and you wish to put it aside for a while, picture the wrapped up parcel in its safe place and turn your attention to something else . . now picture yourself gently getting up from this meditation and getting on with whatever you wanted to clear your mind to concentrate on . . now do that, moving gently and focussing your attention on what you are doing.'

Taking a short mental and emotional break from a problem may give you renewed energy to face and deal with it in reality. Sometimes the solution to a problem surfaces of its own accord when you stop thinking about it. However, it is important with a 'shelving' exercise such as this to give yourself time to reopen the problem and face it, if the solution has not surfaced since you put it aside.

Mental treats: daydreams often comprise memories of good times or imagining something positive happening to you. Here is a structured daydream fantasy to revive pleasant memories and to give you a rest from uncomfortable feelings you are experiencing in the present.

Meditation script no. 9:

'Ensure your position is upright, open, relaxed . take a couple of slow, deep breaths using the abdomen . . . . let your breathing become normal, relaxed . notice how you are feeling right now, your emotional reactions to the situation you have just experienced . . now conjure up memories of times you have felt the opposite, if you are bored think of times you felt excited, if you are anxious think of carefree times, if you feel unloved think of times you felt loved, and so on . . . revive the memories of each occasion, remember the little details as well as the main details, the place, the people or space from people, the colours, shapes, sounds, smells, tastes, textures, touch, temperature . . remember how you felt then . let the pleasant feelings suffuse your body . . you can stay with one memory or move on to others in which you felt good . . if you find painful memories or feelings coming into your mind, acknowledge them and put them gently aside, returning to your theme of pleasant memories . . re-experience the good times . . . remembering feeling good (one minute silence) remembering feeling good (two minutes silence) remembering feeling good . . let the good feelings suffuse your body . you can take this positive energy with you back to your real life situation and use it to nurture and comfort yourself while you deal with the difficulties you are faced with . stay with the positive energy yet put your attention gently back to the difficulties . later give yourself time to look back and review this exercise.'

Everyone has experienced something positive in their lives, and reflective daydreaming is one way of tapping the resources which these experiences have given us. The same structure can be used to conjure up imaginary positive situations instead of memories.

Free fantasy as a mental treat may be easier when you are feeling good, since the mind is more likely to develop pleasant imagery. For instance, if you are enjoying good weather in a garden or park, just ensuring that your body is as relaxed as possible may well allow the free fantasy to flow.

Sexual fantasies may come under this heading. It has long been accepted that men have sexual fantasies, and examples are extensively published in books and magazines. Only recently has the fact been more widely acknowledged that women also fantasise in this way. Nancy Friday's book, which documents women's sexual fantasies, may have had some influence in this respect (5).

Increasing self-awareness: fantasies can be used to enable aspects of oneself to surface from the unconscious mind to conscious awareness. These aspects may be positive, negative, neutral or a combination. Two examples of structured fantasies for increasing self-awareness are given in this section.

These are based on the notion that we often project aspects of ourselves or feelings about ourselves on to significant objects or other people. Considering what we like or dislike about these objects or people can sometimes help us to face the positive or negative aspects of ourselves which we have hidden in our unconscious minds. The mental mechanisms which keep these parts hidden can be quite strong, so notice in these exercises when you censor or deliberately adapt the images which come into your mind. You need to have pen and paper beside you for these exercises.

Meditation script no. 10:

'Sit in a comfortable, open, relaxed and upright position . take a couple of slow deep breaths using your diaphragm . . . . let your breathing become relaxed and rhythmic . . allow yourself to picture in your mind's eye an object which you particularly like . hold that memory of the object in your mind . notice what exactly it is about the object which you enjoy . . what qualities does this object have that you like? . . . . now write these qualities down on the paper, leaving a space between each line, switch the tape player off now, and then on again when you're finished the list . now go through the list, delete "it has" or "it is" and write "I have" or "I am" before each of the qualities and substitute "me" for "it" in midsentence; as you do this, stop to reflect on what each statement tells you about yourself, even the ones which sound ridiculous. You can rewrite the statements to incorporate the meaning it has for you if you wish. You can turn the tape off now.'

An example of a list produced in this exercise is as follows:

Object: guitar
It has a nice shape. (I have a nice shape.)
It's really important to me, I've had it a long time. (I'm really important to me, I've had me a long time!)
It gives me the chance to express myself, to let off steam. (I can give myself the chance to express myself, to let off steam.)
It has a pleasant battered look about it, with quite a lot of scratches and cracks that have been mended. (I'm ageing pleasantly, I have quite a few lines and scars that have healed.)
I've only recently started playing it again after putting it aside for quite a few years and I'm really enjoying rediscovering it again. (I've only recently started paying more attention to myself again and I'm really enjoying what I'm discovering about myself.)

The exercise can be adapted to use an object you dislike, or a person you like or dislike. In my experience, nurses have little trouble pinpointing what they dislike about themselves, but need plenty of practice in accepting their positive points.

Meditation script no. 11:

'Sit in an upright, open and relaxed position . let your spine elongate effortlessly . balance your head with minimum effort . take a couple of slow, deep breaths using the diaphragm . . . . breathe normally . allow your thoughts to slow down and clear like clouds thinning out . as they clear allow an image of a rose tree to come into your mind, hold the first rose tree you thought of as I said the word, picture the rose tree . picture the environment in which the tree is growing, the season, the surrounds . . picture the shape, colour, condition of the rose tree . . . what do the branches bear? . . what condition are the roots in, are they near the surface or do they grow deeply? . . who looks after the tree? . . what else do you notice about the tree? . . . . . . now write down a detailed description of the tree, leaving a line between each line you write, switch this tape off and then on again when you've written the description. Go back over the list and cross out the "it's", referring to the tree, and substitute "I have", "I am", "me" or "myself". Reflect on what the rewritten statements tell you about yourself, even the ridiculous ones. Perhaps rewrite the description to incorporate the meaning it has for you. You can turn the tape off now.'

An example of what can arise from this exercise is this description of a rose tree: 'This tree is climbing around the door of a cottage. It's summer and (it's/I'm) covered with red flowers. (It/I) look(s) a bit of a shambles, (the/my) flowers are weighing down the smaller branches, but (the/my) main stems are well supported. (It's/I'm) not a wild rose but (it's/I'm) not a florist's dream either, the flowers open out a lot and grow in clumps. (It's/I'm) quite healthy, only a bit of blackspot and no greenfly, because (it's/I've) been sprayed every now and then. (It/I) get(s)

fed and watered too: (it/I) need(s) extra feeding and watering, because (the/my) roots are next to the house, along with a lot of other (plants/people), all crowded into that particular spot. The owner of the cottage (does/I do) the spraying and feeding and watering when (she/I) remember(s). (There are/I have) a lot of thorns; the ones on the main branches are quite big, but they're right back against the wall behind the foliage. Some of (the/my) smaller branches flop across the doorway a bit and (the/my) thorns can scratch and tear people or their clothes if they're not careful.'

This nurse's analysis of the relevance of the exercise to her present state showed that she saw herself as giving off the impression of disorganisation but that the important things in her life, her support system, were well organised. She was taking quite good care of herself, in a haphazard way, although her home, which was very important to her, became too crowded at times. She was managing to keep her nastiest traits under control, but sometimes the people closest to her got hurt if they did not treat her with care. Generally, it was a sunny phase in her life and she was being creative and productive.

Analysis of free fantasies and of dreams can also increase self-awareness.

Allow yourself to relax physically and to fantasise freely without structuring or censoring the way the fantasy develops. When it comes to an end, or when you have had enough, take time to reflect on the fantasy; or when you wake up and remember a dream, take time to work on it. Remember as many of the details as you can, particularly the emotional tone. Making notes or drawing a picture may help you to remember. According to Gestalt psychologists, each detail of the fantasy or dream symbol-ises a part of yourself at that point in time. You can learn about those parts by systematically turning your attention to each detail in the fantasy or dream. Imagine you are that object or person, and describe yourself, your feelings and the way you change during the fantasy or dream. For instance, if your fantasy con-sisted of imagining yourself walking through a dark forest, you would not only relive the experience of being yourself walking through the forest, but also of being the trees, the fallen branches, the floor of the forest, the damaged tree which had been struck by lightning, each animal and bird, the darkness and the sky.

One nurse's example: 'I am the trees, I'm crowded and tall and struggling to get light. I form a canopy of leaves and branches high above the ground. I feel protective towards the animals and particularly towards the small person walking on the ground. I don't like the darkness I've created because it frightens people walking through, but I'm overcrowded. If someone would come along and thin me out I'd let in more light . . . .'

Then going back through each of those identifications, pinpoint what you have noticed about the symbolism of the statements and the way they relate to you in your present life. For instance, from the extract quoted above, the nurse found that the trees symbolised her protective feelings towards the vulnerable people that she dealt with in her family and at work and also, she was surprised to discover, towards herself. The overcrowding symbolised the lack of time she had on her own. The darkness reminded her of how she often cut off from people close to her or got bad tempered with them, because of that lack of time alone. She realised that she was waiting for someone else to give her permission to take time for herself. She decided to use those protective feelings towards herself to do something about having the space and time she needed.

Working in this way with dreams can be especially powerful, since they are less likely than fantasies to be unconsciously censored while they are happening, although of course the censorship can happen by simply not being able to remember them. If you would like to be able to remember dreams more, then working with conscious fantasy may help you to become accustomed to remembering this kind of experience and therefore more likely to remember dreams. Having pen and paper available when you wake up from a dream can help you; you can jot down the main points or draw a picture or diagram. A willing listener can help you put the dream into words. Keeping a diary of your fantasies and dreams, perhaps with your interpretations, can provide you with a fascinating record of your changing state of mind over a period of time. It can also help you to see how much you avoid when interpreting; with hindsight, symbolism you ignored at the time can seem more than obvious.

Enhancing creativity and use of intuition: any of the relaxation and meditation methods can help to reduce the 'chatter' of the mind and allow more abstract conceptualisation and creative use of intuition. In slowing down the left brain, the right brain can be noticed. People often use the expression 'I told myself . . . .'; meditation can help you learn to listen to yourself as well. Each person has an immense pool of experience and knowledge from which wisdom can arise if it is allowed. Living and working in a system as hierarchical as nursing can make us tend to look for answers outside ourselves, believing that someone else must know better. However, you are the only expert in your life, you have specialised in it for a lifetime. The answers to your own particular stresses and problems are within yourself. Other people's opinions and experiences may be useful only insofar as allowing your own opinions and ability to learn from your own experience to surface. Structured fantasies can help you to bypass the blocks which prevent you from being your own 'guru'. The structured fantasy in the creative problem-solving chapter is designed to encourage intuitive problem-solving; it might help you to ask yourself the right questions and to provide some of your own answers.

Releasing potential for healing: nurses often witness the effects of patients' will-power on their physical and psychological condition. Some patients seem to recover when the odds are against them, apparently as a result of their determination to do so. Others 'turn their face to the wall' and deteriorate unexpectedly. It would appear that human beings can exert influence on the defence systems of their own bodies by using the power of the mind, and this influence can have a healing effect. The concept of healing in this sense means a positive effect on the person as a whole. It may include physical improvement or recovery although not necessarily; but it does include a reduction in physical and psychological distress related to the ailment.

The following structured fantasy illustrates an approach to allowing the mind to influence positively your physical defences and correcting mechanisms towards healing any ailment from which you are currently suffering. Again it is described as a script for tape recording a guided fantasy. You will need to use one of the deep relaxation routines, possibly from the deep relaxation scripts in Chapter 3. Then add the following instructions

Meditation script no. 12:

'. . . now that you are deeply relaxed, create in your mind an image of your current illness, it can be anatomically correct or it can be totally abstract and symbolic . hold that picture gently in your mind . . now imagine your body's defence mechanisms, again the picture can be scientifically correct or it can be totally abstract or symbolic . . picture the defences overcoming, controlling or correcting the condition, scientifically or symbolically . . . imagine the defences working successfully to heal you, to correct the condition . . . . if you are receiving treatment, visualise the process of the treatment helping you to overcome the condition, and picture your body defences helping the treatment to overcome the condition . . . . allow healing energy to enter your body, imagine a kind of light suffusing your body . . notice if the light is focussed in one spot or is it flowing throughout your body . . . . allow the energy to flow throughout your body, bathing every cell with healing . . . . let it grow brighter and stronger . . stronger and brighter . . picture yourself totally free of the ailment, well and healthy, hold the image of the healthy you in your mind . . . visualise yourself feeling totally healthy . . . . the exercise is over, now take time to reflect on the experience.'

When you are feeling unwell, this kind of exercise can enable you to feel part of the healing process and take some responsibility for it, rather than feeling helpless and totally dependent on others. It might enable you to get in touch with the healing energy which many meditators experience and be able to use it for yourself and for others. This energy tends to be associated with feelings of deep peace, rest, recuperation, bliss and oneness with everything. Meditators of various religions give this experience of bliss a number of names: the Christians for instance speak of a 'state of grace' while Hindus have names for different types of bliss, such as samadhi and turiya.

Sceptical nurses sometimes dismiss reports of such experiences as probably being of chemical origin, such as a result of anoxia (certainly someone in a deep meditation hardly seems to be breathing at all), or easily explainable in concrete terms by a physicist. However, physicists specialising in the study of energy seem to be moving out of the realms of what has hitherto been held to constitute physics, into metaphysics. For instance, Pearce (1) describes the similarities between the physicist Bohm's theory of energy and the Siddha Yoga model. Western scientists and Eastern mystics are increasingly coming together in their viewpoints (6).

Sensory perception, images and hallucinations

Nurses unused to using imagery sometimes confuse sight, images and hallucinations, usually because of trying too hard in the meditation. If the meditation exercise involves picturing something peaceful, the perplexed nurse may, for instance, find that she could think of a lake but could not actually see it, merely seeing red lights. When you close your eyes, the lights and shapes you see are the impressions received by the retina through the eyelids, with shapes seen recently lingering as recent memories. The imagery used in meditation consists of thought pictures — the thought of the lake in the above example. It is this thought which is deliberately repeated and held in the mind which constitutes the mental picture.

Another nurse might be confused in that she can imagine a scene, but cannot feel that she is actually there. She is using imagery correctly. You aim to be aware, while using imagery, that the experience is going on in the mind and not outside in reality.

A hallucination, on the other hand, is something which is solely a mental image but is believed to be actually in existence in reality outside the person as well as within. Transitory hallucinations are normal during sleep (i.e. dreams), when half-awake, and in extreme emotional states, such as ecstasy or deep emotional pain. They may also occur during meditation, probably because of going to sleep or being in the half-asleep state, characterised by increases in theta waves, as monitored by EEG or biofeedback machines. Strong visual mental images can easily be distinguished from hallucinations by opening your eyes; the retinal image will be clearly perceived and distinguished from the mental image. A hallucination is a mental image so strong that it overrides the brain's reception and perception of sensory stimuli. Strong auditory images are less easy to distinguish from auditory hallucinations unless there is someone else in the vicinity with whom to check out the experience of sound. If transitory hallucinations occur during meditation then it is important to have the guidance of a specialist meditation teacher. If they also occur outside the normal occasions mentioned earlier, or are more than transitory, then of course a medical checkup is necessary since there may be organic causes. When these are ruled out, the support of a counsellor or psychotherapist skilled in the use of imagery can help you deal with distressing hallucinations.

Meditation in a nurse's daily life

Nurses caught up in the 'busy syndrome' may think they have no time to spare for meditation. If this applies to you, you could start by noting the number of times in a week when you are sitting without a specific task to do, for instance as a passenger in a car, train or bus. If you have caught the 'busy syndrome' badly, every one of these potential occasions may be filled up with tasks such as reading, writing, marking or knitting. Pinpoint a couple of those times when you could stop working and give yourself five minutes to practise meditation. Ten minutes per week should be possible for all but the most incurable workaholics. Having found that you can make time for yourself, it will be possible to build up the number of practice sessions to every two days, daily or ideally twice daily. As with any skill, you need to practise regularly to gain expertise. When you have reached the level of skill with which you are content, you may not need to practise deliberately regularly, but will be more able to fit it into your life as and when you need to. Indeed, Eastern meditation teachers encourage meditation students to learn to make their whole lives into a meditation. In theory this is possible even in the most hectic nursing jobs.

Even if you do not aspire to being a self-realised yogi in nurses' uniform, you can at least apply basic meditation techniques to everyday life. For instance, one way of improving concentration is by slowing down the 'chatter' of your mind. Focus gently on whatever you are doing, perhaps repeating silently to yourself 'I'm . . . .' whatever it is you are doing.

Many nurses are anxious about fitting into their busy day the aspects of their role which require a slow, relaxed approach, such as counselling and teaching. Sometimes counselling and teaching courses give nurses a guilt complex about not giving hours of their time to patients and students. It is true that most nurses do not have long periods of time to spare to do in-depth counselling and teaching. This is where meditation practice can save you time and save the energy wasted in feeling guilty. If you are able to give someone your full attention by putting aside your other preoccupations, you are likely to have less demanding patients and junior nurses for a smaller investment of time. Five or ten minutes of your undivided attention will leave a patient or nurse feeling more satisfied than having half an hour of your presence when you seem distracted and they feel they are being a nuisance. You may feel less guilty because you know the quality of your attention has been good even if you cannot give the quantity you would like. You may find it useful to use a mantra when trying to listen and support someone; as your attention wanders, repeat silently to yourself 'I'm listening' and gently focus back on to the person who is talking. Alternatively, you could repeat the person's name silently to yourself.

So you can slow down the mental interruptions which interfere with your concentration. It might also be useful to notice how you respond to outside interruptions. If you tend to respond immediately to every interruption, including the non-urgent requests, it might be worthwhile considering sometimes gently asking people to wait a few minutes while you finish the task you are doing.

Practice in the techniques for external noticing can enable you to become more alert in the work situation. Staying relaxed but opening your awareness to everything that is going on around can help you to fulfil your role as an observer or supervisor without being obtrusive. Meditation can also give you the ability to be calm in the most hectic situations and your very presence can have a calming influence in a tense situation.

Pitfalls in using meditation to prevent or cope with stress

In learning meditation you are likely to make mistakes. As with any other skill, these mistakes are part of the process of learning, provided you notice them and correct them. The very practice of meditation will enable an increased ability for self-acceptance and make it easier to learn from any mistakes you make in your life.

1. *Lack of commitment:* just running once through the exercises in this chapter and then ticking meditation off your list of things to learn will not have enhanced your skills much. You may have high hopes about what meditation can do for you, and after a few attempts at meditating discover that it is not a panacea and abandon it in disgust. Building skills in meditation takes practice so you need to allow regular times to do so, however short.

2. *Over-dependence:* if you learn meditation at a class or use a mechanical aid such as a tape or biofeedback machine, you could become overdependent on the teacher, the group atmosphere, particular meditation tapes or the feedback from the machine.

Thus, it is important to practise meditation on your own and without aids between assisted sessions.

3. *Passivity:* if you rely too much on meditation as a method of coping with stress, you may become increasingly passive in your lifestyle. You could become physically unfit, and increasingly submissive, allowing decisions which affect your life to be made without your participation. Some meditators believe that vast numbers of people meditating can influence the forces for good in this world. This is very probably true, but direct action is also needed to carry through changes for the better. To use a nursing analogy, praying for the recovery of a patient who has had a cardiac arrest may help at some level, but resuscitation attempts are needed too. The health service, the nation and indeed the planet are in need of urgent direct action to save them. Nurses need to be willing to participate in that action, and at least to actively support those who do act on our behalf.

4. *Going to sleep in the car:* meditation tapes should never be played in a car because the driver may become dangerously sleepy.

5. *Hyperventilation:* the deep breathing used to relax and calm you prior to or during meditation needs to be slowly done, and to be temporary. If you are used to breathing quickly, you might find yourself breathing deeply but at the same rate as when you breathe more shallowly. If you feel the symptoms of hyperventilation, tingling extremities and light-headedness, you need to rectify the oxygen overdose and carbon dioxide starvation in the blood by taking some physical exercise, such as shaking your limbs, jogging or jumping on the spot, or breathing in and out of a bag until the symptoms go.

6. *Inflexible meditation rituals:* allowing yourself regular time to practise meditation can be taken to the extreme to the extent of becoming a compulsion. You need to be able to be flexible to some extent in the timing of your practice sessions. It is possible to become overdependent on a certain chair to meditate in, a particular outfit or blanket around you, a special object to focus on, or a place to meditate. While familiarity and routine can help you practise and build meditation skills, and give a much-needed stability in a hectic, changing world, it is important to be able to change the routine at times and still be able to meditate.

7. *Trying too hard:* meditation is supposed to be about allowing, not forcing. The techniques need to be used gently. Some people believe that the mind should be blank to meditate properly, but this is not possible in a living brain. Striving to empty the mind is a fruitless task, as are attempts to create a particular type of meditation experience. You may hear other meditators speak of blissful experiences, or read about transcendental states, think you are not doing it properly, and try to achieve something similar. It may happen that you do have an experience during meditation which is special and beautiful for you, but then subsequently are disappointed with relatively boring or ordinary meditation sessions. It is better to stay with the disappointment and allow it to happen, than to try to recreate a past experience. Sharing meditation experiences with other meditators can be useful, but one pitfall is that you might get into a competitive discussion, competing to show who is the best meditator, or who gets most 'blissed-out'! Meditation techniques are ways of allowing your mind to be the way it really is, and you will have to take the rough and the ordinary, with the smooth and the extraordinary. Another aspect of trying too hard relates to the way meditation is applied to everyday life. People who specialise in meditation and do little else for many years eventually become beautifully serene most of the time. To meet someone like this is a remarkable experience and it is only human to want to model oneself on such a person. But a person who is a relative beginner at meditation and who tries to project a serene image, wafting about with a fixed beatific smile, gazing deeply into everyone's eyes, is easily recognisable as a sham. Genuine serenity will shine through without any effort if and when it occurs.

8. *Ammunition for put-downs:* each of us has probably got a critic inside us eager to grab at any ammunition to shoot down the tentative learner part of ourselves and the learner in other people. Knowledge of meditation might be used in this way too. You might berate yourself for not being the perfect, disciplined but flexible, serene saint you think you should be, and berate others too for the same failing. You need to accept that your use of meditation will be less than perfect; you will make mistakes, but you have the capacity to learn from them. This acceptance leads to ease in accepting other people as they are.

9. *Imposing meditation on other people:* if you find meditation useful, it

can be tempting to get carried away with your enthusiasm and try to persuade all and sundry to take it up, irrespective of their interest. Your meditation experiences may be absolutely fascinating to you, telling you a lot about yourself and it can be very useful to recount the experiences and the self-learning to someone else. The pitfall lies in assuming everyone else will be equally fascinated and boring them silly with endless blow-by-blow accounts. So check that the other person is interested and wants to listen and if so, keep it brief.

10. *Emotional flight:* overusing focussed meditation and fantasy may lead to a habit of avoiding painful emotions so that eventually you are unable to face them. This might lead to passivity and all the other symptoms of repression. People trying to communicate with you are likely to experience you as being not fully present with them, as 'spaced out'. Extreme self-reliance is another form of emotional flight which might be encouraged by overdoing meditation. It might be very tempting for nurses, who as an occupational group have a reputation in psychological circles for being great helpers but for making it difficult for other people to help them, to exaggerate the self-reliance aspect of meditation. While meditation enhances your ability to nurture psychologically, to reassure, to comfort and to counsel yourself, total psychological independence can be dangerous. It might be tempting to avoid emotional involvement with other people, because of the inevitable risks of disappointment, embarrassment, hurt and loss, when the emotional self-support of meditation may seem so much more reliable, especially during a stable or lucky phase of a person's life. The close supporting network of friends which are a human being's insurance against emotional disaster may be phased out. Then when life deals an unlucky blow, and some unexpected stress is piled on, the self-reliance can fail but there are less back-up resources in the form of other people's support upon which to draw; or the ability to accept whatever support is available has been lost.

11. *Negative attitudes about one's own emotions:* mental 'chatter', such as preoccupations with the past or plans for the future, can also be a defence mechanism against uncomfortable emotions which are being experienced in the present, though perhaps unconsciously. When this hyperactivity of the mind is slowed down, repressed emotions are likely to surface. This might mean that some

meditation sessions are unpleasant. Worry, shame or disappointment about this phenomenon might lead you to give up meditation, to believe that there is something wrong with you, or to endure the distress on your own. Emotions are natural human experiences but it is common in this culture for people to be frightened by the intensity of newly-discovered, bottled-up feelings. There is no shame in seeking the support of someone who is experienced in helping people to deal with them. A specialist meditation teacher, co-counselling teacher or counsellor will be able to help. When painful emotions surface in meditation, it is a sign that you are doing it right: you are not kidding yourself that everything in the garden of the psyche is rosy.

References and further reading

1. Pearce J. (1981). *The Bond of Power: Meditation and Wholeness*. London: Routledge & Kegan Paul.
2. Muktananda. (1975). *Siddha Meditation: Commentaries on the Shiva Sutras and Other Sacred Texts*. California: SYDA Foundation.
3. Russell P. (1976). *The TM Technique: The TM Book for Sceptics*. London: Routledge & Kegan Paul.
4. Chaitow L. (1983). *Relaxation and Meditation Techniques*. Wellingborough: Thorsons.
5. Friday N. (1973). *My Secret Garden*. London: Quartet.
6. Bohm D. (1981). *Wholeness and the Implicate Order*. London: Ark Paperbacks.

Where to learn more about meditation

Local adult education institutes and the extra-mural departments of universities and polytechnics may run meditation courses or courses on stress management which include meditation. These include:

The Human Potential Research Project
Dept. of Educational Studies
University of Surrey
Guildford
Surrey GU27 5XH.

Siddha Yoga Dham U.K.
c/o Campenton
Riverside
Temple Gardens
Staines
Middlesex TW18 3NJ
Tel. 0784-64962

Transcendental Meditation
Roydon Hall
Seven Mile Lane
East Peckham
Kent TN12 5MH
Tel. 0622-813243

The latter two of the above addresses are the UK headquarters of international organisations. They have centres throughout Britain.

Many other centres offer meditation courses. Some are advertised in a magazine called *Human Potential Resources* which is on sale in some bookshops or by post from· Maureen Yeomans, *Human Potential Resources*, 35 Station Road, London NW4, Tel. 01-202 4941.

5

Assertiveness

There are two main reasons why nurses need skills in assertiveness; first, so they can act as advocates for patients and colleagues and, second, so they can avoid the exhaustion arising from compulsive helping.

Authority and professional decision-making

Nursing is not only about doing, but about the decisions which affect what we do. Legally and ethically, the nurse is responsible for her actions, yet often she does not have the authority to make the decisions which influence her field of responsibility. Much of our education, training and social conditioning has been based on the inculcation of what we 'ought', 'must' and 'are expected' to do, without much attention being paid to developing our skills in making our own decisions. The conditioning process includes teaching by humiliation: when we step outside what we 'ought', 'must' or 'are expected' to do we are often blamed and punished out of all proportion to the severity of the 'mistake'. This tends to create an inappropriately high level of fear of making mistakes and the buck is passed up the hierarchy. This causes stress since one of our basic human emotional needs, that of making decisions for ourselves (see Chapter 2), is being denied, and indeed we deny it of ourselves. Thus the nurse suffers the added stress of being in the horns of a dilemma; she is responsible for an area of work in which her actions can have a great impact on the lives of the people involved, yet she often has little authority in that area.

Lip service is often paid to the concept of the nurse being a 'professional in her own right' while some members of the medical profession and some nurse managers compete to gain control over the nurse's professional decisions. This is illustrated by one GP's complaint about nurse managers; he refers to them as 'matriarchs' who forbid district nurses to carry out certain clinical procedures (1). The point at issue here is not whether or not the tasks should be carried out, but that the district nurse should make the decision. Dr Ashworth seems to want to take over the district nurse's professional decision-making, since he goes on to say that '. . . because of the resistance of nursing officers . . . we are obliged to employ our own treatment nurse *over whom we have direct control*' (my emphasis). This doctor/manager struggle indicates a strong need for district nurses to think and speak for themselves as professionals in their own right, and occurs in all branches of nursing.

Advocacy

Nurses often speak of the stressful experience of being caught between the patient and a health care system which is not geared to the patients' needs. Standing up for the patient not only serves an altruistic function, but helps us to feel better about ourselves and the care we are able to give. Most patients and their families are in the social categories of people who are most disadvantaged in terms of health care, and therefore are most in need of advocacy: the working class, women, the elderly and the chronically and terminally ill.

It has been shown that people from the working classes have higher morbidity rates, yet receive less good health care (2). Often they are in awe of professionals and find it difficult to articulate their needs. Middle-aged and elderly women can suffer from the results of sterotypical attitudes held by some doctors, who dismiss them as being neurotic, depressed and unable to cope with crises. Indeed, physical disorders can be neglected in women since their symptoms can be dismissed as psychogenic and proper investigation and treatment is delayed. Likewise, elderly patients of either gender may receive inadequate attention since their problems may be dismissed as being due to their age and due to lack of resources.

Many patients and carers have difficulty in gaining information about medical diagnosis and prognosis. Doctors may be insufficiently skilled in coping with the emotional aspects of chronic or terminal illness, and to protect themselves, avoid disclosing information which might put them in a position of having to deal with someone who is upset. As an advocate, the nurse can help patients and carers to persist assertively in their attempts to gain appropriate treatment and information, and when necessary to act on their behalf towards these ends.

Advocacy is also part of the UKCC's ethical code; the nurse is advised to speak up on behalf of colleagues and the staff for which she is the manager. It is every nurse's responsibility to challenge unsuitable working conditions, high workloads and inappropriate policies and procedures — anything which is detrimental to the maintenance of high standards of care (3).

If nurses are to be seen as equal members of the health care team, we need to act as self-advocates and assert our right to make our own professional decisions. Being able to stand up for those who may be relying on us is also an essential part of our caring role. Yet being assertive can be particularly difficult when you are under stress.

Stress and confidence

Stress can often result in lower self-confidence, which can make it more difficult to be assertive. Non-assertive approaches can lead you to further stress, because of lack of respect from other people, not having your needs met and from feeling bad about yourself. This reduces self-confidence and the cycle goes on. If you can find ways of breaking into this vicious circle, you can transform it to a positive cycle of realistic self-confidence leading to being able to

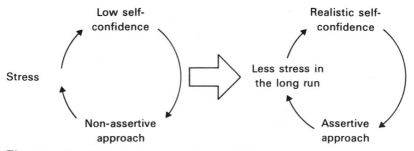

Fig. 5.1   *Breaking out of the stress/low confidence trap.*

be more assertive, leading to less stress, leading to realistic self-confidence and so on. One way of interrupting the negative cycle is to learn some techniques for consciously developing a more assertive approach. (The negative cycle can be penetrated and broken by other methods too; for instance, methods such as co-counselling can help increase self-confidence.)

A useful first step towards regaining your confidence when

Table 5.1 *Assertive rights.*

1. I have the right to state my own needs and set my own priorities as a *person* whatever other people expect of me because of my roles in life.	**and**	You have the right to state your own needs and set your own priorities as a *person* whatever other people expect of you because of your roles in life.
2. I have the right to be treated with respect as an intelligent, capable and equal human being.	**and**	You have the right to be treated with respect as an intelligent, capable and equal human being.
3. I have the right to express my feelings.	**and**	You have the right to express your feelings.
4. I have the right to express my opinions and values.	**and**	You have the right to express your opinions and values.
5. I have the right to say 'Yes' or 'No' for myself.	**and**	You have the right to say 'Yes' or 'No' for yourself.
6. I have the right to make mistakes.	**and**	You have the right to make mistakes.
7. I have the right to change my mind.	**and**	You have the right to change your mind.
8. I have the right to say 'I don't understand'.	**and**	You have the right to say 'I don't understand'.
9. I have the right to ask for what I want.	**and**	You have the right to ask for what you want.
10. I have the right to decide for myself whether or not I am responsible for another person's problem.	**and**	You have the right to decide for yourself whether or not you are responsible for another person's problem.
11. I have the right to deal with people without having to make them like or approve of me.	**and**	You have the right to deal with other people without having to make them like or approve of you.

Adapted from *A Woman in Your Own Right* by Anne Dickson (4) under stress can be to remind yourself of the rights you have as an individual person when communicating with other people, who, in turn, also have rights. Many nurses have found it helpful to carry around or post up a copy of the rights outlined in Table 5.1 and to refer to it when feeling stressed.

Under stress, which of these rights in Table 5.1 do you find the most difficult to remember (a) with respect to yourself and (b) with respect to other people?

Distinguishing between assertive, aggressive, manipulative and submissive approaches

Who makes the decisions?

To clarify the meaning of 'assertiveness', we could distinguish it from three other non-assertive approaches: being aggressive, being manipulative or being submissive. One important difference between the four approaches is related to decision-making. Being assertive means that you are deciding for yourself and allowing and enabling other people to decide for themselves. If you are aggressive, you are making decisions for yourself and not allowing others to decide for themselves, very obviously making their decisions for them. The manipulative, indirect approach involves making decisions for yourself and other people while giving the impression of allowing them to think for themselves. Being submissive means that you are allowing others to decide for you. What this means in terms of what you do with your life, expressing your wants and needs, saying no, stating your opinions, giving and receiving criticism and giving and receiving compliments is outlined in subsequent sections of this chapter.

Body language

Before we go on to look in more detail at the 'what?' of assertiveness, we need to look at the 'how?' of assertiveness. Often it is not so much a matter of what is communicated, but how it is communicated. Take the following situation: a staff nurse has already asked Dr Smith to see a patient, Mrs Brown. He agreed, but seems to have forgotten; he is working on something in the office. The staff nurse goes into the office to remind him. She makes a straightforward request using the words 'Dr Smith, I would like you to have a look at Mrs Brown now'. These words might sound assertive, but they may come over non-assertively because of the tone of voice and body language. For instance:

1. Marches into office, hands on hips . . . loudly:
'*Dr Smith!* I would *like* you to *go* and have a look at Mrs Brown! Now!' . . . immediately turns on heels and leaves office. (Aggressive approach.)

2. 'Ah! Dr Smith' . . . winning smile . . . 'I *would* like you to go and have a look at Mrs Brown.' . . . more smiles, then just as he is about to reply she says 'now?' . . . raised eyebrows, fluttering eyelids. (Manipulative approach.)

3. Softly . . . 'Er Dr Smith?' . . . pause . . . 'umm, umm, I would like you to er, go and have a look at Mrs Brown? Now?' . . . defeated posture and facial expression. (Submissive approach.)
These contrast with the assertive approach:

4. Gently but firmly . . . 'Dr Smith?' . . . waits for him to look up . . . 'I would like you to go and have a look at Mrs Brown now.' . . . . waits for a response.

Body language can communicate very well the strength of feeling involved in the situation. As we have seen in Chapter 2, because of stress, that strength of feeling may be out of all proportion to the real life situation. One skill in assertiveness is to allow appropriate strength of feeling to come through in the non-verbal communication. The relaxation training suggested in Chapter 3 can help develop the body awareness and the use of non-verbal communication in building assertiveness skills.

In the majority of situations, a relatively calm but firm approach is usually most appropriate. Consider the body language which one group of nurses suggested for each of the four categories, listed in Table 5.2 on the following page.

There seems to be a direct two-way flow between body language and emotion; non-verbal behaviour may not only reflect emotion but also restimulate emotion.

Try using some of the aggressive body language while describing something stressful, perhaps into a mirror or to someone else as an exercise. If you keep it up for a minute or so, you are likely to notice quite a lot of aggressive feelings coming up inside you. Next, if you adopt some of the submissive non-verbal features and

Table 5.2 *Body language of the four approaches.*

Assertive body language

Posture is relaxed, well balanced, upright, facing the other person, calm and relatively still. Gestures are open and relaxed and related to the points being made, otherwise the hands are relatively still. Eye contact is direct but relaxed, and at the same eye level whenever possible. Facial expression is relaxed, firm, open and pleasant without inappropriate smiles. Distance from the other person is at an average, comfortable proximity. The voice is relaxed and relatively low pitched, with a firm but gentle tone, enough volume to be heard clearly.

Aggressive body language

Posture may be tense and erect, possibly trying to get physically higher than the other person, chest and shoulders possibly over inflated. Gestures such as hand on hip, pointing, waving and poking movements with the finger. Chopping movements with the hands, clenching fists and tapping or shuffling feet may come over as aggressive. Eye contact may be staring, glaring with a hard, uninterrupted gaze. It may involve looking down from a height. Facial expression may be tense, including frowns, gritted teeth, pursed lips, angry smile, narrowed eyes. The distance may be uncomfortably close at times, or at a considerable distance at which it would be difficult to respond. The voice may be sharp, threatening and over firm.

Manipulative body language

Posture may be over relaxed, too 'laid back', over-friendly, coy, flirtatious or exaggeratedly elegant. Likewise, the gestures may be exaggerated in elegance or friendliness. Signs of indirect aggression may include hand-crunching handshakes and over-hard jocular slaps on the back. There may be patronising touching or patting. Eye contact may be direct but may also be part of the exaggerations, looking out of side or the top of the eyes or avoiding eye contact at crucial moments. The facial expression may also be exaggeratedly friendly, innocent or concerned. The proximity may be too close for comfort as part of the exaggerated friendliness, or it may be too distant for the other person to easily make a response. The voice may also be exaggerated in its friendly, sweet singing tone. It may have a tone of veiled threat, criticism or sarcasm.

Submissive body language

Posture may be slumped, defeated-looking or tense and agitated, allowing oneself to be towered over. Gestures may be nervous, fiddling, touching the face a lot, covering mouth while speaking. Eye contact may be poor, looking away. Facial expression may show defeat and tension or a desire to placate with pleading smiles. Proximity may be distant, or allowing the other person to come uncomfortably close. Voice is quiet, shrill, hesitant or obsequious.

keep it up, after a while you are likely to feel defeated and lacking in confidence. Conversely, if you consciously adopt an assertive stance and use some of the relaxation breathing mentioned in Chapter 2, after a while you are likely to feel more confident and find it easier to be assertive.

Take this example: Sylvia, a clinical nurse specialist, found that when she went to see the senior nurse manager, he always offered her a low comfortable armchair, while he sat on an upright chair behind his desk. She found that she slumped because of the shape of the armchair, and felt at a disadvantage because she was at a lower eye level and had to look up to him. Although she came in with good intentions to be assertive about getting across a particular point of view, she found very quickly that her confidence drained away and that she could not get herself across very clearly. When she realised this, she decided to prevent it at her next visit: as she walked into the office, she picked up an upright chair near the wall and took it to the side of the desk so that she felt at a more equal level and could sit more assertively. She began to make her point and found herself becoming increasingly more

confident as she realised that her body was projecting a more assertive impression.

Talking assertively

Although the non-verbal aspects of communication have an important influence on the approach conveyed, the way things are phrased affects the impression given. There are some common features in assertive statements.

Study the examples in Table 5.3 and pick out the features which are common to most of them (imagine each statement is being said using assertive body language and tone of voice).

Table 5.3   *Some examples of assertive statements.*

Giving positive feedback

I liked the way you did that. You were so patient with her.

I really appreciated your help yesterday when I felt so terrible. Is there anything I can do in return?

I like your taste in clothes. You look great.

Thanks for lending your ear yesterday. I feel so much better now, you helped a lot by listening.

I admire the way you handled that situation. You seemed to get across your message loud and clear without putting him down. He certainly knew where he stood with you.

Responding to feedback

Thanks. I was pretty pleased with myself too, it went much better than I expected.

Thank you for the compliment. That makes me feel really good.

Yes, that's true, I did forget to tell the patient. I'll put that right straightaway.

I do admit I did forget that one arrangement we made, but I don't make a habit of it. So, no, I disagree with you, I'm not a total scatterbrain.

No, I don't think that's true. On the contrary, I think I work very hard. What made you think I was lazy?

Making a request

I'm not satisfied with the work done on my car. Please put it right without further charge.

Could you return the £5 you borrowed last week?

(continued)

Could I join you and Mildred for lunch?

I'm taking half an hour's lunch break. If anything crops up, could you wait till I come back rather than disturb me?

I think we've reached a deadlock here. Could we sit down and talk it through?

Saying 'No'

No, I am not doing it for you this time. I'd like you to do it on your own. Take your time, I'll wait for you.

That's not really my responsibility. Please find someone else to deal with it.

No thank you, I'm not interested in your double glazing.

No it's not really convenient for you to come this weekend. How about next weekend instead?

No, I'm not prepared to lend you another £5.

Setting limits

Thank you for your concern, but I'd like to make my own decision.

I don't like the way you said that. It sounded patronising to me. I'd prefer you talked to me as an equal.

This is a non-smoking area. Please put your cigarette out.

Mildred's my friend and I don't like you talking about her like that. Please stop.

I don't like being ignored. I'd prefer you answer me when I speak to you.

I don't like racist jokes. Please avoid telling them when I'm around.

I don't like it when you make commitments for me. I'd prefer you consulted me first.

I really don't like you touching me like that. I find it offensive.

I don't like what you're doing. Please stop it.

You may have noticed that most of the statements were directly to the point, positive and involved speaking in the first person.

Go directly to the point: it is common for people not to come to the point of what they want to say, but instead to merely hint, use a general statement or add unnecessary flannel.

Write some assertive alternatives or pick out the statements in Table 5.3 which could replace each of the following:

Hinting:

'Er, how are you off for money these days? It's just that since I lent you that £5 I've been a bit short.'

'You'd like to stay this weekend? Well, let's see, I've got a committee meeting Friday evening, and Saturday we're going to finish decorating the spare room, then Saturday evening we were going to Sandra's party so, er, you get my point?'

'Cough, cough, smokey round here, isn't it.'

Too general:

'You're always so nice to your staff.'

'I'm fed up of you people always talking down to me as if I were an imbecile.'

'Try not to bother me for a while.'

Unnecessary flannel:

'I'm sorry to let you down, I know you wouldn't ask unless you really needed it, but I'm pretty broke myself and anyway you still owe me £5 from last month.'

'Well, come to think of it, now you mention it, perhaps I did forget to tell her. But I've been ever so busy, it's been one thing after another, you know how it is. I'm sure you must understand, don't you?'

'I was wondering, well, whether you and Mildred were having a working lunch to talk about something in particular, well, if you're not, would I be intruding if I joined you? I know you don't get much chance to talk together.'

Be positive: a positive statement gives the other person a clear message about exactly what you want — rather than what you do not want. It helps them to conjure up a definite picture of what you are trying to get across. Thus they know where they stand with you and can understand more readily. Lack of clarity and difficulty in understanding can cause anxiety and frustration on both sides, and reduce the chances of assertive cooperation or negotiation.

For instance, if a nurse says 'Don't spit it out' to a child or a mentally handicapped or confused adult whom she is feeding, he is likely to spit it out because that is the immediate picture which is conjured up in his mind. However, if she encourages him to 'chew this carefully and swallow it', he has a more positive picture of what is wanted and is more likely to cooperate. A 'don't' request puts the wrong picture into anyone's mind, however sophisticated their brain functioning is.

Write some assertive alternatives or pick out the statements from Table 5.3 which could replace each of the following:

Too negative:

'Don't ask me, that's not my job.'

'You've done it again. For goodness' sake don't make commitments for me.'

'Don't do that, I don't like it.'

Speak for yourself: when you speak for yourself, using the first person, you show you respect yourself, your own right to have opinions, feelings, impressions, wants and needs, and you indicate you expect respect from the other person too. It also indicates that you are taking responsibility for those opinions etc. This has been called the 'language of responsibility'. It also indicates humility in that you are acknowledging the individuality of your viewpoint, rather than pretending you are 'right', 'objective' or dressing up your opinion as an indisputable fact. It also helps to avoid blaming and putting words into other people's mouths. Thus you leave open the possibility that the other person might also have their own unique opinion, feeling etc. and avoid putting them down. It is particularly important when expressing uncomfortable emotions, e.g. 'I feel cross when you keep me waiting' — rather than 'You make me cross', an approach which blames the other person. It is also particularly important when criticising or praising somebody, e.g. 'I don't like the way you handled that patient, I think your approach was much too rough' — rather than 'You're a very rough person', which labels the person and is unconstructive.

Write some assertive alternatives or pick out the statements in Table 5.3 which could replace the following:

Blaming

'You make me so angry when you ignore me like that.'

'Your mechanic's hopeless, he's made a right mess of that service on my car.'

'That's why the atmosphere's so bad in this place — people like you are always bitching behind other people's backs.'

Distancing from own feelings, opinions

'Yes, you do feel good when it goes well, don't you?'

'Everyone's been saying how good you look today.'

'We don't like that kind of joke round here.'

Put-downs

'You're really stubborn, aren't you?'

'Get your hands off me, you little pervert.'

'Mind your own business, I'm quite capable of thinking for myself, thank you very much.'

Trying to put words into other people's mouths

'Don't you think we've reached a deadlock here? Do you think it would be a good idea to sit down and talk it through?'

'Don't you think it would be a good idea if you put your cigarette out considering this is a non-smoking area?'

Irrational beliefs

Beliefs can affect the way we act. It can be difficult to be aware of all the beliefs which affect your approach since most are totally unconscious. However, it is possible to examine your own beliefs and, if appropriate, to restructure them for yourself.

Pinpoint any beliefs in Table 5.4 which you find you believe to some degree, and which you would prefer not to believe. Formulate a rational counterpart to each of these. Write the counterpart in the space, and cross out the irrational version, e.g. Irrational belief: it is uncaring to be assertive. Rational counterpart: being assertive indicates I care enough about the other person, and myself, to treat us both with respect. It also means I can stand up for people who depend on me. (When you write out this exercise, cross out the irrational belief.)

Add any other irrational beliefs which apply to you and write their counterparts.

Making requests

In most situations in nursing, it is more appropriate to make a request of someone than to give an order (emergencies would be exceptions). You have the right to state what you want, as others have the right to refuse. In trying to clear your mind of anxieties about the possibility of refusal, you could try to remind yourself that having a request turned down is not the end of the world: you are not being rejected as a person, you are merely having your request turned down. On the other hand, you may be surprised at how often your requests can be granted. In any case, if you are not getting what you want or need, then you have nothing to lose by asking.

1. The first step is to work out exactly what you want (not what you don't want). This may well be the most difficult step if you are not used to considering yourself.
2. Work out a statement which clearly and concisely expresses what you want with the relevant strength of feeling — remembering to go directly to the point, to be positive and usually using 'I'.

For instance; a district nurse has called to see her GP colleague to discuss something important about a patient. As is his wont, the GP continues to busy himself with tidying up his surgery while they are talking and she is finding this distracting, and the fact that he is towering above her while she is seated is rather

Table 5.4 *Some common irrational beliefs related to assertiveness.*

Irrational beliefs	Rational counterparts
1. It is uncaring to be assertive.	
2. It is part of my role as a nurse to meet everyone else's needs.	
3. My definition of a team is a group of people who do as I say.	
4. I have no right to change my mind; neither has anyone else.	
5. When something goes wrong, somebody must always be to blame for it.	
6. I must be liked by everyone and they must all approve of what I do.	
7. There's nothing I can do about shortage of staff or money for vital resources.	
8. If someone turns down my request, it is because they do not like me.	
9. It would be a disaster if someone turned down my request, so I will not take the risk of asking. I will just hope that somehow I will get what I want or need.	
10. I have no right to express my opinion about the care given to any particular patients. The doctor's decision is final and I must do what he says without question.	
11. I ought to be tough at all times and never show my vulnerability.	
12. I must keep the peace at all costs.	

intimidating. She realises that she wants him to sit down and give her his full attention.

3. Attract the person's attention and make sure you have it before you proceed. Using their name and allowing a silence may give them time to switch their attention from whatever was on their mind. Touching an arm or shoulder might be appropriate sometimes.

An example: the district nurse says, gently but firmly: 'Dr Andrew . . . . .' (he looks around at her) 'Dr Andrew, I'd like you to sit down and give me your full attention while we discuss this problem.'

There are a number of possible responses to a request, some easier to handle than others.

- Immediate agreement (you may be surprised how often this can happen).
- Direct refusal.
- Agreement but postponed to another time.
- Suggested compromise.
- No direct refusal but a series of blustering excuses.
- Request ignored — no response.
- Attempts to sidetrack you with manipulative or argumentative bait.
- Sarcastic put-downs.
- Sulks.
- Churlish complaints.
- Aggressive attack.

Faced with a difficult response, if you are serious about your request and it is important to you, there are two techniques you could use to help you to persist.

Persistence

1. *'Sticking to it':* this simply involves repeating your request over and over again until it is heard properly. Taking the district nurse and GP situation again:

Dr Andrew replies to her request with 'All in good time. Goodness me, what's all this mess doing here? Now, what were you saying about Mrs Smith?' and continues to busy himself. So she repeats her request: 'Dr Andrew, I'd like to discuss Mrs Smith with you sitting down and giving me your full attention.'

2. *'Fielding the response':* this technique involves listening carefully to what the other has to say, and responding briefly to relevant questions or summarising what has been said, while always ending up with your 'sticking to it' statement.

For instance, Dr Andrew again: 'Aha, I've got the measure of you! You've been on one of these assertiveness training courses they're sending all the nurses on these days. Waste of time. They should let you get on with the work, there's enough to do, don't you think?'

District nurse: 'Perhaps you don't think much of our assertiveness training, but the point is, I want to talk to you about Mrs Smith with you sitting down and giving me your full attention.'

The techniques for persistence help you to keep clear about your request when faced with difficult responses, particularly manipulative or argumentative bait. Here are some more examples:

A senior nurse asks a state enrolled nurse: 'Mrs Evans, could you work on B ward until lunch time, they're desperate with Sister and two students off sick. SEN: 'You're always picking on me, why is it always me who has to go?'
Senior nurse: 'I know this is the second day running, but nevertheless I'd like you to go to B ward till lunch time.'
SEN: 'Why don't you send the student? Why me?'
Senior nurse: 'You're more familiar with B ward so I'd like you to go over there till lunch time.'
SEN: 'Oh all right.'

Two colleagues join Ann at the table where she is eating her lunch. They both light up cigarettes. Ann is a non-smoker and hates having smoke wafting around while she's eating.
Ann: 'I just want to say something. I like chatting to you over lunch, but could you put your cigarettes out while I'm eating.'
Colleague 1: 'Oh sorry, look we can keep the smoke away from you, no bother.'
Ann: It's still affecting me and I'd like you to put the cigarette out till I've finished my lunch.'
Colleague 2: 'What's all this holier-than-thou stuff, Ann? You used to smoke like a chimney when we were students.'

Ann: Yes, I did, but now I just want you to avoid smoking while I'm eating.'

Colleague 1: 'OK Ann, got the message. I didn't realise it bothered you.'

It is important to be deliberate in regulating the strength of feeling expressed each time you use these techniques. Usually, it is appropriate to stay in the same 'gear', i.e. to keep the same gentle, firm tone of voice each time, rather than getting increasingly sarcastic, strident, apologetic, aggressive, parental or churlish at each repetition.

Practise writing persistent request statements for the following situations:

Eleanor lent David £5 two weeks ago and she wants it back urgently so that she can buy some lunch and pay for her journey home. David uses four responses to her persistent request before coughing up:

1. 'Er, well, I've only got £5 on me right now and I've got to get my lunch and pay the train fare too and I've forgotten my cheque book again.'

2. 'What am I supposed to do? Starve and stay here all night?'

3. 'Oh come on, I promise to let you have it tomorrow when I've been to the bank.'

4. 'What are you getting so het up about? Calm down, it's only a fiver.'

Mary is a staff nurse on an Intensive Therapy Unit. She has asked to be sent on a particular short counselling course, and has already outlined her reasons very well in a report to the senior nurse (giving references about the needs of bereaved relatives and stress amongst staff on ITU). She and the senior nurse have just finished discussing something else and Mary comes in with her repeated request:

Senior nurse's responses:

1. 'Well, I don't see the relevance to your job. Why not go on that study afternoon on drugs instead?'

2. 'I've heard some weird stories about some of these counselling

courses and the things they get up to. I wouldn't touch it with a barge pole myself.'

3. 'But you're already very good at this sort of thing. I got a letter only the other day from John Brown's wife saying how sympathetic you'd been. Really singing your praises she was.'

Saying 'no'

This is one of the most anxiety-provoking aspects of assertiveness and nurses can usually bring to mind very easily all the possible things that can go wrong if they say 'no'. To redress the balance we need to also consider the possible negative effects of *not* saying 'no'. These could include:

- Degrading the other person by assuming they cannot cope with your refusal.
- Being exploited and treated as a 'pushover'.
- Not getting the respect you deserve from others; hating yourself for being so weak.
- Resenting the people who ask you to do the things you unwillingly agree to do.
- Doing whatever you've agreed to do badly, late, grudgingly or not at all because you don't have the time or motivation.
- Spending your time on other people's priorities and carrying out their responsibilities, rather than your own.
- Getting little satisfaction out of your job/life because you spend your time doing other people's cast-off tasks (usually the mundane or unpleasant ones) and can't spend enough time on the things you are good at, interested in or that would challenge you and help you to develop your talents.
- Exhaustion and despair at being unable to succeed at being 'all things to all people'.
- Depression as the backlog of resentment gets turned in on yourself.
- Losing any self-identity you had because you forget who you really are, and others only consider you for what they can get out of you.
- You may bring out the worst in even the nicest people around you, as your 'victim' or 'martyr' role drives them to distraction, or your lack of limits brings out the bully in them.

So saying 'no' may be risky in that you may have an uncomfortable situation to deal with in the short term, but the long-term risks of not saying 'no' are even more formidable (5).

There are six stages to consider when saying 'no':

1. Notice your gut reaction to the request and take that into account when deciding to agree or not. For instance, if you get that sinking feeling as the request is made then the chances are that you really do not want to agree to the request.
2. Notice if 'oughts', 'shoulds' or 'musts' come to mind and check if they are consistent with what you *really* want.
3. Make sure you have all the information you need to make the decision.
4. If you are undecided, take time to make your decision.
5. When you turn down the request, make it very clear that is what you are doing, preferably using the word 'no': go straight to the point without any flannel, and show you mean it by using assertive body language and tone of voice.
6. Persist in your refusal by sticking to it and 'fielding the response' and keeping in the same 'gear'.

Consider the relevance of various possible additions to the word 'no'.

1. *Giving a reason:* try to avoid white-lie excuses which could tie you in knots, for instance, refusing to lend money because you say you have none with you, then finding that you dare not go to lunch in case the person sees you buying something. Consider whether the person is entitled to a reason or not. It might be that in a work situation if you refuse to do something which is normally accepted as part of your job (e.g. helping to lift a patient), it is appropriate to give a reason (e.g. you have hurt your back). However, with something more personal you have every right not to give any other reason than that you just do not want to agree to the request (e.g. someone asks you to go to a party with them or to babysit). On most occasions it is probably appropriate to give a reason if you have one, otherwise you may come over more bluntly than you intended. But having given a reason once, there is no need to repeat or defend it. Beware of expert manipulators who will try to invalidate your reason. In the following example, Fatima manages to say 'no' for once, and wants to soften the refusal with a reason. However, she begins to lose ground when she starts to defend her reason.

Fatima: 'No, I can't babysit for you tonight, I've got an essay to write.'

Edward: 'No problem, just bring your books. The children won't be any trouble once you've got them to bed.'

Fatima: 'But I need all my own things around me to be able to concentrate — my stereo and so on.'

Edward: 'Well, bring your records too. I'll pick you up so you won't have to carry them.'

It may be the case that giving a reason makes it easier for you to refuse, but be prepared to abandon giving reasons if you are getting manipulated.

Fatima: 'No, I just don't want to babysit tonight.'

Edward: 'Why not? You get on so well with the kids, they're always asking when you're coming again.'

Fatima: 'The answer's no, Edward.'

2. *Making an apology:* most books on assertiveness are written by Americans (e.g. Clark (6), Smith (7) and Alberti (8)) and advocate never apologising unless you are absolutely genuine about it. This probably makes sense to all but the Southern English, who are often accused of being insincerely over-apologetic. (Have you ever found yourself saying 'sorry' to someone who has bumped into you?) If you are used to apologising and find it easier to say 'no' by putting in an occasional 'I'm sorry' to soften the blow, then it may well be appropriate for you to do so. However, notice if you begin to overdo it and to slide towards being submissive or manipulative, then cut out the apologies and stick to your 'no' message.

Examples: genuine apology: 'No, I'm really sorry, I've already got appointments booked for that day. I'm very interested in supporting your project though, when does the working group meet again?'

'Polite' apology: 'I'm sorry but I'm not prepared to lend you any more money.'

3. *Suggesting an alternative:* if you really would like to agree to the request but the time or place is inconvenient, then it is appropriate to suggest alternatives which would suit you. You may also wish to suggest someone else to do it. In this case, try to avoid passing the buck to someone who you know would not like to be asked, and try to avoid offering to arrange the alternative. For instance, Jill was asked by the senior nurse to sit on a particular

committee, an offer which she definitely did not want to take up. She knew Tom liked committee work and offered to contact him. Tom couldn't do it, which left Jill in the position of having to inform the senior nurse and at this point she weakened and agreed to do it.

If the person making the request rejects your alternative, stick to your 'no', and avoid trying desperately to think of a lot of alternative suggestions to solve their problem (this is likely to degenerate into the 'Why don't you ... yes but ...' game described by Eric Berne). Examples of assertively suggested alternatives: 'No, I'm not prepared to swop my day off on Sunday with you on Monday. How about asking Alison, she said there was something she wanted to do on Monday but couldn't because she's on duty.' 'No, I can't spare any staff this morning, but I could after 2 p.m. Would that help?'

4. *Not intending to hurt:* if you are concerned the other person might be hurt by your refusal, it might be worth explaining that you are not intending to be hurtful. Example: 'I'm sorry if you're hurt because that's not what I'm setting out to do. I'm only turning down your request, not rejecting you personally.'

5. *Sharing how you genuinely feel about saying 'no':* if you feel bad about refusing, it might sometimes be appropriate to say so, while sticking to your 'no'. Example: 'I feel really guilty about saying 'no' to you again, but still I have to.' 'I find this really difficult to say, especially as it's you, but no I can't help you out right now.'

Beware of the manipulator or aggressive person who will pick at your vulnerable spots when you reveal them like this.

Assertiveness and cooperation

'But what happens if two people are both being assertive, don't you get a deadlock?'

Assertiveness is often linked in some people's minds with being non-cooperative. Although it may indeed be appropriately assertive to refuse to cooperate, the two are not inseparable.

Assertive cooperation	Assertive compromise	Assertive non-cooperation
Non-assertive cooperation	Non-assertive compromise	Non-assertive cooperation

Fig. 5.2 *Assertive non-cooperation and five other options.*

Figure 5.2 shows six possibilities in relation to the assertive/non-assertive and cooperative/non-cooperative dimensions. Consider the following examples:

1. A student nurse is asked by a staff nurse to help to lift a patient. She sees that the patient's comfort is more important than the task she is already doing. She agrees. This is assertive cooperation.
2. A ward sister agrees unwillingly to accompany the surgical registrar on a ward round even though he has disturbed her while she is talking to some bereaved relatives. Afterwards she grumbles to a colleague that he is quite capable of finding the notes and talking to patients himself and that she is fed up of having to drop everything to help him. This is non-assertive cooperation.
3. A health visitor is faced with a manipulative client who is trying to persuade her to write a report supporting her claim for a day nursery place. The health visitor does not feel her circumstances warrant a special report and declines to write one, but offers to help fill in the application form and also to give her details of a good local private nursery. This is assertive compromise.
4. A nurse who is getting married soon asks a colleague to swop a day off. The colleague grumbles and bulldozes the nurse into agreeing to reciprocate by swopping another day off the following week even though the nurse knows she will have to change arrangements to have the dress fitted and to talk to the priest. This is non-assertive compromise.
5. A doctor asks the staff nurse to give a dangerously high dose of a drug to a child. The staff nurse refuses and sticks to her refusal under pressure. This is assertive non-cooperation.
6. A nurse comes to a ward to borrow a piece of equipment. The sister knows her and sidetracks her into chatting about what's been happening since they last met. The nurse leaves empty-handed having forgotten what she originally came for. This is non-assertive non-cooperation on the part of the sister.

When both people in an interaction are being assertive, there is no guarantee that a deadlock will not occur, but it is not inevitable. Nurses quite often speak of the need to keep 'good relationships' with colleagues as a reason for not being assertive. This avoidance of conflict actually creates bad relationships: keeping the peace at all costs means that someone is giving way or compromising too much of the time. It is a healthy sign if conflict occurs at times.

People respect the person who sets her limits and makes them clear, even if they sometimes find it inconvenient.

At the other end of the scale, when cooperation can never or very seldom be achieved then the people involved need to sit down and work out what is going wrong. For instance, it may be that their expectations of each other are unrealistic, the manner of the demands is unhelpful or there is some basic underlying problem between them. Some relationships just cannot be made to work, so the personality clash needs to be acknowledged and the protagonists to agree to keep out of each other's way.

Giving and receiving compliments

Conscientious nurses suffer from 'performance anxiety' at times: they worry about whether or not they are doing their job well enough. In order to reduce unnecessary anxiety we all need feedback from other people, both positive and negative. Genuine compliments, assertively expressed, can help to build the genuine self-confidence which is needed as a firm foundation on which to build improvements in performance. Unfortunately many nurses report a dearth of compliments in the communication they have with each other: they hear when they have made a mistake or are not working up to scratch, but rarely when their work is going well. When compliments are made they often come over as patronising, embarrassingly exaggerated, insincere ego-boosting to get something out of you, sarcastic, or as a prelude to a telling-off. On the other hand, even well-expressed genuine compliments can be thrown back in the face of the giver because the nurse is so unused to them that she is too embarrassed or suspicious to accept them graciously. This tends to deter the giver from giving that person a compliment again.

So, giving compliments can be risky and stressful to some extent. To reduce the stress of taking that risk, you could try to remember the three main features of assertive statements when phrasing the compliment: be direct and to the point, positive, and speak for yourself. Try to comment only on what has been done, or the way it was done, not the person's personality. (See Fig. 5.3.)

For instance, a sister explained a complicated procedure to a student very clearly, using improvised teaching aids and checking the student understood each step before moving on to the next.

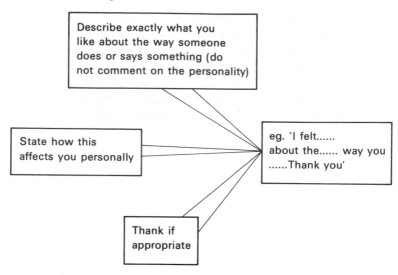

Fig. 5.3   *Giving compliments assertively.*

The student said, 'Thanks, sister, you explained that clearly. What a relief, I've grasped it at last with your help.'

The following example indicates how a change in feedback habits can affect the atmosphere at work. Suzanne was a relatively new sister on a busy surgical ward where morale was low because an influenza epidemic had decimated the numbers of staff available for duty in the hospital. Those on duty were working flat out, and Suzanne was concerned about falling standards, finding that she had to keep an eagle eye on everyone to ensure acceptable standards. As far as compliments were concerned, she thought that 'grown men and women did not need a pat on the head every time they did their job the way they were supposed to'. Also, it had not crossed her mind ever to compliment her senior nurse manager, although she knew the manager was bending over backwards to get more staff, and was helping on the wards herself. When she came across the idea of assertive compliments, she thought the phrases 'I liked the way you . . .' and 'I appreciated your . . .' sounded like useful ways of starting off assertive, as opposed to patronising, compliments. She decided to make a point of looking out for instances of good nursing practice in addition to the slips, and immediately genuinely complimented her staff whenever she noticed them. If it was not appropriate to speak at the time, she mentioned it when they reported to her before going off duty. She continued to pull them up on instances of unsatisfactory work, but found that these instances became fewer and the general atmosphere had become more positive than at any time since she took over the ward. Her staff were tired but had a sense of achievement and satisfaction from coping with the staffing crisis. She also found her relationships with the senior manager had become more human since she had shown her appreciation for the manager's efforts. Suzanne herself felt she was getting more job satisfaction from being more conscious of her own and her staff's day-to-day successes, whereas she had previously taken these for granted.

Receiving compliments assertively is like accepting a gift with pleasure (as opposed to throwing it back in the donor's face). If you want to say more than a direct 'thank you', the key is to stay positive. Share any positive feelings you have about yourself, what you did or how it feels to be complimented. For instance, a patient compliments a nurse on her care and the part it played in his recovery. '. . . Thank you, I'm pleased to have been able to help you get better.' A nurse manager compliments her colleague on the way she chaired a particularly difficult committee meeting. '. . . Thanks a lot. I must admit I'm pretty pleased with myself too, all things considered.' A nurse researcher compliments her colleague on a paper she had published recently. '. . . Thanks. Actually I'm feeling pretty proud of myself to get it published by that journal.' Avoid playing it down, passing on the credit to someone else, putting yourself or the other person down, or giving a compliment in return. Just accept it.

Seeking compliments assertively when you need them can be very healing when you are feeling vulnerable about the way others see you, or the way you see yourself. Share how you are feeling and make your request for positive feedback assertively. For instance. Heather, a tutor of only one year's standing, had had some difficulties with her senior tutor. These difficulties had centred around some mistakes which Heather had made. Heather acknowledged the mistakes but felt the senior tutor had over-reacted out of all proportion to the severity of the 'crimes', including reporting her to the Director of Nurse Education. This incident had passed, but Heather found herself concerned about what the DNE thought of her work. She went to see him and said 'Bob, I know that incident with Francis has blown over now, but I'm left feeling something is unresolved. I know you've heard about the mistakes I've made during this last year, but what I'd like to know is what have you heard or seen about my work that's positive?' Bob: 'Well, there's been no problems lately so I've assumed your work is perfectly satisfactory now.' Heather: 'But what have you actually seen or heard about what I've done well.' Bob: 'Hm . . . er . . . Well, come to think of it, I did hear from some of the senior nurse managers that they were impressed with the way you organised that working group on the nursing process. Oh yes, and last week . . .' The DNE was unused to giving positive feedback, but Heather helped him by her gentle persistence. She got what she wanted and felt much more acknowledged for her achievements, which helped to heal the hurt she had felt about the senior tutor's over-reaction to her mistakes.

Giving constructive criticism

The way you phrase a criticism should include the main features of an assertive statement: getting straight to the point, being positive about what you want, and speaking for yourself. It could be merely a statement of what you want, or with one or more additions (see Fig. 5.4).

Some examples:
Elspeth, a ward sister, considered how to approach Mac, an auxiliary nurse about his continual lateness. Using various combinations from the diagram, her options included:
1. 'Mac, I'd like you to start work on time from now onwards.'

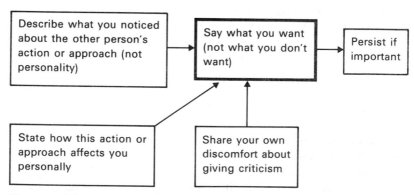

Fig. 5.4   *The main elements of assertive criticism.*

2. 'Mac, I've noticed that you've been late for the last four days. I'd like you to be on time from now onwards.'
3. 'Mac, I'm getting increasingly irritated by your continual lateness. I'd like you to be on time from now onwards.'
4. 'Mac, I'm a bit embarrassed to bring this up again since I myself was a bit late yesterday, but I notice you have been very late for work for the past four days. I'd like you to be on time from now on.'

She expected Mac to respond rather defensively so she chose the second option, keeping the others up her sleeve in case she needed to persist. In the event, he agreed to be on time and he was.

This next example is a common situation, though not many of us can find the courage to deal with it as well as Wilmark did. Wilmark was a student mental handicap nurse and often worked in partnership with his student colleague Liz, who had BO. He had heard a number of people commenting on this although no one seemed to have spoken directly to her about it. He hated working with her because of the smell, but otherwise liked her a lot. He decided to bring up the subject when they were alone. Wilmark: 'Liz, I feel really awkward about saying this, but I'd like you to find a way of reducing your body odour because I find it difficult to work with you because of it.' Liz: 'Are you trying to tell me I've got BO?' Wilmark; 'Well, Yes.' Liz: 'Are you kidding? Is this supposed to be a joke?' Wilmark: 'No, Liz it's not. Oh, heck, I feel really terrible about upsetting you but it had to be said. I just want you to find a way of reducing your body odour.' Liz: 'You feel terrible, what the hell do you think I feel?' She rushed off to the empty day room. Wilmark found her crying, but they were able to talk it over and there was subsequently a considerable improvement in the situation. They remained friends.

Using the constructive criticism diagram, try to phrase statements in the following situation as more assertive alternatives to what the nurse says:

Mrs Green is a patient who is an expert manipulator. Her technique is to run down all the other nurses apart from the one with her, then to indirectly talk them into carrying out various favours. Nurse Jenny Adams has fallen for this before but this time she does not want to have to listen to the malicious gossip.
Mrs Green: '. . . and that posh one, she's so high and mighty,

Lady Muck's not in it. Wouldn't deign to dirty her hands in a million years. Not like you, pet, you're so good to me.'
Jenny: Non-assertive criticism: 'You shouldn't go on like that about the other nurses. It's not right.'

What would a constructive criticism statement be?

Mrs Green: 'Well, you've got to talk to someone haven't you? You're the one person I can trust, I know it wouldn't go any further, not like that black one, you know she told lies about me to your supervisor? Terrible. Not having her near me again.'

Jenny: Non-assertive criticism: 'Oh for goodness' sake, don't be so nasty. I've told you before.'

What would a constructive criticism statement be?

Mrs Green: 'Oh, all sticking together are we? You just can't win when all you nurses gang up together. Huh. Come on, let's get it over with. Where's my pink flannel?'

Dealing with criticism

Nurses often find it very stressful to be on the receiving end of criticism, not least because most people make a mess of giving it. The frequency of instances of over-reaction are disturbing: official reports are made to senior management rather than face-to-face confrontation of the 'miscreant'; disciplinary or grievance procedures are over-used; there are 'trigger happy' outbursts at appraisal time; there is public humiliation and so on. Every single nurse who has discussed the topic of criticism with me has experienced situations like this at some time in their careers. It would appear that the number of these instances is increasing as nurses in positions of authority over other nurses become more and more anxious about actual and imaginary legal implications of nursing actions. Bitterness is often expressed at the discrepancy between the effects of minor mistakes made by nurses (involving some of the over-reactions mentioned above) and major mistakes made by other professionals, such as doctors and pharmacists (apparently brushed under the carpet). Apart from the anxiety generated by difficulties in understanding the complex legal background to nursing and lack of clear-cut answers from legal advisors, one fundamental cause of this problem seems to be lack of opportunity to learn the skills of assertive face-to-face criticism.

Readers who are still smarting from bad experiences arising from such lack of skill may think I am adding insult to injury by suggesting that learning how to handle criticism assertively may actually help the other person to learn how to give it more assertively. Aside from such altruism, you can feel better about coping with the stress of dealing with criticism by using some techniques from assertiveness training.

The first is to work towards a balance between emotion and reason. This means noticing, acknowledging and accepting your own emotional reaction to the criticism. Feelings of hurt, as outlined in Chapter 2, may or may not be totally related to the present situation; they may relate more to past experiences of destructive criticism. However realistically self-confident, assertive and self-accepting we become, each one of us is likely to retain some vulnerable spots — 'crumple buttons' as Anne Dickson calls them. These are words, tones, or areas of criticism which make us crumple inside, and make the situation stressful and hard to handle.

Listening to criticism and protecting yourself

You need to balance (not repress) the emotional reaction with some reason. Reason suggests that criticism can be useful: it can tell you something about yourself and about the effect you can have on others. If you are interested in improving your abilities and performance, then you need criticism to help you do so. It can tell you about the other person's perceptions, values, vulnerabilities and limits. Thus, you have more information about them and this can positively help the relationship. It is reasonable to protect yourself against destructive criticism.

So, assertive techniques can help you to make the most of useful criticism, to protect you from unhelpful criticism and to deal with your emotions appropriately. First, try to distinguish between three types of criticism.

1. Valid — criticism which you agree with, which is true.
2. Not valid — untrue, or you disagree with.
3. Partially valid but overstated — some truth or agreement, but exaggerated or including something that is untrue or something that you disagree with.

If you need time to react, to decide what category the criticism falls into, then try to take the time you need and respond to the person when you have decided. Having decided, respond to each form of criticism by either agreeing or disagreeing.

1. *Valid:* state that you agree and repeat the truth of the critic's statement, e.g. 'Yes, that's true, I did forget to tell the patient.'
2. *Not valid:* state you disagree and contradict with a positive statement about yourself. This can be difficult if you are not used to being positive about yourself. Avoid contradicting so much that you go the other way and put yourself down, e.g. 'I disagree totally, I'm not lazy. On the contrary, I think I work very hard' is more assertive than 'On the contrary, I think I'm a bit of a workaholic'.
3. *Partially valid:* acknowledge the truth in the criticism and reject what is not true, e.g. 'Well, I know I was a bit sharp with Mrs Engels when she pulled my hair suddenly, but generally I think I've got a polite manner with patients, friendly but not rude.'

To practise this initial response to criticism, try the following exercise. List some imaginary criticisms of yourself under the following headings (try to write them out in full in the way someone might express them to you): valid criticisms, not valid criticisms and partially valid criticisms. Then write a response statement for each criticism following the guidelines, e.g. Brenda's list.

Valid criticisms

Response

1. Brenda, you've taken two hours to get that report written.

Yes, that's quite true, it did take me ages to write the report.

2. You didn't fill in the patient's fluid chart.

You're quite right, I did forget to fill his fluid chart in.

Not valid criticisms

Response

3. You're always late.

That's not true, I don't remember ever having been late on duty on this ward.

4. You don't show any interest in teaching the students.

I disagree. On the contrary, I take every available opportunity to teach the students. They often tell me how grateful they are.

Partially valid	**Response**
5. You look a real mess.	Well, I think my hair's probably due for a trim, but otherwise I disagree with you, I think I look quite tidy and smart.
6. You're always changing your mind.	I admit I sometimes change my decisions, as I did about the off-duty, but I disagree with you. On the whole, I think I am fairly consistent.

Try to practise using the responses by having a friend read out the criticisms, for you to respond to. Ask for feedback about your tone of voice and body language and keep practising until you come across as relaxed but firmly assertive.

Next consider what else you might say apart from the agreement or disagreement. Remember that sometimes it may be appropriate to just leave it at that rather than blustering on. At other times, that might be too blunt and extra comments might be appropriate, for instance:

1. Giving a reason: you might feel better or you might clear up a misunderstanding if you give an explanation. But beware of defensively justifying yourself and trying to deflect criticism that is valid.
2. Asking for more details, examples or an explanation: this is helpful if the criticism is general or apparently untrue. You might be able to clear up a misunderstanding, or get some more useful feedback.
3. Stating what, if anything, you are prepared to do about the situation.
4. Asking the critic what effect your actions or approach has on her.
5. Sharing how you feel emotionally about the criticism: this might include a genuine apology for a mistake, or your reaction to unjust or badly given criticism.

Whatever you add, be prepared to make it short and to allow a silence at the end of it, even if it feels uncomfortable. Blustering out of nervousness will lead you into a submissive, aggressive or manipulating approach.

Now go back through your list and add something else to your responses, but only if you think it is appropriate, e.g. additions to Brenda's list:

1. We've been short of staff today so I've had to help out with the patients quite a lot.
2. I'm sorry. I'll do it straightaway.
3. Can you think of a particular occasion when I was late?
4. I'm upset you think I'm not interested. What makes you say that?
5. (no further comment)
6. Did it upset you that I changed the off-duty?

Asking for criticism

Many people find it hard to come out with something which might sound critical at the time, yet harboured resentments will seep out somehow. If you think someone is holding something back, it can be worthwhile asking for the criticism and getting it over and done with. Or if you think you could have done something better, it might be useful to have the opinions of the people involved or observing. Anne Dickson calls this 'negative inquiry'. Some examples:

- 'Have I put my foot in it in some way?'
- 'Have I said or done something to offend you?'
- 'How does my mistake affect you?'
- 'I don't think I dealt with that situation too well but I can't work out what I did wrong. What do you think?'
- 'I get the impression I make you feel uncomfortable. Is there something in particular that I do or say which bothers you?'

Summary

Table 5.5 summarises the main differences between the assertive, aggressive, manipulative and submissive approaches. You could refer to it periodically to review your progress in reducing non-assertive tendencies and becoming more assertive.

Pitfalls in using assertiveness to prevent and cope with stress

As with any skills development, mistakes will be made when learning more about assertiveness.

1. *'The worm has turned':* if someone has been submissive about something for a long time there is likely to be a backlog of suppressed resentments which can sometimes result in the would-be asserter coming over as much too aggressive for a while until she gets the hang of controlling her tone of voice and body language. Try to avoid making widespread and radical changes in your approach to everyone but instead take it in small steps. It is much better to practise the techniques in situations which are not too emotionally charged and with people who do not know you well, rather than turning your established relationships upside down. For instance, you could practise when dealing with difficult shop assistants or pushy door-to-door salesmen, rather than immediately trying to reverse twenty years of submissiveness in your marriage. New relationships give you the ideal chance to start the way you mean to continue.

2. *Self-consciousness:* it is common to feel a little embarrassed when first becoming aware of your behaviour and approach. Sometimes nurses think that if they are aware of what they are doing, then nothing they do will ever be spontaneous again. Being aware is just a matter of noticing, allowing and accepting (see 'noticing' meditation techniques). Even when we are being spontaneous and 'natural', we have made a decision to act in that way; that decision is made in a split second, though is often unconscious. Learning to be aware of those decisions helps you to restructure the neurological pathways which lead you to act in certain ways. So your decision-making when trying to be deliberately assertive can feel comparatively slow and contrived, but with practice you become more 'natural' as you adapt the techniques to suit your own style of self-expression.

3. *Slavishly following the form of words suggested in assertiveness books:* if you do not adapt the techniques to your own culture and style you can sound a little odd. For instance, when using the 'fielding the response' technique, 'I hear what you say, man, yeah, right on' can sound fine coming from someone from Los Angeles but a bit contrived from someone with a Geordie accent.

4. *Anti-anything-American prejudice:* at the other end of the scale, some nurses seem to have an irrational prejudice against anything new which originates in the USA (the nursing process is a case in point). Assertiveness training was developed at first in the USA but is now widely used in Britain. As stated in the previous point, it is important to adapt it to our own culture. (Think about ways

Table 5.5   *Summary of the main differences between the four approaches.*

	Assertive approach	Aggressive approach	Manipulative approach	Submissive approach
Decision making	Decide on what you think is right in each situation, basing the decision on your own carefully considered priorities, having taken into account those of others.	Decide what is right for you irrespective of others' priorities.	Decide what is right for you and pay lip service to other people's priorities. Try to persuade them their priorities are really the same as yours.	Decide according to other people's expectation/ priorities with no regard to your own.
Making requests	State what you want/need with appropriate strength of feeling. Listen and enable others to state likewise. Persist when it is important to you.	Demand. Give orders when a request is more appropriate. Blame for not having fulfilled wants/needs in the past. Make threats.	Use insincere ego-boosting to try to get what you want. Try to convince others they really want to do as you want. Try to make others feel guilty. Drop hints. Give the impression that some significant other person wants it (e.g. someone in authority). Make veiled threats.	Hold back from stating what you want/need. Grumble because you are not getting it. Fail to consider what you want/need. Make requests in an unconvincing way so the other person does not realise how important they are to you. Give up if the initial response to your request is not positive.
Saying no	Make a clear refusal with appropriate strength of feeling. Persist in your refusal when it is important to you.	Refuse for the sake of refusing. Attack the person for asking. Refuse with inappropriately high strength of feeling.	Try to talk the other person out of their request. Avoid making a direct refusal but give a lot of excuses and side tracks in the hope that the other person will retract the request. Try to make them feel guilty for asking. Cite someone else or a policy as an excuse for refusal. Agree but fail to come up with the goods.	Agree to what you don't want. Initially refuse but in an unconvincing, over-apologetic way and allow yourself to be talked into it.

Giving compliments	Give a clear appreciation with appropriate strength of feeling.	Avoid acknowledging positives about the other person. If acknowledging, do so grudgingly and with complaints about previous negative points.	Give the compliments as though surprised. Infer that there is no need for disapproval at this time, hinting there is at others. Patronise. Use insincere compliments to get your own way.	Hold back from giving compliments. If giving a compliment, overdo it and over-inflate the other person.
Receiving compliments	Accept valid compliments and agree. Reject manipulative compliments.	Demand compliments as your right; attack the person for not giving it before.	Put the credit on to someone else.	Become over grateful for any crumb of approval. Respond as if it's the giver who deserves the praise.
Giving criticism	Challenge what the person has done or said with appropriate strength or feeling. Persist when the challenge goes unheeded.	Attack the personality of the recipient of your criticism. Drag up the past for ammunition.	Become sarcastic. Make jokey put-downs. Hint at disapproval. Make veiled threats. Cite other people's concern or disapproval.	Avoid the person. Grumble or bitch behind their back.
Receiving criticism	Accept valid criticism and learn from it. Reject invalid criticism.	Retaliate. Not listen to valid criticism. Blame someone else.	Try to talk your way out of facing the criticism. Hint it's someone else's fault. Try to talk the other person into changing their mind.	Absorb all criticism whether valid or not. Use it to feed your negative self-image.
Stating opinions	Make a clear statement of your own opinion, not allowing frequent interruptions. Allow others to state their opinions without interruptions and show respect for their right to have their own opinions.	Insist your own opinion is 'right'. Prevent others from expressing theirs. Interrupt a lot. Put other people's opinions firmly down. Show you think they have no right to express their opinion.	Try to convince the other person that your idea is their idea. Try to talk the other person round to your point of view. Make jokey or sarcastic put-downs of others' opinions.	Hold back, not expressing an opinion. If you do express your opinion, do it in an unconvincing way. Allow self to be interrupted and put down. Allow self to be swayed by strong opinions which are really contrary to your own. Seek approval for your own opinions. Adapted from Bond (9)

in which we have adopted and adapted the motor car: most nurses' cars are smaller, more economical and less flashy than those of our American counterparts, yet the automobile was originally developed in the USA.)

5. *Unwillingness to invest in increased short-term, comparatively minor stress for significant long-term benefits*: undoubtedly, it can be difficult to pluck up the courage to speak or stand up for oneself in a hierarchical set-up which depends on the submissiveness of subordinates to maintain the fragile egos of autocratic seniors. However, that investment is likely to have long-term pay offs when people are aware of your limits and no longer try to push you beyond them.

6. *Using assertive techniques to manipulate or be more subtly aggressive:* sales personnel are trained to use some of the techniques outlined in this chapter but without the 'respect for other people's rights too' philosophy. Their aim is to persuade you to buy what you do not really want. It is not the purpose of this chapter to give you ammunition to 'get one over' other people: if you do, you will be causing yourself more stress in the long term since the trail of suspicion and resentment you leave in your wake will result in lack of cooperation and overt or covert retaliation.

7. *Becoming a 'hard nut':* assertiveness is often misunderstood as being to do with appearing superconfident, cool and incisive all the time. That is not what I have intended to convey: it often involves sharing your own vulnerability, humility and warmth. For instance, the 'speaking for yourself' principle means you are often sharing your own feelings and feelings can be confused or soft just as often as the opposite.

References and further reading

1. Ashworth H. (1981). 'Where's Nurse?' *Nursing Times*, September 23, p. 1654.
2. DHSS. (1980). *Inequalities in Health ('The Black Report')*. Norwich: HMSO.
3. UKCC (1984). *Code of Professional Conduct for Nurses, Midwives and Health Visitors*, 2nd edn. London: United Central Council for Nursing, Midwifery and Health Visiting.
4. Dickson A. (1982). *A Woman in Your Own Right*. London: Quartet.

5. Bond M. (1982). 'Dare You Say No.' *Nursing Mirror*, October 13, pp. 40–42.
6. Clark C. C. (1978). *Assertive Skills for Nurses*. Rockville, Maryland: Aspen.
7. Smith M. (1975). *When I Say No I Feel Guilty*. London: The Dial Press.
8. Alberti R., Emmons M. (1974). *Your Perfect Right*. London: Impact Books.
9. Bond M. (1985). Assertiveness in District Nursing. *Journal of District Nursing*, February, pp. 20–25.

Where to find out more about assertiveness

Local adult education institutes and extra-mural departments of universities and polytechnics may offer courses (for instance, The Human Potential Research Project, Dept. of Educational Studies, University of Surrey, Guildford, Surrey GU2 5XH).

There are independent courses run privately by individual facilitators. For a list of facilitators trained by Anne Dickson, write to Redwood, 83 Fordwych Road, London NW2 3TL, enclosing a stamped, addressed envelope.

You can arrange a course yourself and hire a facilitator. To find one, you could contact one of the organisations listed above, or you might find that some local nurse tutors have been trained to teach assertiveness.

To learn how to teach assertiveness, contact Redwood at the above address (though this is for women facilitators only) or me, Meg Bond, at the University of Surrey.

6

Receiving and giving support

The need for more give and take in nursing

This chapter is about support between nurses with the emphasis on peer support. By peers I mean people who feel equal in status to one another; in nursing this is usually restricted to nurses at the same level of the hierarchy.

Outside observers and nurses themselves report that the climate in the nursing culture with respect to mutual support is decidedly chilly. While we are seen as being caring towards patients, we seem to be uncaring towards each other. Sheila Hillier found that the nursing culture 'inhibits the development of close personal and supporting ties amongst nurses', and that we use shame and ridicule as a means of maintaining acceptable codes of behaviour rather in the same way as the 'shame' cultures of some North American Indian tribes (1). Peter Hingley discovered a lack of constructive feedback about job performance among nurses, and few opportunities to meet and share concerns (2). Penny Crawley describes a tribal concept of nursing culture, in that when a nurse becomes ill, 'the minute she stops being one of Us and starts being one of Them, she's thrown out of the tribe' (3). Nurses often complain that when they themselves become hospitalised, they are almost ignored by colleagues, sometimes given a side ward and administered the necessary physical care but little human support.

Chenevert goes as far as to suggest that at times nurses act like a flock of chickens; when one individual displays a sore spot, the rest peck at the sore until it dies (4). Certainly the way the disciplinary procedure can be wielded as an over-reaction to a nurse making a mistake is horrifying. Nurses often quote examples of potentially lethal mistakes made by doctors and pharmacists, yet their colleagues close ranks and support the individual who has slipped up. The converse seems to be the case in nursing. So we have a poor reputation for giving each other support. But giving cannot be done without someone else receiving, and nurses can seem remarkably difficult to help, particularly if one is used to helping patients who are non-nurses. Most patients welcome support with open arms since they have a socially-defined role in which it is acceptable to be vulnerable and to need help. It is easy and satisfying to support patients. Not so with nurses. We seem to have great difficulties in allowing ourselves to be vulnerable enough to receive support. There may be social and psychological reasons for this.

The role of the nurse consists of the expectations of her behaviour and qualities held by those around her and her own expectations of herself. A nurse is often expected to be the solid idealised parent figure, the rock upon which those around her can base their stability (rather than their finding their own stability within themselves). Nurses often report that when they allow themselves to crumble a little, they are met with expressions of surprise, dismay or even contempt from colleagues, family or friends. They also have within themselves feelings of failure, from not having lived up to their own ideal image of perfection. Whether we create expectations in other people by setting ourselves up to be seen as able to cope with anything, or whether we internalise these ideals because of other people's expectations is rather like the which-came-first-the-chicken-or-the-egg debate.

It has been suggested that people in the caring professions to some extent choose their line of work because of a mental defence mechanism called reaction formation. We may have missed out on some aspects of our own need to be cared for, and project that need into giving others what we most need for ourselves. This is rather like parents wanting to give their children what they themselves never had, and often going overboard in the other direction. For instance, someone who has suffered at the hands of authoritarian and restrictive parents may give their own children too much freedom, while denying themselves freedom by living in a stifling marriage or in a highly regulated job.

As nurses we may be pouring care and support onto other

people but denying it for ourselves by keeping potential supporters at bay. This can be done by not asking for support, or
when offered it, rejecting it in a way which will not encourage that
person to offer support another time, or by giving the impression
by what we say or by body language that we do not want to be
offered support. This creates a kind of invisible but intuitively felt
barrier through which someone who cares may not see the real
need for support, may find it too risky to offer it, or may not wish to
intrude out of respect for the nurse's desire to keep her defences
intact at that moment.

To what extent do you find it difficult to receive support? Do any
of the above explanations apply to you at all? How do you think
you might keep potential supporters at a distance?

Trust between nurses

It takes trust to be able to receive support. I have found in working
with groups of nurses that there is often considerable anxiety
about this issue. It seems to be highest among groups where the
members actually work with each other. One recent group
described some examples of the sorts of things that colleagues do
which prevents trust developing or damages trust that has already
been built:

- Destructive criticism
- Cynicism
- Sarcasm
- Dishonesty (including white lies)
- Breaking confidences (whether confidentiality is explicitly
  agreed or assumed)
- Breaking an agreement/promise
- Not doing what I expect them to do
- Being critical about other people behind their back
- Inconsistency
- Joking at someone else's expense
- Unwilling to reveal anything about themselves
- Agreeing with anyone, not stating own opinions
- Manipulating
- Being over-chummy/charming
- 'Pollyanna' syndrome: always going on about how everything
  is going well, dismissing real problems

- Getting aggressive, bossy
- Superior attitudes
- Reporting to someone else, often a senior, rather than criticising face to face
- Overreacting to situations or things said

Trusting someone is always a risk; no one is 100% reliable. Some of the points made in the above list are likely to apply to everyone. For instance, it is impossible to live up to everyone else's expectations, indeed many expectations are unrealistic.

It is also impossible to be totally consistent; as time passes, one tends to change opinions, moods and approaches. Often there are misunderstandings about confidentiality; what one person assumes will be kept confidential, another might assume to be available for general circulation. Nurses, in common with other human beings, are naturally curious and often take pleasure in discussing details of other people's lives. But this gossip can be a sign of affection and interest, or an expression of relief that the gossipers are not the only ones with problems or failings. Nurses who discover their lives have been talked about behind their backs often assume the intention was malicious. This may be true but it is not always necessarily so; it depends on the manner and tone in which it was done. You can make a fair prediction of how you will be talked about by a particular person by the way she talks about other people with you.

It seems that nurses often have an all-or-nothing approach to trust; a particular person might be seen as either totally trust-worthy or totally unreliable, with no grades in between. If X lets down Y over one issue, Y often assumes that X will let her down over everything else and does not trust her again with anything. This is one way in which potential sources of support are written off. It would be more realistic to accept that each person can be trustworthy in some respects but not in others, and to accept some types of support from one colleague and other types of support from another.

Trust-building ground rules

Whatever support is being sought or offered, it can often be useful to clarify some ground rules. Human interaction involves a myriad of ground rules which are mostly taken for granted. For instance, the legal system lays down that in relating to one another we should not steal, intentionally injure or slander. Apart from these more obvious rules, there are many less definite rules, with great variation between individuals' unstated expectations. There can be misunderstandings and loss of trust when expected ground rules are merely implicit or assumed. I have found it useful when working with groups of nurses to negotiate explicit ground rules along the lines of the following:

1. *Confidentiality:* anything personal which anyone shares is kept confidential unless permission is given to pass it on. If it is difficult for personal information to be kept confidential, you seek support for your own anxieties without revealing the information.
In some extreme exceptions where information must be passed on (e.g. a colleague whose drug problem is putting patient's safety at risk), then the person concerned is given the chance to reveal it to the relevant person or, if that fails, informed that this will be done on her behalf.
2. *Autonomy and choice:* each person is responsible for choosing for themselves whether or not to join in any discussion or activity, and how much to disclose or keep private. Therefore, probing, pushing, group pressure or unwarranted advice is to be avoided. Each person is also responsible for saying what they want, and opportunities will be made for this to be heard and understood.
3. *Speaking for self:* each person speaks for themselves, preferably speaking in the first person (e.g. 'I think/feel/imagine . . .', 'In my opinion/experience . . .', 'It seems to be . . .'), rather than

generalising or being dogmatic (e.g. 'all nurses . . .', 'you . . . don't you', 'one does . . .' 'you are feeling . . .', 'the group . . .', 'what you're really saying . . .' 'we nurses . . .'). The exception would be when one person has been elected to represent a particular group.

4. *No put-downs:* everyone has the right to have an opinion and to find their own individual right answers, therefore avoid judgments (e.g. 'you shouldn't feel . . .' 'that's stupid', 'don't be silly . . .' 'rubbish') or labels (e.g. 'typical neurotic/hysteric', 'chauvanist pig', 'inadequate'). There is opportunity for disagreement but not put-downs.

An agreement between all members of the group is sought that each will try their best to stick to the ground rules and will share responsibility for reminding each other if they start to be broken.

Types of support between nurses

The effectiveness of support can be maximised by the potential giver and receiver clarifying what type of support is needed and acceptable and who the most appropriate person is to give it. Below I have outlined the main types of support for which nurses have expressed a need, and have divided them into three main categories: ordinary conversation, direct support and facilitative support (see Table 6.1).

Table 6.1 *Types of support between nurses.*

Ordinary conversation

Direct support
    open expression of loyalty
    practical help
    sharing information
    joint action
    advice
    encouragement
    feedback

Facilitative support
    providing opportunities to talk
    listening
    allowing
    facilitative questioning

Ordinary conversation

The purpose of ordinary conversation is to help the participants to feel noticed, to feel they belong, to share ideas, information and experiences, to get to know each other and to have a period of light relief to take their mind off deeper issues. Ordinary conversation can be supportive to someone who is feeling stressed, especially if direct attempts are made to encourage her to join a group of nurses talking, to understand what the topic under discussion is about, and to join in the conversation. A nurse who is going through a difficult time may particularly need to feel noticed, to feel she belongs and to have a little light relief.

Yet often nurses feel embarrassed and helpless when a colleague is under stress, and normal conversation becomes difficult, or they might feel it is inappropriate but do not know what to substitute in its place. For instance, one nurse reported: 'When I came back to work after I lost my husband, it was awful. I felt like a leper. Every time I went up to a bunch of people talking, they just went quiet as though they'd been talking about me or something, then found excuses to go off and do something. The only person who would talk to me normally was one of the nursing auxiliaries. She gave me the chance to put things out of my mind for a while and concentrate on being back at work. You really find out who your friends are at a time like that.' So, if you are chatting with a group of people and feel embarrassed about talking normally when you see a colleague approaching who you know is going through a bad time, help her to join in by:

1. Waving her over to join you, making a space or pulling up a chair next to you so she can join the group properly.
2. Quietly telling her about the topic of the conversation.
3. If she does not join in of her own accord, eventually ask her a question related to the topic.

Try to avoid putting the whole group's attention on her just as she joins the group; this is added stress. Also be sensitive to her responses; she may not feel like joining the group or taking part in the conversation, so avoid being too pushy.

If conversation is to fulfil its functions and be supportive then everyone involved needs to have equal opportunity to join in fully. Often imbalances occur when one person mostly listens and another mostly talks. This can lead to frustrations on both sides.

The good listener may feel unnoticed, taken for granted, or that the other person is not interested in her. The enthusiastic talker may wonder what the listener is thinking, and resent her keeping her opinions and ideas to herself, leaving the talker to expose herself more by talking on. If you find yourself doing most of the listening, you may have to interrupt to get a point across. It can be useful to lead in gradually before making the point in order to give the talker a chance to switch her attention to you: 'can I/I'd like to make a point here', 'I'd just like to say something', 'did I tell you about . . .', 'I've got something to add to that . . .', 'what you said about . . . reminds me of . . .', 'going back to what you said earlier . . .', 'something similar happened to me . . .'. The talker's mind may still be in full swing on her own train of thought, and she may interrupt you. Ignore the interruptions for a while, or explain that you have not yet finished, and stick to your story or wait until you have come to the end without raising your voice. When you have finished your point, ask a question related to what you have just said. The longer you leave your assertion of space in the conversation, the more problematic it is likely to become. Indeed it can become more difficult to think of something to say, the mind goes blank, possibly because of repressed resentment. You may have to break into the conversation a few more times to assert your right to equality. Most people eventually get the message that you want to take a more active part and want them to do their share of listening. Unfortunately, some people do not however hard you try. If you want to continue the relationship, then this can be raised as a problem (not a blame session) which needs to be tackled by both sides.

When doing most of the talking, try to find ways of holding back some of the things you want to say, though without stifling your enthusiasm or strength of feeling. For instance, at the end of each point or story, leave a silence so that the other person can think out what they want to say and get it said. You may think much more quickly, or find it more difficult to bear a silence than the other person. Some of the mini-relaxation exercises in Chapter 3 may help to curb impatience. As an alternative to a silence, you could ask a question related to what you have just said: 'what do you think?', 'has anything like that ever happened to you?', 'how do you deal with situations like that?' If you are doing more than your share of interrupting, some listening techniques might enable you to cut them down. One is the 'I'm listening' method mentioned in the meditation chapter. Another is attempting to preface your point by specifically referring to something the other person has said first. For example, instead of the usual 'But . . .', you could start with 'I take your point about . . . but . . .', 'I agree with what you said about . . . but . . .', 'What you said about . . . reminds me of . . .' The 'abouts' are important here since they make you discipline yourself to really listen to be able to reiterate something which was said. Perfunctory prefaces such as 'Yes, but . . .', 'With respect . . .', 'I take your point, but . . .' are often interpreted as mere attempts to pretend that you are listening. You could open up the issue by acknowledging that you are doing most of the talking, and asking if the other person wants to say something on any of the topics covered. You then need to sit back and listen.

If you realise you have been talking more than the other person, try to notice any signs that she is tired of listening. This is not necessarily because she is bored or does not care, it is just not humanly possible to listen for long periods. On average, the brain switches off at least every three minutes or so, and apart from that, she may be preoccupied with her own concerns. Signs of tiredness might include looking at the watch, fidgeting, posture slumping or looking as though she is about to move away. Draw your point to a close, give her the chance to speak or check whether she wants to do something else.

Think back to a conversation in which you did most of the listening. Categorise each of the following statements according to the degree to which they applied to you: yes (applied to me), no (did not apply at all) or partly (applied to some extent). Note that it is possible for two contradictory statements to apply at once.

I was content to mostly listen, it wasn't just habit or not bothering.
I was really interested in what she had to say.
I wanted to show I cared.
I've talked more on previous occasions so this time it was Y's turn.
Y seemed to need to talk a lot so I was happy to give attention.
I waited for gaps to get a word in but there weren't many.
I waited for Y to ask me a question or show some interest but she didn't.
I didn't try to interrupt.

When I tried to say something I let the interruptions shut me up.
The things I wanted to say didn't seem important or interesting
enough to be put into words.
I didn't really want to listen for so long but I seemed to get
trapped.
I couldn't get away.
I've got into the habit of doing most of the listening when I'm
with Y.
I like to be considered a good listener.
I wasn't really listening, I was miles away, but I kept up a good
pretence.
I couldn't think of much to say.
I didn't want to risk saying something I might regret.
My mind went a complete blank.
I dropped hints that I wanted to get away but they didn't get
noticed.
I couldn't be bothered to say much and wanted Y to make all the
effort.
I thought it was up to Y to keep me entertained.
I preferred staying aloof with Y just then.
Staying aloof gave me a feeling of getting one over her.
I wanted Y to feel uncomfortable because of my silence.
I wanted to find out as much as I could about Y without saying
much about myself.
I was sulking.
I became so fed up with Y not taking an interest I ended up not
wanting to tell her anything at all.
I deliberately egged Y on so she would rattle on and make a fool of
herself.
I'd just come back from the dentist and I had a frozen tongue.

Consider what other statements would describe your side of the
situation. Looking back over the conversation:

1. What was the most positive aspect of your doing most of the
listening?
2. How might you begin to create a more equally balanced conversation another time?

Now, think back to an ordinary conversation in which you did
most of the talking. Categorise the following statements as before.

I was really pleased to see X.
I had saved up a lot to say to X.
I felt strongly about the topic.
I was stimulated and excited by the conversation.
I was thinking quickly and getting lots of interesting ideas.
I wanted to contribute to the discussion. X seemed interested in what I had to say so I went on.
I wanted to get my ideas into words before I forgot them.
I left silences but X didn't often say anything.
I asked questions to find out what X had to say but she didn't say much.
X usually does most of the talking so on this occasion the balance was redressed a bit.
The conversation flagged and I kept it going.
I spend most of my time listening to other people so I deserved the attention on this occasion.
I needed to chatter to get my mind off something that was bothering me.
I thought it was up to me to keep X entertained.
I talked so much I probably overwhelmed X to some extent.
I found the silences hard to cope with.
I didn't leave many silences.
I interrupted a lot.
I didn't ask many questions to find out what X had to say.
I didn't think to notice if X was getting tired of listening.
I wanted to impress X with my intelligence/wit.
I didn't really want to talk much with X at that precise moment so talked a lot to cover it up.
I wasn't particularly interested in what X had to say.
I knew X had just come back from the dentist with a frozen tongue so I kept the conversation going.

Consider what other statement would accurately describe your side of the situation.

Looking back over the conversation:
1. What was the most positive aspect of your doing most of the talking?
2. How might you begin to create a more equally balanced conversation another time?

Direct support

This category of types of support includes those in which someone does or says something which has a direct bearing on the stresses experienced by the nurse needing the support.

1. *Open expressions of loyalty:* nurses speak of needing people to stick by them. This seems to mean making direct statements about the value and worth of a colleague usually when that colleague is being criticised, and also refuting unjust criticism while not denying the validity of just criticism. For instance, if a nurse has been criticised by a patient, manager or doctor, colleagues would be showing loyalty by directly telling the critic how much they genuinely appreciate the nurse's good points and strengths. Where there are extenuating circumstances, such as understaffing or a personal crisis, loyal colleagues might ensure that these are known and acknowledged by the critic, with the permission of the victim. The loyalty is most effective when the vulnerable nurse knows about it, and also has the validations said directly to her.

When a nurse has made a mistake or has had a weak point in her job performance highlighted, open expressions of loyalty can help her to gain the strength to develop her abilities to prevent further mistakes or improve on her weak areas, rather than falling into despair. Too often excellent nurses leave nursing after having fallen down once, usually in times of great personal stress or when working in impossible conditions. In any other occupation such an occurrence would be seen as a natural hiccough in an otherwise successful career. However, it seems that a nurse's level of self-valuing plummets to zero when a fault is discovered, and any colleagues who disagree with that zero rating melt into the shadows. Metaphorically speaking, we often seem to 'barrier nurse' someone who is down, keeping them at a distance in case it is infectious. Nurses have often reported a great sense of betrayal when they have been under attack and their managers and colleagues have given no indication of loyalty. They are not asking for mistakes or faults to be overlooked, merely to know that they are valued in some way by somebody.

Here are some ways of openly demonstrating loyalty:

i. Tell a colleague who is feeling bad about having been criticised how you feel about the criticism, whether you agree or not (be honest), and emphasise some of the other things you value and appreciate about them.

ii.   Remind the critic of your colleague about her good points, and extenuating circumstances if you have permission to reveal personal details. Inform the critic if you honestly disagree. Let your colleague know you've done this if she is aware that she had been criticised, and that you are willing to do it again if necessary.

iii. If someone is criticising a colleague in front of you but not directly to the colleague, suggest they speak to her face to face. Refuse to carry critical messages from one person to another. If you agree with the criticism avoid getting into a 'bitch' session: you may be destroying any trust your 'co-bitchers' have in you, since they can assume you would talk this way about them given half a chance.

2. *Practical help:* nurses often help each other by sharing work. For instance, when one nurse or group of nurses feels overburdened, another colleague or group which seems less 'busy' may take some of the work. This apparently simple phenomenon involves a number of significant issues, each of which need to be taken into account for this type of help to be given and received freely. First, the nurse needs to be assertive enough to ask for help — this means feeling confident enough to be able to admit that she cannot maintain her standard of care with the workload as it stands. Second, there needs to be trust between the colleagues, based on a mutual understanding and agreement of what is meant by 'busy'. This issue can be fundamental to their working relationship, and depends on how each sees her role. For instance, a nurse who values only clinical tasks as 'real work' would have problems sharing work with another who also values the counselling, teaching and management aspects of her role. The third important factor is the willingness of the nurse to admit to a temporary period of being 'not busy' and to be caring enough of her colleague to offer to help out.

Sometimes colleagues will, in emergencies, step in to give practical help with problems outside work. Obviously this is easier when colleagues are also personal friends. Nurses seem to find giving practical help one of the easiest forms of support, and colleagues can usually be relied on for some kind of help in this way. For instance, one nurse reported: 'I once collapsed on the ward. It turned out I had bronchopneumonia. I was in a state because I'm on my own. I had no-one to look after the children and I was worried sick. I was trying to stop them keeping me in hospital because of the children. An enrolled nurse, I didn't know her very well, just dropped everything, collected them from school and moved in with them while I was in hospital. She was single, didn't have any ties, but it's amazing that people can be so kind.'

3. *Sharing factual information:* being in a situation where you are unaware of what is going on can be very anxiety provoking. Therefore, it is important in nursing that information about patients, changes in staffing situations, meetings and so on is disseminated as effectively as possible. It is particularly important with regard to colleagues who are new members of staff, or have recently returned from annual or sick leave. In addition, it is useful to share professional knowledge such as that gained from study days and professional journals.

In-service training budgets have been cut in many areas, so opportunities for each individual nurse to attend updating sessions are thin on the ground. Nurses also often find they cannot make the time to read the nursing journals. Nurses can create specific opportunities to share knowledge with colleagues by having 'do-it-yourself up-dating' sessions. Each person brings a brief summary of what they have learnt from a study day, or of a relevant article from a recent nursing journal, and shares the information with colleagues, giving the stimulus for discussion. This can enable nurses to be more selective in reading the professional journals, saving time and maximising the value of scarce study days. Many nurses have extra training and experience in specialities about which their immediate colleagues have little knowledge. Making your knowledge known to others and sharing it with people who want to learn is not arrogance; some nurses tend to hide their light under a bushel out of unnecessary modesty.

Knowledge contributes towards a feeling of personal power; someone who is feeling insecure may find it difficult to share information, because of an unconscious wish to achieve greater status or security in a group by knowing they have more knowledge than the others in certain topics.

4. *Sharing personal information:* When nurses share personal information with each other, about their own experiences, feelings, problems, reaction to stress and so on, it can reduce the sense of emotional isolation which is common in nursing. A nurse may feel

inadequate or a failure because she is finding something difficult; when she hears that colleagues have the same or another equally difficult problem she can feel less alone. For instance, a student nurse found support in knowing colleagues felt the same as she did: 'I was getting quite a thing about that particular staff nurse, she made me feel stupid whenever she talked to me, and I kept dropping things when she watched some of my procedures. I thought it was just me, I didn't say a word to anyone for ages, then when I did say something to one of the other students, it turned out that evidently she's upset a lot of people. It was a relief to know I wasn't the only one.'

5. *Joint action:* many nurses have said that they have been reluctant to state their point of view or to take some kind of action, for fear of being branded as a 'trouble-maker' and being victimised. It would appear that in many cases this fear is unfounded, but unfortunately there are situations in which this fear is rooted in reality. One method of helping to reduce this anxiety is for colleagues to get together to take some kind of joint action such as joint reports or joint statements. This form of peer support requires trust and determination to stick to your commitment to support. All too often nurses report that they have been elected as the spokesperson to put forward a controversial point of view at a staff meeting on behalf of their colleagues, then at the meeting find that they are left high and dry when the rest of the group renege on their promise to speak up in agreement.

6. *Advice:* nurses often seem keen to give advice or make suggestions when a colleague has a problem. Advice can be very useful, particularly if it is about a factual topic in which the giver has more knowledge or experience than the receiver. Paradoxically, poor advice can also be helpful: the person with the problem situation realises she is not the only one to be unable to think of an ideal solution, and it can help her to eliminate some of the options since she can see more clearly exactly what she does *not* want to do.

However, advice-giving is fraught with pitfalls. Bearing the following points in mind may help to avoid them:

i.   Check that the person *wants* some advice.
ii. Make it clear that the advice you are giving does not have to be taken, that the decision is the responsibility of the person with the problem.

iii. 'Soft' advice: this is appropriate for most situations. You give the advice as a suggestion and phrase it tentatively: 'I suggest . . .' 'You could try . . .', 'You may/might . . .', 'Possibly . . .', 'One option/possibility is . . .'.

iv. 'Hard' advice: this is for use only when you feel strongly about the course of action you are suggesting. You express this strength of conviction, but still as a suggestion, not as an order. For instance, 'I strongly advise/urge/suggest you . . .', 'I think it's vital/very important/essential that you . . .'. Spell out the consequences of not carrying this out.

v. When you are using the 'If-I-were-you . . .' approach, try to be honest! It is very easy to look at another person's problem situation and imagine yourself handling it perfectly, because you do not have the emotional history of the situation to contend with. If you try to put yourself into another person's shoes, you would be showing more empathy by imagining yourself feeling as concerned about it as they do. On the whole it is probably better to avoid this approach and use the 'soft' or 'hard' advice format instead.

vi. Avoid asking for a response to your advice, but instead give the person a chance to think about it. Advice phrased as questions, for example, 'Have you tried/thought of . . .', 'What about . . .', 'Why don't you . . .', demands an immediate decision and this is not fair on someone who is finding something difficult.

vii. Do not be too attached to your advice. In a nurse's urge to support and help in a useful way by giving advice, she may become overanxious about her advice being taken and hound the poor recipient with reminders and unnecessary follow-ups. When you feel hurt that your advice has not been taken, or that the recipient has gone also to other people for advice, remember that you may have helped by enabling your colleague to pinpoint what she does *not* want to do and so clarify what the best answer is for her. Her seeking further advice is not a bad reflection on the way you helped, she is likely to be collecting a range of ideas and options from which to choose her own answer.

If you are going to ask for advice, the following points may be useful to bear in mind:

i. The responsibility for your decisions and actions is yours. Your advisor is not to blame if the outcome is negative, nor is she your saviour if it goes right: *you* decided to accept and act on the advice.

ii. Give yourself time to think about any advice given; just because you asked for advice does not mean you are obliged to take it.

iii. Sometimes under stress, nurses believe that there is one ideal solution to a problem if only they could find it. Usually there is not, otherwise the situation would not have become a problem in the first place. If you are asking for advice and the advisor comes up with a less than perfect solution, try to avoid showing resentment.

Advice from a group of colleagues can be useful, but is often time-consuming as the discussion may delve into the pros and cons of each option, or go off the point altogether. One way of saving time is to structure the session. Ask a group of colleagues if you can pick their brains about a difficult situation you are facing. If they all agree, outline the main relevant details of the situation. Ask the group to think silently for a while, and then to write down their suggestions and give them to you. This method helps to ensure that you collect all the ideas in the group. Unstructured group advice may result in the quickest thinker, or the most eager

talker getting her suggestion aired first and others not having time to formulate ideas or not speaking up.

7. *Encouragement:* a nurse under stress may find it difficult to think positively about herself and her own achievements and may notice only the negative aspects. She can be encouraged by being reminded of the positive aspects, while not having her difficulties negated. For instance, a student who is stuck with an essay may say she 'can't even get it started', but questioning will reveal that she has done all the background reading, has made a plan, and has copious notes. She can be encouraged by having someone point out that she is already at least halfway through the process of writing an essay, that she has in fact achieved a lot.

Having someone put into words what has already been achieved, however small those achievements are, can give the positive impetus for moving forward. Day-by-day routine achievements are often unacknowledged in nursing. For instance, if ten tasks need to be done while the person in charge of a ward is away, and nine are completed by the time she returns, then only the tenth is likely to be commented on. One student nurse compares the encouraging approach of a staff nurse with the discouraging approach of the sister: 'That staff nurse, he was good. He always saw what you'd done. He'd say something like "Fine, so you've done such and such, now could you do such and such". I really enjoyed working with him. The sister was awful though, however much you did she'd always pick holes in it. I dreaded it when she was on.'

8. *Feedback:* every conscientious nurse is likely to suffer from performance anxiety at times: wondering if her standard of work is good enough, being concerned about possible lapses, mistakes or work that could have been done to a higher standard. Under stress this anxiety may grow to unmanageable proportions, or the nurse may repress the anxiety and attempt to pretend to herself and possibly others that her standards are perfect and there is no need for improvement. Frequent positive feedback and constructive criticism can help to achieve and maintain a healthy balance. However, few nurses have had opportunities to learn how to do this and there are many pitfalls.

Some suggestions for giving and receiving feedback are given in the assertiveness chapter. In addition, some structures for requesting and giving feedback are offered here:

i.   Liked most and liked least. Colleagues could give each other feedback about what they liked most and liked least about each other's handling of specific situations (*not* commenting on personality). For instance, a psychiatric nurse asks a colleague what she thought of the way he handled an aggressive patient, and asks her to specify what exactly she liked most and liked least about his approach. Her reply: 'Well, what I liked most was the way you listened to what he had to say and kept your voice calm, and I liked least the way you kept trying to hold his arm when he seemed oversensitive to touch in that state.'

ii.   Structured self and peer evaluation. Some groups of nurses regularly meet with colleagues at the same level to help each other with self-evaluation and to give feedback. This form of performance appraisal indicates a high level of professionalism: the nurses are taking responsibility for their own professional development, for developing explicit criteria for excellence and using colleagues to regulate each other's standards of performance rather than depending on one-way control down the hierarchy. It is a valuable adjunct, if not replacement, to the usual staff appraisal system, which seems to have a poor reputation among nurses. As with any appraisal scheme, there are pitfalls. The following structure can help nurses to learn the skills of self and peer evaluation and avoid or minimise possible mistakes (5).

- A number of nurses who are at the same level in the nursing hierarchy form a group to carry out self and peer evaluation. The ideal number is between four and eight people. In order that this can be truly a peer group, it is essential that no one in authority over any of the members of this group be present. If they want a facilitator, this should be someone who has no supervisory responsibility over them, e.g. a tutor from a different field.

- The group make a contract with each other to abide by the ground rules suggested in the 'trust' section earlier in this chapter, or they can negotiate their own adaptation and/or additions to these rules.

- A common aspect of their work role is chosen as the focus of the evaluation. This is done by allowing each person to list or show diagrammatically on a large sheet of paper how she sees her own role. All the sheets are displayed, and an aspect of work common to everyone is chosen for evaluation. For instance, one group of five ward sisters and charge nurses from different departments had varying perceptions of their roles, partly because of the differences in the nature of their work. However, each included teaching, so this was chosen as the area to evaluate.

- The group then brainstorm a list of criteria of excellence in the chosen area. They can crystallise their thoughts by having the following questions written up: 'What abilities/ skills/qualities/approaches/knowledge/attitudes/actions make for a high standard of . . . (e.g. teaching) in our work?' A list is made of any points which come to mind, without discussing or judging. Then at the end of the brainstorming session, questions are asked to clarify meanings of particular terms. The ward sisters/charge nurses group came up with the following list of criteria for good teaching:

    Able to explain things clearly.
    Finds out what students/whoever is being taught knows already.
    Finds out what they want to know in particular.
    Does not overload with information
    Patience.
    Willing to say 'I don't know' or 'I don't remember'.
    Making time to teach.
    Using student's own knowledge.
    Setting a good example, doing what you preach.
    Interested in the student.
    Willing to learn perhaps from the student.
    Knowing your field.
    Keeping up to date.
    Demonstrating procedures slowly.
    Letting students have a go, have responsibility as appropriate.
    Careful supervision to ensure safe practice.
    Encouraging, giving praise where it's due.
    Getting the right balance between the need to give patients high standard of care and allowing students to learn.
    Pointing out mistakes tactfully.
    Approachable, not making students feel stupid for not knowing something.
    Using knowledge and skills of other staff.

Having relevant books and articles on hand.
Good liaison with the school of nursing.
Finding out what students have been taught.
Giving students time to learn, not just using them as pairs of hands.
Ensuring they get relevant experience.

- Self-evaluation: each person then studies the list of criteria. Of the criteria with which she agrees, she picks out the three which she believes are her strongest points and the three which are her weakest, writing these down with comments, preferably on a large sheet of paper to display to the others in the group. Then a realistic step-by-step plan is made to maintain or improve each of these. One ward sister's self-evaluation:

Weakest points

Criterion	Comment	Plan
Good liaison with school.	Don't like the tutors or the clinical teacher for my ward.	Make an effort to talk more to clinical teacher when she comes on the ward and find out what the students are being taught.
Does not overload with information.	Sometimes tell them too much and they get confused.	Next time find out or assess what they most need to know. Give them information in small chunks.
Using knowledge and skills of other staff.	Don't give other people a chance to teach much. I like teaching so tend to hog the show a bit.	Ask other nurses and doctors to talk to the students. Will plan some sessions like this. Will teach the staff nurses and senior students more about teaching.

Strongest points

Criterion	Comment	Plan
Knowing your field.	I think I know my stuff in oncology.	Will go to the library more often to

Strongest points – cont.

Criterion	Comment	Plan
	I've done the right courses and go to study days when I can.	catch up on journals, weekly if possible. Will practise skim reading more and not get distracted by irrelevant articles.
Making time to teach.	There's a good system of teaching sessions in the afternoons. I make time when I possibly can for on-the-spot teaching when particular things come up.	Using other staff to teach will help make the best use of the time.
Patience.	I think I'm pretty good at being patient with students. I understand their difficulties with getting used to an oncology ward because I felt that way too, and the ward sister's patience with me helped a lot.	Continue as before. Perhaps tell them a bit about what I felt as a student.

- One person presents her self-evaluation to the group, display-ing her notes if written on a large sheet. A time limit for presentation could be set, perhaps five or ten minutes.
- The following peer evaluation structure is used. Each person has a copy of the structure and phrases feedback using only the words suggested in the outline. Each section has a time limit (e.g. two minutes) which is adhered to as much as possible, in spite of uncomfortable silences, until participants become accustomed to thinking out what they want to say more quickly. One person writes down each of the comments made by the group from step (ii) onwards. The possibility of

projection is highlighted, and each person is encouraged to notice the comments she makes to the self-evaluator and to consider whether they also apply to herself. The self-evaluator bears in mind that feedback from colleagues may highlight something useful about herself and be totally appropriate. At the other extreme, the feedback may not be relevant at all to her; the colleague giving it may have misunderstood something or be projecting her own issues. Third, the feedback could be a combination of the two. Another vital point to bear in mind is that the self-evaluator is in control of this structure; she decides which steps will be carried out and how long they will last. If she wishes to stop the peer evaluation at any point she is perfectly free to do so, with no criticism or pressure to continue. Note that after step (i) the self-evaluator does not verbally respond to any of the feedback. This can be difficult at first but participants who have adhered to this format find this of great benefit. It avoids getting into discussions, giving explanations or defensive justifications, and improves the ability to listen with concentration to the feedback since you do not have to work out what you are going to say in reply.

Examples taken from the oncology ward sister's feedback are given with each step outlined here.

i. Clarification questioning. Self-evaluator responds. 'Could you expand on . . .', 'Tell me more about . . .', 'What did you mean by . . .', 'How . . .', 'Where . . .', 'When . . .' For example: 'Could you tell me more about not liking any of the tutors or clinical teachers?'

ii. Responses to self-assessment. Self-evaluator does not respond. 'I agree/disagree with . . .' 'I'm delighted/surprised . . .' 'I'm sure/not sure . . .', For example: 'I agree with the statement about not having good liaison with the school.' 'I'm surprised you say you don't involve the other staff much in the teaching, because I've seen you give them good training in ward management and I've seen you involve them in that way.'

iii. Supportive challenging questioning. Self-evaluator does not respond. 'Do you really think . . .' 'Did you notice the contradiction . . .' 'When did you last . . .' 'What makes you . . .' 'Are you aware . . .' For example: 'Do you notice any contradiction between your obvious interest and ability in teaching and your poor liaison with the school?'

iv. Supportive negative feedback. Self-evaluator does not respond. Commenting on action/approach, not personality. 'I think/don't think . . .' 'I get the impression . . .' 'It seems to me . . .' 'I dislike/like least . . .' 'I felt . . . when you . . .' For example: 'I get the impression you get a bit jealous of anyone else doing any teaching on your territory, in your ward.'

v. Devil's advocate. Self-evaluator does not respond. Acknowledge own imagination or perception as possibly exaggerated. 'I imagine . . .' 'My worst fear/fantasy is . . .' 'If I let my imagination run riot, I can picture . . .' For example: 'My worst fear is that you hate the guts of any tutor or clinical teacher just because they are teachers.'

vi. Alternative suggestions. Self-evaluator does not respond. Soft advice: 'Perhaps you could try . . .', 'One option/alternative/possibility could be . . .', 'You might/may . . .' Hard advice: 'It's very important that you . . . otherwise . . .' 'I strongly urge you to . . .' For example: 'I suggest you get to know the new post-basic tutor. She's worked in oncology and I think you'd get on well.'

vii. Positive feedback. Self-evaluator does not respond. Commenting on action/approach, not personality. 'I like . . .' 'I value . . .' 'I appreciate . . .' 'I felt good when you . . .' For example: 'I really like it that you're so keen on your subject and on teaching. I think I'd enjoy being a student on your ward.'

Having heard the feedback, the self-evaluator has the chance to debrief by stating what she noticed about her internal reactions throughout the feedback session and how she feels now that it is over. Most nurses who are trying this for the first time are usually pleasantly surprised at how supportive the feedback feels when expressed according to the structure.

Each person in turn shares her self-evaluation and goes through the feedback structure. Often, after having had sufficient practice in using the phraseology suggested, the structure is adapted by amalgamating some of the steps and by shortening the time limit as people find they can think of what they want to say more quickly.

- Time is taken for each person to evaluate the feedback. Going through the list of recorded comments, she categorises each as Yes (on target or comment accepted), No (off target or comment not accepted) or Perhaps (something in it, will bear it in mind). For instance, the oncology ward sister categorised the examples of feedback shown above as follows: (ii) yes (iii) yes (iv) no (v) perhaps (vi) yes (vii) yes.

• The group members then review their self-evaluations in the light of the feedback, making any necessary changes. Each person in turn makes a brief statement indicating any changes to the self-evaluation. The sister in the example added: 'Will try to get to know post-basic tutor and look out for tarring all teachers with the same brush' to her first plan.

• The group fix a date to meet again to review each person's progress in implementing her plans and to do further self and peer evaluation on other aspects of their work performance. All the paperwork is kept to be used and displayed again at the review meeting.

• Before the group parts, the ground rules are looked at again to remind each other of the contract made at the beginning of the meeting: the confidentiality rule is particularly important to remember at this stage.

Facilitative support

This type of support is less active, less obviously giving, yet it can enable someone to sort things out for themselves and can often be the most effective form of help. However, it may feel less rewarding in that less gratitude comes your way. If a nurse's self-image is sharply focussed on the 'sleeves-rolled-up-solver -of-all-problems' stereotype, then she may gain no personal satisfaction from helping colleagues to work through their difficulties in their own way. But if she can let go of that image, a lot of satisfaction can be gained through *being with* a colleague who is feeling stressed rather than trying to do something for her.

Another common reason for wanting to rush in and solve a problem may be the desire to alleviate your own uncomfortable feelings which have been stirred up by hearing of the other's difficulties. Equally often perhaps, a nurse's motivation to do something or give advice comes from a desire to demonstrate tangibly that she cares. However, if she can learn and adapt facilitative counselling skills to extend her repertoire of ways of showing that she cares, then the caring can be more appropriate and more effective.

Unfortunately, most nurses have little opportunity, if any, to learn the skills of facilitative support. These sparse opportunities usually come in the form of occasional workshops of only a few hours' or a few days' duration. During those workshops, the structured exercises which are necessary for building the required skills often leave nurses with the feeling that counselling is a stilted, false way of showing caring. The workshops are often too short, too infrequent or with too little follow-up in the work situation for the nurses to develop beyond awkwardly and self-consciously using techniques and on to easily and self-awarely using skills as expressions of care. A book has even less chance to help a reader move from just using techniques mechanically to becoming skilled in counselling. Therefore some ordinary ways in which nurses facilitate each other are outlined here to enable you to pinpoint what you already do supportively to facilitate colleagues. As a result you can perhaps become more aware of how you are helping, and use your existing skills more intentionally, hopefully avoiding most of the pitfalls.

'Thank you so much for helping, I'm feeling a lot better now. I've decided to . . .' 'But I didn't do a thing!' Most nurses have had the experience of being thanked for letting someone talk or let off steam, and have perhaps been puzzled about the reason for its effectiveness when they did not remember having actually done or said anything.

If this has happened to you, look back over the most recent situations. What you were probably doing was (a) providing the opportunity to talk, (b) listening, (c) showing that you understood or were trying to understand, (d) allowing the person to talk, cry or whatever without criticising her for doing so, and without interrupting, (e) enabling her to untangle her thoughts by asking an occasional facilitative question. The effectiveness of these methods of facilitative support can be enhanced by using them awarely and appropriately.

The following sections of this chapter enlarge upon these ordinary methods. Although they may have some principles and applications in common with various psychotherapy and counselling methods, there are some crucial differences. In peer support between nurses, there is usually no contract for a psychotherapy or a therapeutic counselling session. The facilitative support which is usually needed and wanted is an extension of ordinary conversation between two equals. Probing is not appropriate.

1. *Providing opportunities to talk:* often facilitative support between nurses happens after a period of ordinary conversation when trust has developed. The supporter may not actually say anything, but gives the impression from her calm manner that she has enough time and interest to listen. Opportunities can be offered by showing care and concern or opening up a subject.

'Are you alright?' and 'What's the matter?' are probably the most common openers. Other examples are: 'Is there something bothering you/worrying you/on your mind?', 'Is it true that . . . ?'' 'I understand such-and-such happened to you', 'Do you want to talk about that?' and 'If ever you want to talk it over you know where I am.' Whatever words are said, the main message comes over in the body language and tone of voice; if you seem to be in a hurry, or critical, then this will not come over as caring concern or a genuine offer of support. It is vital to respect the person's right to choose when and from whom to receive support: the opportunities you offer may not be perfectly timed, or you may not be the most appropriate person.

2. *Listening:* listening is more than keeping quiet while the other person talks. It is a process of paying attention to the talker as a human being: not only attending to the words said, but to the way they are said, the meanings which are intended and conveyed, and to the emotions accompanying the words. It includes *being with* the person, at some level feeling their emotions with them.

Everyone needs attention, at whatever age, and particularly when feeling vulnerable, and nurses need it too. But in an uncaring culture this need is often dismissed as immature, and there is a scarcity of caring attention. So just listening with full undivided attention can be a rare and valuable gift.

For the listening to be of value, the talker needs to know that the listener is in fact doing just that; therefore the listener needs to show that she is listening by her body language.

i.   Eye contact: when two people are talking, it is usual for the talker to often look away while talking, probably to remember or imagine an event or to find the right word to express what she wants to say. She will then tend to look at the listener at the end of each point that she is making to check that she is being listened to. The listener needs to be looking at her whenever she does this otherwise she will give the impression of not listening. So the listener needs to maintain almost continuous eye contact in a relaxed way without staring. Some nurses find this difficult to do, particularly if they have been brought up in a family in which continuous eye contact is considered rude.

ii.   Facial expression: a listener would be demonstrating empathy and that she is giving attention when her facial expression mirrors the mood of the talker, for instance, a smile at hearing of a happy event, laughing with funny stories, a sad expression on hearing of an upset and so on. If the talker is speaking about something serious and is feeling vulnerable, she can be discouraged by or misinterpret an inappropriate facial expression. Sometimes nurses think they should smile all the time to be pleasant and show interest, but this fixed smile can be misinterpreted as derision, patronage or sadistic enjoyment of the other's plight.

iii. Posture: the listener needs to look relaxed but alert. Often a listener will mirror to some extent the body language of the talker. For instance, if the talker is leaning forward with the right hand supporting her chin, the listener may also be forward with her left hand to her face or supporting her chin. This mirroring can be a sign of empathy.

iv.   Nods and grunts: a nod and/or 'hmm' at the end of each point made can demonstrate attention and give encouragement to continue. Too many of them can give the impression of impatience or false listening.

v.   Proximity: each of us has our own personal space, the invisible area around our bodies within which we keep at our own comfortable distance from other people. The listener needs to be careful not to invade this space by getting too close when it is unwelcome, but to be close enough to show attention.

Listening exercise: this highlights the importance of demonstrating relaxed, attentive listening by appropriate non-verbal responses. You will need at least one willing partner for this. Decide who will be the talker and the other will be the listener. There are three consecutive stages:

Talker	*Listener*
1. Speaks non-stop for one minute on the topic 'My journey here', giving a blow-by-blow account.	Without speaking, exaggerates the body language of someone who is not listening.

2. Speaks for one minute on the topic 'Unpleasant journey(s) I have experienced'.

Without speaking, exaggerates the body language of someone who has just finished a counselling course and is over-anxious to show intent listening. Looks sickeningly sympathetic.

3. Speaks for one minute on the topic 'Pleasant journey(s) I have experienced'.

Without speaking, relaxed, attentive, listening.

After all three stages have been completed, you could debrief by sharing how you each felt during each stage and what you noticed about the listener's body language and its effect on the talker. A third person to act as observer can give useful feedback on what she noticed. Swop roles so each person has the chance to experience both sides of the coin.

3. *Understanding:* everyone needs to feel understood or at least that other people are trying to understand. There are two levels of understanding: understanding the situation and understanding the emotional reactions to the situation. Nurses sharing difficulties related to being a nurse with other nurses can often feel understood and supported because the other nurses may have had similar experiences or at least understand the background to the situation. Emotional understanding, or empathy, can be received from someone who has felt similar emotions, though perhaps for different reasons. So a nurse who has suffered a personal bereavement can still receive a lot of emotional understanding from another nurse who has never had anyone close to her die, but who has experienced sadness, anger and anxiety in other situations. Nurses who do not allow themselves to feel their own emotions cannot have emotional understanding with other people.

Often when one nurse talks about her problem to a colleague, the colleague will share similar experiences or emotions, and the support becomes a two-way process. Each feels understood and less alone. This reciprocity is desirable and usually preferable in peer support. It is one of the ways in which peer support differs from formal counselling or psychotherapy: if the counsellor or therapist spends half the time talking about their own problems, the client quite rightly feels cheated. In contrast, support between nurses is enhanced by reciprocity.

You can show you are trying to understand when you ask clarificatory questions, e.g. 'Do you mean that . . .', 'What did you mean when you said . . .', 'Are you saying that . . .'. Also, summarising the main point(s) of what is being said can show you are understanding or trying to understand. There are two main ways of summarising; each depends on your intention. You may intend to demonstrate factual understanding, or to show emotional understanding. The former requires a summary of the main facts, events or opinions recounted by the talker. The latter needs a summary which highlights the main emotions expressed or implied. For instance, take the following account of a nurse's problem: 'I had a terrible time on the round this morning, you know. Mr Mitchell, one of the consultants, he was so pig-headed. We were standing round this old boy Mr Everett, and Mr Mitchell tells him he can go home today. Well, he'd never discussed it with any of us first, so I piped up and told him, Mr Mitchell that is, that Mr Everett still needed 24-hour care and I tried to say what care he needed and he says "Thank you Staff Nurse, your opinion will be sought as and when it is required" or something like that, and off he swanned with his entourage in tow. I was livid, so livid I was speechless. Wish I could think of the right things to say at times like that, but I think I'd blow my top if I opened my mouth.'

A factual summary might be along the lines of 'He really put you down by dismissing your opinion like that', whereas an emotional summary might be 'You must have felt furious with him'. A combination of the two might be: 'You must have felt furious with his putting you down like that. No wonder you got tongue-tied'. One common pitfall in summarising is to embellish what has been said as a result of your own experience. For instance, a nurse who has had a similar experience, but whose main problem was the embarrassment she felt at being humiliated in front of other people, might have summarised by saying 'You must have felt really embarrassed that he showed you up in front of everyone else like that'. Here, she is imposing her own experience on the talker, whose main emotion was not embarrassment but fury, and whose main point was not being conscious of other people but her inability to speak.

You could practise these methods of summarising by doing the following exercises:

Write three brief summaries of the following account, giving a summary of the main factual point made, one of the main emotions expressed and one which combines the two.

'What a day. Staff nurse off sick and three new students starting today. I spent ages showing them round, telling them everything they need to know about the ward and I thought "Great, now I can get on with things" but no, every five minutes they're pestering me, asking where this and that is. Honestly they're the end, I wish students would think for themselves a bit more, I never thought we'd get done today with all the time I had to spend nurse-maiding them.'

Scan through some novels and pick out some passages of dialogue which describe someone's own experience, or use some of the other quotations in this book, and practise writing the three types of summary. Compare your answers with someone else's.

With a partner, ask her to describe a recent event in her life, and practise the three types of summary. Check with her if you correctly summarised the main point and the main emotion she was experiencing and assess the extent to which you put your own interpretation on the situation rather than summarising what was actually said.

4. *Allowing:* you can allow someone to relate their problem in their own way by giving space, time and attention with minimum questions or interruptions. Although your desire may be to understand, it is not necessary to grasp every detail immediately. Usually if the person is allowed time to explain in their own, albeit sometimes chaotic way, you can usually grasp the general gist of the situation. If you need to comprehend certain details which are unclear to you, these can be clarified after the talker's main explanation comes to an end.

An essential ingredient of allowing is being non-judgemental; accepting the person and their predicament as they are, without criticising. 'Don't be silly, that's nothing to worry about' and 'That was a stupid thing to do' are common examples of criticisms which could result in the talker feeling judged and dissuaded from continuing to talk. A nurse who finds it difficult to accept herself, her feelings and failings, will be unable to accept others. Anyone who is interested in developing their ability to give facilitative support to colleagues needs to begin with themselves.

A full training in co-counselling (a specific method of two-way reciprocal peer counselling, the fundamental skills being learned on a special course of at least 40 hours) is one structured and safe way to learn about emotional release or catharsis, primarily for your own use but also to learn how to help others in this respect. However, not everyone may be able to do this training and many nurses have expressed how inadequate they feel in coping with colleagues or patients who are upset. Some of the ordinary ways we can support people who are upset by allowing them to let go are outlined below, with suggestions about enhancing their effectiveness.

The most important principle is that of following cues and not pushing. Trying to 'make someone cry because it'll do them good' is unhelpful if not dangerous. These guidelines may help you to allow someone to let off steam if they so wish, and involve mainly listening.

i. Listening and being with the person silently: this can be very difficult, particularly if, in general, you find it hard to allow yourself to release your own feelings. You will have a backlog of bottled-up emotions, so seeing someone else doing what you really need to do for yourself can be unbearable. The urge to interrupt by asking for factual information, giving advice, giving false reassurance or making her drink tea can be great. The most helpful and supportive action for someone who is releasing emotions safely is silent, attentive inaction. Pay attention to the emotions she is expressing and tune into those; do not become preoccupied with trying to understand the facts and details of the story. If you really need to know them, wait until she has really had the chance to get all the emotions she wants to off her chest first.

ii. Gentle touch can be helpful in many instances: it is important that your touch is gentle; a tense hand grasp or bear hug is likely to communicate your desire for her to be quiet. Some people do not like to be touched so this needs to be respected. An angry person may interpret touch as provocation or attempts to restrain.

iii Giving permission: often someone who is upset will berate themselves for feeling the way they do or for expressing that feeling. Comments such as 'it's only natural to feel that way', 'you have every right to feel angry', 'it's OK to cry', 'you've been through a lot, no wonder you're upset' can help. Sometimes after a nurse has finished letting-go with a colleague, she may feel embarrassed about the episode. You might be able to forestall this by commenting positively on her catharsis shortly after she has finished. For instance: 'I think you were wise to get that out of your system', 'you were right to let go like that, it needed to come out', 'I admire your ability to get things off your chest and then get on with life', or whatever feels natural to say.

iv.　Distracting attention: after the person has had a chance to let go, and seems to have finished, it can be helpful to distract attention away from feelings. This can be done by going for a walk, having a cup of tea, encouraging her to talk about mundane events of the near future or about the surroundings. One very useful way of helping her to think positively is to remind her of something positive which she herself has said (avoid trying to think of something positive on her behalf — it will sound like a platitude).

5. *Facilitative questions:* these are questions which encourage the talker to express opinions and emotions, and to begin to untangle her thoughts so clarifying things for herself. They are usually open as opposed to closed questions.

Open questions are those which encourage the other person to give more than just a brief reply, and which do not indicate any expectation of what the answer will be. They can be helpful when seeking general information, e.g. 'What's it like to work on that ward?', when giving someone the chance to express an opinion, e.g. 'What do you think about the way the consultant and the nurses relate to each other?', or to give someone the opportunity to express emotions, e.g. 'How do you feel about the support you get from the sister?'. They are not helpful if you are seeking specific factual information; closed questions are more useful in this context.

A closed question is one which could be answered by a brief factual reply or a 'yes' or 'no'. They are not helpful if you want to encourage the other person to talk and think things through for herself. You may end up asking a lot of questions and appearing overbearing or nosy, e.g. 'How long have you worked on the ward?', 'Were you transferred there from another ward?', 'When did you start?', 'Have you worked in this field before?', 'Had you spoken to the district nurse about the patient?'. Closed questions can put words into the talker's mouth, e.g. 'Don't you think the sister should have backed you up?', 'Do you like her?'.

Some questions cannot be easily categorised as being totally open or totally closed but are a bit of each. For instance, some of the 'openers' which provide an opportunity for someone to talk and are listed earlier in this chapter are both open and closed. 'Do you want to talk about it?' strictly speaking can be answered with a 'Yes' or 'No', but if it is a 'Yes' then the talker tends to continue talking. If the reply is 'No' that often closes that part of the conversation.

Open ├───────────────────────────────┤ Closed

Exercise: on a scale representing open at one extreme and closed at the other, classify the following questions according to whether you consider they look open or closed. (Obviously the degree of openness is affected by the body language and tone of voice, but in print we have to work with the words alone.) For instance, if you think (1) is totally open, write (1) on the left side of the scale; if you think (2) is closed, write (2) on the right; if (3) is half and half, write (3) in the middle.

1. What's on your mind?
2. Have you had a bad day?
3. Did you have another row with the registrar?
4. Have you seen the charge nurse about it?
5. Would you like a cup of tea?
6. What does that mean to you?
7. How do you feel about that?
8. You do feel better now, don't you?
9. Did you have time to eat your lunch?
10. Do you want to leave?
11. You do know about the complaints procedure, don't you?
12. What do you think about early discharges after surgery?
13. What made that situation difficult for you?
14. What would you like to say if it ever happened again?
15. What's your next step?
16. Is there anything else you want to talk about?
17. Don't you think we should go now?

Both open and closed questions can be useful in facilitative support, but open questions usually need to be used more often.

Open questions can either lead or follow what the talker says. 'Leading' open questions introduce a new topic, or a new direction in the existing topic. 'Following' questions pick up a point made by the talker and give her the chance to expand. For instance:

Listener: 'What's up?' (leading). Talker: 'Oh, I feel awful. Heck, sometimes I wonder if I'm really cut out for nursing. Perhaps it's all a big mistake after all.' Listener: 'What makes you say that?' (following). Talker: 'Well everything's going wrong. I just don't think I'm good enough. My mother always said I wouldn't make it, that I'm too soft. I get too involved. You can't be a good nurse if you get involved, can you, that's what she always says. I suppose she should know, she's been at it for years.' Listener: 'What was your last ward report like?' (leading). Talker: 'Oh, it wasn't too bad, the sister said some quite nice things, actually. I was surprised, I didn't think she liked me much.' Listener: 'What did she say that was nice?' (following).

On the whole, nurses seem to be adept at using closed questions when talking to each other but find open questions more difficult, particularly open questions which follow. Practice in using open questions can be extremely useful, while not forgetting that closed questions also have their value.

Exercise:
With a partner, try to find out what she thinks and feels about her nurse training, using only open questions beginning with:

'Tell me about . . .'
'What did/do you think . . .'
'How did/do you feel . . .'
'What did/do you most/least . . .'
'To what extent . . .'
'In what way?'
'What made/makes you . . .'
'What else . . .'

Set a time limit for the exercises, e.g. 3–5 minutes. Give yourself time to phrase the questions, and do not worry about sounding stilted — this is only an exercise to practise using open questions. Try to remember which questions you asked; better still, ask a third person to observe and note the questions. After the discussion, assess to what degree the questions were open or closed and whether they were leading or following. You could repeat the exercise, using another topic, and after the talker has said something (perhaps as a result of an open leading question), try to ask only 'following' open questions.

In helping someone to sort out a problem and move towards a decision, you could use the spiral outlined in the problem-solving chapter. Your open questions can help the other person to clarify some of the stages in the cycle without your having to give advice. It may be helpful to familiarise yourself with the use of the spiral by applying it to your own problems and decisions before trying to use it with someone else. There are exercises in the problem-solving chapter for doing this.

Open questions can be used when enabling a colleague to achieve a balanced self-evaluation. It can be very easy on a bad day to run oneself down, looking only on the negative side. Conversely, on a good day it might be tempting to become over-confident and overlook the areas which could be improved. A colleague can be very supportive by helping to maintain the balance. For instance, the conversation given earlier as an example continues:

Talker: 'Well, um, she said I was friendly and popular with the patients and staff.'

Listener: 'What do you think about that?'

Talker: 'Well, I suppose I am quite friendly. It has its drawbacks though, everyone seems to ask me to do things for them or talk to me rather than the other nurses. It gets embarrassing when you're not allocated to those particular patients.'

Listener: 'What else do you think you're good at as far as being a nurse is concerned?'

Talker: 'You sound a bit like that tutor we had in introductory block: "Think-positive-Charlie", we called him!' (laughs) 'OK, let me see, actually, one thing that really surprised me was that I could cope with emergencies. I thought I'd go to pieces, but I don't.'

Look back over the various types of support nurses could give and receive, as listed in Table 6.1. Pinpoint a situation in your current life which you find stressful to some degree. At the top of the sheet of paper write 'I can cope with . . . . but I could probably cope better if I had the following support: . . .' Then list the types of support which might enable you to cope a little better, and list beside each point the people who might possibly be able/willing to give each type of support to you if you asked or gave them a chance to offer. Look at the 'making requests' section of the assertiveness chapter and formulate request statements you could make to ask for the relevant support, and then try them out. Be prepared for the fact that they may not be able/willing to help just at that moment: if this is the case, you have lost nothing by asking. However, you may be surprised by how much support is actually available to you, provided you do not burden one or a few people with all the various types of support you need.

Combining the various types of support

Usually the types of support mentioned in this chapter happen in various combinations: it would certainly feel unnatural most of the time for only one type of support to be given. For instance, this is illustrated by the following account of two nurses talking over lunch.

Bridget was sitting at a table and was just about to eat her lunch. She saw Vanessa entering the dining room, caught her eye, and signalled for her to join her. When Vanessa sat down, they chatted about the food and Bridget's day off (ordinary conversation). After a silence, during which Bridget realised something was bothering Vanessa, she asked if anything was on her mind (opportunity to talk). Vanessa said there was not, and changed the subject back to Bridget's day off (ordinary conversation). She asked about Bridget's relatives, whom she had visited on the day off, and Bridget told her about her aging aunt and uncle (sharing personal information). Then Vanessa began to talk about her mother, who had been depressed and unhappy when she had visited her the previous day. Bridget said nothing for a while (listening), then suggested Vanessa talk it over with her brother (advice). She did not really listen to the advice and seemed to want to just talk it through, so Bridget continued to listen. After she had talked for quite a while, Bridget was a bit confused about the details of the situation though she understood what Vanessa's feelings were about the situation. So Bridget tried to summarise the main points of Vanessa's account (understanding). She did not quite get the details right, so Vanessa corrected her, then went on talking. She said a lot about feeling responsible for her mother and guilty that she could not cheer her up more. Bridget explained that she had had similar problems with her aunt (sharing personal information). Bridget could see another colleague approaching so she steered the conversation back to the food and asked what Vanessa thought of the new wholefood campaign the catering manager had instigated (leading open question).

Support groups

Nurses have a lot of ability, some of it latent, to support each other in day-to-day contact and in structured support groups. Although the group dynamics of a support group can be complex, I believe that if nurses are given the opportunity, they can build the skills of using and running peer support groups without the need for an 'expert' to be in charge. I am rather concerned by the numbers of albeit well-meaning psychiatrists, psychotherapists and psychiatric social workers (mostly male) who wish to lead support groups for nurses without being willing to pass on their skills and make themselves redundant and who seem to encourage dependence in the group members (mostly female). Peer support groups can be a healthier and more effective form of self-help.

In setting up a peer support group the following suggestions may provide a useful structure.

1. *Decide on membership of the group:* is the group just for nurses or for others as well? Will it have a fixed membership and be closed once it has started or will it be a totally open drop-in and come-when-you-please group? What size of group do you want? (I suggest meetings with a maximum of 12 attending seem to work best; although not every member can always attend each meeting, so the actual membership may be larger.)

2. *Decide the main purpose(s) of the group:* what types of support are you aiming for?

3. *Set a time span for the group:* this can be renewable. It is easier to commit yourself to a group if the duration of the commitment is specified.

4. *Discuss leadership issues:* is one person going to lead every meeting, or will you take turns? Do you need to have a specified leader each time: perhaps you could just let the person who is feeling

most like doing it at the time take the lead? Apart from the actual meeting, there are other leadership tasks such as organising the venue, informing members of changes and buying the tea and buns.

5. *Agree on a contract with each other:* the ground rules mentioned in the trust section of this chapter could be adopted or adapted and added to. It is important that each person takes equal responsibility for reminding each other of the ground rules.

6. *Discuss decision-making strategies:* are you going to use democratic voting, consensus or let's-see-what-options-have-the-most-energy-behind-them-as-we-discuss-them? Each have their advantages and disadvantages.

7. *Use some structured group activities to get the group cohesion going:* this is particularly important at the begining of each meeting. Examples include 'rounds': each person takes a turn to make a short statement, perhaps on a positive theme such as 'two good things that I have noticed/experienced since we last met', or 'trust circle' and 'lifting and rocking' (6).

8. *Learn some structures which can be used during the meetings:* the 'rounds' can be used to ensure that each person gets a word in about a particular topic before the enthusiastic talkers in the group jump on to another topic. Various other 'games' can be used to open up topics for exploration or to provide a change of activity to prevent boredom and to aid concentration (7).

Many groups of nurses have come together to support each other using these sort of structures, such as the self and peer evaluation group mentioned earlier in the chapter. ITU nurses, health visitors, psychiatric nurses, district nurses, ward sisters/charge nurses and hospice nurses are among the groups I have come across who have met specifically for emotional support. Some have had training in co-counselling and also belong to the Co-Counselling International network of peer support groups.

Co-counselling

This is a form of mutual support which is based on a specific course of training (which takes about five to six days). People who have done the course can then meet up with others in the national and international network, to co-counsel in pairs or groups. Co-counsellors take turns to be 'client' and 'counsellor' with each other, and abide by strict ground rules about the techniques to be used. The techniques learned on the basic co-counselling course are mainly to do with working on your own emotional blocks, safely releasing bottled-up feelings, restructuring your own beliefs about yourself and the world at large, and changing unwanted behaviour patterns. The training for the 'counsellor' role involves mostly undoing 'compulsive helper' habits and learning how to assist the co-counselling 'client' rather than to lead her. See Townsend and Linsley (8) and Self and Society (9).

Other self-help groups

Specific stress problems can often be coped with by receiving support from people who have also experienced the same type of problem. Indeed, joining such a group can give you the chance to give some support as well as receive it. There are literally thousands of such groups throughout the country: there is probably a group for every identifiable medical or psychiatric problem and social minority group.

Pitfalls in receiving and giving support

1. *Lack of reciprocity:* colleagues can fall into 'helper' and 'helped' roles, resulting in the former not allowing herself or not being expected to need support, and the latter becoming dependent or demoralised. It is not necessary to reciprocate immediately, but rather to create a balance over a period of time.
2. *Not asking for support:* sometimes the word 'manage' in nursing means 'battle on in impossible situations'. If you find you are a good 'manager' in this sense, it might be worth stopping occasionally to consider what type of support would be useful and asking for it. Notice if you fall into the martyr role: nobody's-noticed-I-need-help-oh-woe-is-me-no-one-cares-about-me. Someone may have noticed and may care but may assume you do not want help because you have not asked. Some nurses like to adopt a 'mother hen' or 'earth mother' role and then complain when no one notices their own need for help.
3. *Refusing the support you need:* when much-needed support is offered, nurses often brush it off claiming they can cope. When someone offers support, it does not usually mean that they think you are inadequate or cannot cope. The chances are they care and

know you can cope, but that you might be able to cope better with care and support. Ungratiously brushing off the offer of support can feel like a slap in the face to the person who wants to help.

4. *Feeling obliged to take unnecessary support:* at the other extreme, you might accept support which you genuinely do not need because you want to avoid hurting the other person's feelings. The section on saying 'no' in the assertiveness chapter may help with this problem.

5. *Wrong type of support requested/wrong person/wrong time:* if you are feeling vulnerable or upset, it can be difficult to think logically about exactly what type of support you need, who would be the most appropriate person to give it and how to get the timing of the request for help right. When the mistake has been made, notice whether it was a merely logical mistake (not thinking it through clearly enough) or was it a pattern of behaviour which feels familiar. Examples of the latter include the myriad of ways a person can set themselves up to be rejected by unconsciously creating the scenarios for the rejection, e.g. starting to talk about something important just as the listener is about to go; asking for help at the worst possible moment for the potential supporter; manipulating the person ('you're the only person in the world I can count on') into giving all the support you need until they can take it no more and push the manipulator away; repeating mistakes which should have been learnt from, such as disclosing private information to someone who you know from previous experience cannot keep it to herself.

6. *Wrong type of support or support given at the wrong time:* nurses often have a tendency to assume that support and caring must be demonstrated in a tangible way, by giving practical help or advice. Although these can on occasions be the most appropriate support, many other types of support are also good but are often not considered by nurses. Indeed, practical help and advice can make the person being helped feel inadequate, as though the supporter considers her incapable of doing or thinking things through for herself. It can also lead to dependence.

The other types of support can also be used inappropriately. For instance, doggedly rabbitting on in ordinary conversation when you know a colleague is feeling upset, without giving any opportunity for her to talk about the problem, can be interpreted as being callous.

Information-giving can be badly timed. For instance, if someone is distracted or upset, they may be in no fit state to take in information. Feedback, particularly negative feedback, can be unhelpful if given at the wrong time. If the person is feeling very vulnerable, such as after a difficult appraisal interview, it can be hurtful to pile on the negative feedback.

Facilitative support can be frustrating when direct support, such as specific advice or information is needed, or it can be embarrassing when given at the wrong time, such as asking a colleague how she is feeling about a deep emotional upset when you meet her in a busy corridor or dining room.

7. *Badly given support:* with the best of intentions it is possible to make mistakes when giving support, particularly when there has been little opportunity to develop supportive skills. The concept of loyalty may be misunderstood as including covering up. Trying to save an incompetent colleague (such as someone with a drink or drug problem) from the personal consequences of her actions can be counterproductive for her in the long term, not to mention dangerous for patients.

Ordinary conversation may become a platform for one person to air their views while others meekly listen. Or it may become a competition between participants, each trying to get the upper hand by saying the most, or by being the best listener.

Information can be unclearly explained or too much can be given at once. It may be something the recipient already knows, or does not wish to know. Advice also may be imposed on someone who does not want it, or who is capable of working it out for herself. The advice might be given in a way which comes over as critical, and thus stimulate a rebellious response. Eric Berne (10) describes an interpersonal game called 'Why don't you' . . . 'Yes but . . .', which seems common among nurses. The 'why don't you' can sound critical, the 'yes but' prefaces a rejection of the advice. The advisor tries to think of some other solution, phrasing it the same way. The other person rejects it again, and round it goes till one breaks it off in frustration.

Encouragement can sound patronising if it is insincere, over-done or given with a tone of condescending surprise, e.g. 'Good-ness me, we have got a lot done while I was away. Good girl.'

Feedback can be destructive if it is unwelcome or badly done. There may be an imbalance between criticism and compliment, perhaps a machine-gun effect with too much criticism at once, or over-inflation when criticism is also warranted. It may involve

attacking her or attributing fault, putting her down, being sca-
thing or critical of emotion or saying hurtful things as a joke. It
may involve humiliation by being given inappropriately in front
of other people.

Facilitative support may be overdone. The supporter may try
to play psychotherapist or be a compulsive counsellor. It can be
quite disconcerting to find oneself being 'worked over' by a colleague or friend when all that is wanted is a bit of supportive chat.

Another interpersonal trap described by Eric Berne which is
common among nurses is 'Ain't it awful': It involves agreeing
with all a colleague's moans and groans and helping her to
become even more miserable. It could also involve agreeing with,
and compounding, her blaming of others.

8. *Lack of limit-setting:* in the urge to support colleagues, there is a
danger of going too far. You might end up spending so much time
and effort helping them with their concerns and responsibilities
that you have no time for your own. You might take on the role of
supporter when you are not the most appropriate person to do so.

References and further reading

1. Hillier S. (1981). Stresses, Strains and Smoking. *Nursing Mirror*, February 12, pp. 26–30.
2. Hingley P. (1984). The Humane Face of Nursing. *Nursing Mirror*, December 5, pp. 19–22.
3. Crawley P. (1983). Interviewed by Anne Shearer, in 'Angels in Hell'. *The Guardian*, June 29.
4. Chenevert M. (1978). *Special Techniques in Assertiveness Training for Women in the Health Professions*. St. Louis: C. V. Mosby.
5. Kilty J., Boud D. (1983). *Self and Peer Assessment for Educational Staff Development (A Workshop Facilitators Guide)*. Guildford: Human Potential Research Project, University of Surrey.
6. Stevens J. (1971). *Awareness: exploring, experimenting, experiencing*. Chapter on 'Group Activities'. London: Bantam.
7. Brandes D., Phillips H. (1979). *The Gamester's Handbook*. London: Hutchinson.
8. Townsend I., Linsley W. (1980). Creating a Climate for Carers. *Nursing Times*, July 3, pp. 1188–1190.
9. 'Co-Counselling I and II' Special Issues of 'Self and Society, The European Journal of Humanistic Psychology', A.H.P., 62 Southwark Bridge Road., London SE1 0AS.

10. Berne E. (1967). *Games People Play*. Harmondsworth: Penguin.

Where to learn more about support

Local adult education institutes and university and polytechnic extra-mural departments sometimes offer courses on counselling, self-help and self and peer evaluation; for instance, the Human Potential Research Project, Dept. of Educational Studies, University of Surrey, Guildford GU2 5XH has pioneered and specialised in such courses.

Your local in-service training tutor may be able to give you information about local opportunities.

You could organise a course yourself and hire a facilitator from, for instance, one of the above organisations.

The local Citizen's Advice Bureau or local authority information centre should have details of the thousands of self-help groups.

A list of co-counselling contact people who can give local information can be obtained from Jean Trewick, Westerly, Prestwick Lane, Chiddingfold, Surrey.

If you are going through a crisis and want one-way counselling to help you through it, contact CHAT Service (Counselling Help and Advice), Royal College of Nursing, 20 Cavendish Square, London W1M 0AB, tel. 01-409 3333. Their counsellors hold sessions in many parts of the country (for any nurse). Also, The British Association for Counselling, 1a Little Church Street, Rugby, Warwickshire, will provide a list of approved counsellors. Details of special local counselling services (e.g. pregnancy counselling) can be obtained from advice or information bureaux.

7

Creative
problem-solving

Rational and intuitive thinking

Problem-solving techniques are usually least represented in the methods nurses cite for coping with stress (in contrast, for example, to groups of top business executives). This may be due to the conflicts arising out of prevailing values about the way we use our brains to solve problems. Rational problem-solving is overvalued and intuitive problem-solving is undervalued. If the majority of nurses have greater skills in intuitive thinking, but little confidence in their value, this would explain why problem-solving techniques are not often reported among their ways of coping with stress. On questioning, I usually discover that nurses have often used intuitive methods but did not think they were worth mentioning. If this applies to you, the aims of further self-training could be for you to become more aware of the intuitive methods you use, value them more, use them more intentionally and expand your range of problem-solving strategies by also incorporating logical structures into your repertoire.

Before we go on to look at some practical methods, it might be useful to expand a little on the differences between rational and intuitive thinking. Table 7.1 summarises and adapts some good points made by Robert Ornstein (1), and Fig. 7.1 illustrates the differences in mental processes.

Neurological research has shown that rational thought occurs in the left cerebral hemisphere and intuitive in the right. The two hemispheres are linked by the corpus callosum. In effect, we have

Table 7.1 *Two extreme styles of thinking.*

Rational	**Intuitive**
Connected thoughts	Disconnected thoughts
Organised	Chaotic
Concerned with detail	Concerned with overall context
Thought of as masculine	Thought of as feminine
Deliberate	Spontaneous
Verbal language	Body language
Analytical	Hunches
Numbers	Pictures
Initiates	Reacts
Concerned with analysing the past and planning for the future	Concerned with each moment as it occurs
Convergent thinking	Divergent thinking
One-track mind	Scatterbrain

two minds which can operate simultaneously. We even use the expression 'I'm in two minds', when there is a conflict between 'head' (left brain) and 'heart' (right brain). In the Western culture, skills in using the left brain are valued and encouraged more than those of the right so the left brain has become identified with the conscious mind, and the right with the unconscious. If you have been 'successfully educated' in the traditional system, you will be more aware of what goes on in your left brain than in your right. However, many nurses do not see themselves as educational successes, since they are mostly educated in the middle streams during secondary schooling. If this is the case with you, you may be in a more favourable position than a highly academically trained nurse to develop a balanced use of your mental potential

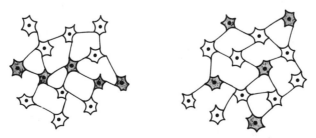

Fig. 7.1 *Rational and intuitive thinking.*

for coping with stress, provided that you can overcome your blocks to developing your intellectual as well as intuitive potential. On the other hand, if you are an intellectual, you have probably had more positive experiences of learning and could transfer your enjoyment of learning to developing your intuition, provided you can accept the value of doing so.

The importance of valuing and using both areas of the brain could be illustrated by the following analogy. Suppose a busy surgical ward has two separate groups of staff, the day nurses and the night nurses. They seldom communicate with each other. The day staff seem very efficient: they use a strict routine to get through the nursing procedures, treatments, pre-op preparation and post-op observations, ward rounds, meals, visiting times, reports and teaching sessions. They make all the decisions about nursing care and ward policies. However, they are often puzzled by the frequent mistakes they make in assessing patients' needs and conditions — patients they thought were doing well die suddenly and vice versa, and patients they thought were ready to be discharged are rushed back as emergencies. The night staff have few routine tasks to do, but tend to deal with the patients

who cannot sleep and want to talk, with the mysterious changes in patient's conditions, and the deaths. They are very sensitive to atmosphere and can accurately predict a change in a patient's condition even though physical signs are stable. They know when a patient has started to fight the illness or has given up. They know when she is really ready to go home or not, irrespective of the practical facilities available. However, they leave the ward in a mess and often forget to do the routine observations. The patients are anxious in the mornings because of the apparent chaos. The night staff keep their points of view about the patients and ward policies to themselves because they will not be listened to due to lack of hard data to back up their intuitions. The two groups of staff have such different styles of working that they anticipate only conflict if they began to communicate. So the patients suffer because the staff are not willing to learn from each other.

Likewise with rational and intuitive problem-solving — under-using your potential in either sphere can mean you end up by suffering from unnecessary stress, and restricting your personal and professional development. The aim is to increase your capacity to use both rational and intuitive thinking simultaneously, to cope with the inner conflicts which can arise, and to be able to focus on one or the other at will, as appropriate.

Practical techniques

These are suggested here in a sequence with increasing amount of structure.

Allowing

This involves postponing a decision by distracting attention away from the problem until the answer just comes without trying. For instance, an ITU sister reported: 'I'd been battling with the problems on that unit for two years. I hate to give in or run away but I knew I'd tried absolutely everything and would have to do something drastic but kept putting off any plans for the future. I just took each day as it came. One day, when X was being thoroughly unpleasant to everyone as usual, I suddenly thought "I don't have to be here" and immediately felt a peace of mind I hadn't had for a long time. So I left and I found this job and I'm a different person now. It was the best decision I've made.'

Sleeping on it

Rather like the previous method, this involves putting off a stressful decision until after a good night's sleep (or two or more). It requires the ability to put aside anxieties about the problem to allow yourself to get to sleep. One way of enabling the anxieties to subside is to trust in the power of your sleeping brain and just before going to sleep to allow the thought 'I wonder what to do about . . .' to be repeated very slowly and gently as a mantra, without pushing to find an immediate solution. When anxieties about finding a solution creep in, just slowly repeat the phrase and allow yourself to stay in a state of wondering.

Structured fantasy

This can help you to learn to listen to the part of your mind which has the intuitive answers which are right for you. The following script describes one such structure and can be read out to you or recorded on a tape. Each full stop represents a pause of about five seconds.

'Sit in a comfortable, upright, open position with your spine upright . imagine the spine effortlessly extending, your head balanced with minimum effort . take a couple of slow, deep breaths using your diaphragm . . . . allow your breathing to become relaxed . let your mind settle, slowing down . . in this fantasy you will be going on a journey . imagine the starting point for your journey, the place you are leaving behind . . picture yourself taking the first step, then the next few steps in your journey . . picture the mode of transport that you take, are you going under your own steam or being carried by a vehicle? . . visualise your journey, how you feel, the scenery as it passes by . . . . . after a while, you meet a person on your journey, an old, wise woman or man, picture this old, wise woman or man . . notice the first thing that comes into your mind after my next instruction: you ask the old, wise woman or man a question, what is your question? . . . again, notice the first thing that comes into your mind after my next instruction: the old, wise person gives you an answer to the question, what is the answer? . . . . take time to reflect on the meaning of whatever question and/or answer came to mind . . . . now imagine that you leave the old wise person, you have reached the goal of the journey, you are about to return . picture the journey back, is it the same route or a different one, the same type of transport or a different one? . . how do you feel on this stage of the journey? . . notice the scenery . . . soon you will finish the journey, picture the place you finish the journey, is it the same as your starting point or different? . . picture yourself at the end of the journey . . how do you look and feel compared to when you started out? . . . . the exercise is over now, take some time to reflect on the experience.'

The old, wise man or woman in that fantasy symbolised that part of you which has the knowledge and experience to give you the answer which is most appropriate to you at that point in time.

If no question or answer surfaced then perhaps the exercise was not appropriate for you at that time. Using it again another time may be more fruitful. Sometimes the question and/or answer which comes to mind may seem irrelevant or incomprehensible. Given time, relevance or meaning may become clear to you. John Stevens describes similar structured fantasies which he has entitled 'Wise Man' and 'the Search' (2).

Making a thought map

One way of starting with intuitive thinking and working towards interpreting it with rational thinking, is to adopt a method suggested by Tony Buzan (3). It is based on the anatomy of the brain. The millions of cells have millions of connections, and thoughts whizz around the brain at great speed. The electrical activity of the brain occurs so quickly that we cannot be conscious of every thought. This method of collecting your thoughts helps to slow down the thinking process and involves drawing a sort of thought map. (See Fig. 7.2.)

1. The first step is to write the topic you want to think through in the centre of a sheet of paper.
2. Then write the thoughts this heading stimulates, around the central point, putting a circle round each other and linking each to the central heading.
3. Expand on each of the thoughts.
4. Then see if any of the thoughts under separate sections link together, and draw a line between them. Add any further thoughts that arise from each link. Emphasise any useful plans or comments you make to yourself, either in a different colour or with a bolder border.

i.

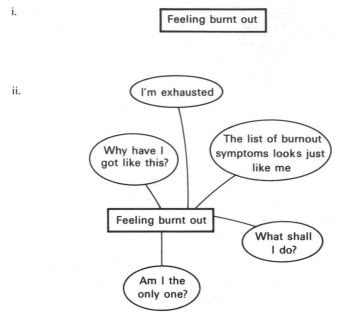

Fig. 7.2   *Making a thought map.*

Making the most of a 'to do' list

A lot of nurses find that the simple method of making a list of everything they need and want to do, then deciding on priorities, helps to clear the mind. Sometimes just pinpointing the highest priority item and getting on with it helps you to get started and everything else falls into place. A common pitfall in list-making is to only include the tasks which other people want or expect you to do and to forget about your own needs and priorities. Alan Lakein (4) has some useful exercises for establishing your personal priorities, some of which have been adapted here.

This first exercise is for setting your lifetime goals. At the top of a piece of paper, write 'What are my lifetime goals?'. Set yourself two minutes to write furiously anything which comes into your head in response to the question. Do not censor. Take into account personal, family, social, financial, community and spiritual goals as well as career. Allow ridiculously impossible things to be included such as single-handedly rescuing the National Health Service, or becoming world cream gateau eating

iii.

Fig. 7.2 *Making a thought map (continued).*

champion. The goals can also be expressed as non-competitive achievements, such as having a peaceful life or five nights sleep in a row without being disturbed by the children. Bear in mind that you are not committing yourself to any of the goals by writing them down; this is merely a brainstorming exercise and most will be discarded.

After two minutes, give yourself another two minutes to add anything else. Consider the implicit goals in your present life patterns. For instance, if you regularly watch the TV news, your unspoken goal may be to be able to hold your own in discussions about national and international affairs. Many of the goals in this

Fig. 7.2   *Making a thought map (continued).*

answer may be expressed in general terms, so the next two stages of the exercise may help you to clarify goals in more specific terms.

On another sheet of paper, write the question 'How would I really like to spend the next three years?'. Again, list as many uncensored answers as you can in two minutes. Then have another two minutes to add further answers.

The third stage is to write the question 'If I knew I was going to be struck dead by lightning six months from today, how would I live till then?'. Assume that everything related to the death, such as a will and funeral expenses have already been planned. Just list the points which come to mind about how you would really like to live for those six months. Give yourself a two-minute deadline for scribbling anything which comes to mind, then two further minutes for additions.

Look back over all three lists and give yourself two minutes to notice any links. Then spend a further two minutes picking out the most important three goals on each sheet. You now have a list of nine lifetime goals which are important to you today. They are likely to change, so it can be useful to repeat the exercise a number of times during the course of, say, a fortnight, in order to clarify those which are consistently the most important. If you use a notebook, you can more easily keep a record of your ideas which can be interesting for long-term comparison.

The next step is to make a list of small tasks which would contribute towards each goal. Think of each task as a five-minute 'bite' at the larger tasks involved in achieving the goal. For instance, one nurse's goal was to own her own flat. Her lists of tasks included: 'Ring Chris and ask him about mortgages. Stop at estate agents on the way home from work and get a list of the lowest priced flats to get an idea of current prices. Invite Betty for supper to talk about the possibility of jointly owning a flat so we can both get a foot into the market. Ring building society and ask for pamphlets on mortgages. Talk to Eva about her flatmate: how much does the rent she gets from the flatmate pay towards the mortgage repayments?' You now have a list of small tasks which contribute towards your own personal goals. Ensure that at least one of these features as a priority on every 'to do' list.

You can decide on the sequence of priorities on your list either by dividing the tasks into As, Bs and Cs, or by numbering them in order of priority. Lakein points out that it is not essential to complete every task on every list, but actually leaving the low priority tasks undone is often a better use of time. He writes of the 80/20 rule: 80% of the value of your effort comes from only 20% of the tasks. We do, however, need to be aware that some low priority tasks (Lakein suggests only one in a hundred) can create crises if they are left permanently undone, so notice when low priority tasks begin to creep higher up the scale of priorities.

A problem-solving spiral

Figure 7.3 shows a step-by-step process of working through a problem to enable you to untangle your thoughts when under stress. It incorporates the opportunity to use intuition as well as reason. Although it is expressed in a certain sequence, you will probably have to go back a stage or more at times, particularly between the first two stages. The problem which actually needs to

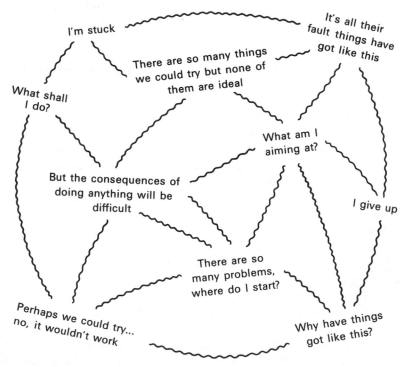

Fig. 7.3   *From tangled thoughts to a step-by-step problem-solving spiral.*

be tackled is often one of the factors contributing towards the initial problem, so the presenting problem usually needs to be redefined. Also, usually when deciding on a course of action, the priority goals need to be reconsidered. Table 7.2 lists some questions which you can ask yourself at each stage of the spiral, and gives an example of one nurse's thinking.

This process may seem a long drawn-out way of thinking through a problem. However, not all the stages need to be done at

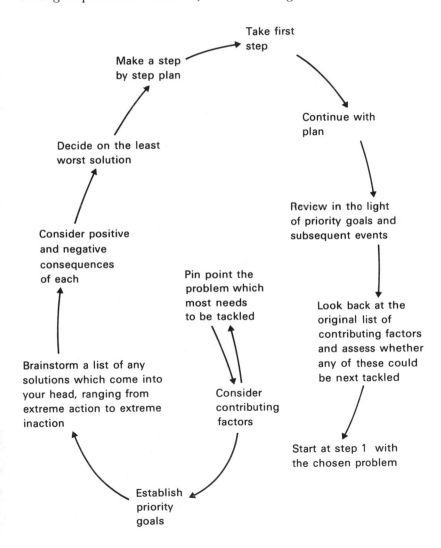

Table 7.2 *Questions to lead you through the problem-solving spiral, with one nurse's replies.*

---

1. What's the problem? What's causing this current stress? What's bothering you?	Acute shortage of staff on my district, particularly next weekend. It's going to be desperate.
2. What do you think causes this problem? What makes it worse? What's behind the problem? Which of these factors do you think should be tackled first?	Financial cut backs because of Government policy. Earlier discharge of patients to the community, without consulting us about our resources to cope. Non-replacement of a colleague who left. Cut backs in numbers of hospital geriatric beds so we have more acutely ill geriatric patients with no increase in staff to cope. Increased sickness rate because of exhaustion among nurses. Clinical nurse manager doesn't seem to understand our position.
What do you think causes *this* problem? What makes it worse? What's behind the problem?	He doesn't seem to accept that our caseloads are heavier. We've told him that although the numbers haven't changed much, that's because we've pruned out the follow-up visits, bereavement visits, cut down on frequency of dressings, etc., so we're left with the heavy patients. He just keeps telling us to reassess priorities in our caseload management.
	As it is there are dozens of patients who need our support who aren't getting any at all, and others who need more visits but we can't fit them in. It's a disgrace.
	The morale of my team is at rockbottom. We're ashamed at the standards of district nursing on our patch and we just get angry with him at meetings. That puts his back up so he tends to avoid us as much as he can. He's always 'at a meeting' when we ring up to complain. Perhaps we're approaching it in the wrong way.

Table 7.2 *Questions to lead you through the problem-solving spiral, with one nurse's replies. – cont.*

3. What are you hoping for/aiming at in the long run? What are your ultimate goals?	Better patient care, more staff.
What short term goals would help towards that end?	CNS understanding our position and making a case on our behalf for more staff.
4. Brainstorm a list of anything which comes to mind as a way of helping towards achieving your goals. Put the most outrageous action at one end and extreme inaction at the other, and fill in all the options inbetween. Then cross out anything which you are definitely not prepared to do under any circumstances whatsoever.	Bop him one on the head! Leave the job immediately. Resign *en bloc*. Go on strike a. Find a job elsewhere and resign giving required notice b. Threaten to resign if nothing's done. c. Refuse to nurse some of the patients. d. Close our books, refuse to take on any more new referrals. e. Work out a dependency scale and write a report showing levels of dependency and the unsafe level of care with our numbers of staff. f. Enlist support of GPs. g. Ask GPs to do something about it. Do nothing and continue to work ourselves into the ground and continue unsafe levels of practice. Forget about it and hope it'll get better of its own accord. Lie down right now and sleep off the exhaustion.
5. What are the likely positive and negative consequences of each of the options you have left on your list?	a. + ease my stress. − feel I'd be running away. b. + gets the message across. − got to be willing to leave if nothing's done. c. + gets the message across, the Health

Table 7.2   *Questions to lead you through the problem-solving spiral, with one nurse's replies.*

	Authority would be forced to provide someone to nurse those patients.
	− feel guilty not giving individual care to some of our patients.
	d. + gets the message across that we can't expand infinitely; puts us on a par with hospital wards which can close their beds.
	− new patients at home would be left struggling on their own.
	e. + gives some figures to help managers argue their case.
	− takes time to work out, I'm not good with figures.
	f. + avoids getting their backs up about our not being able to care for their patient's properly.
	− they might not cooperate.
	g. + they may be listened to because they have more status.
	− likely to put up CNS's back even more. Passes the buck too much; it's up to us.
6. Which are the least worst or most effective solutions bearing in mind your goals?	c., d., e. and f.
7. What's your plan? What is your very first step? Then what next?	We have to do something fairly drastic so:
	a. Get team together this lunchtime to work out dependency scale — Joe's good at figures. Decide how many patients can be safely nursed at the weekend given the few staff we've got. Make a list of patients we cannot safely cover.
	b. Write report tonight about unsafe levels and list patients we cannot cover this weekend, putting the responsibility on the Health Authority to cover them.

Table 7.2 *Questions to lead you through the problem-solving spiral, with one nurse's replies.* – cont.

	Also that any new referrals must be passed straight to the CNS since we cannot cover them. Ring GPs and let them know that we are doing it and that they'll get copies of the report.
	c. After the diabetics have been done, take the report and put it on CNS's desk with a copy on the divisional nursing officer's desk.
	d. Meet team at lunchtime for support in case all hell's let loose!
8. (later) How far were the goals achieved? In retrospect were the goals appropriate?	Yes, the goals were appropriate. An agency nurse was provided for that weekend and the CNS himself went out and did the male patients. We repeated it again for the latter part of the following week and the next weekend because one person went off sick. Plans are now afoot to start a nurse bank for the district: the District Health Authority has agreed to provide funds.
9. Looking back at the factors contributing to the initial problem, is there anything else which could usefully be tackled?	Yes, we could look at this problem of changes in the policies about early discharge and the cutting back on geriatric beds without consulting the district nursing services.

once, and the time invested will save all the time you would probably have spent worrying and dithering about the stressful problem.

Pitfalls in using problem-solving techniques to deal with stress

Mistakes will be made in using any techniques for coping with stress but they are an important source of learning provided you are aware of having made them.

1. *Trying too hard:* forcing yourself to analyse and find solutions when you are tired or upset can lead to poor decisions or exhaustion. Spending too much time mulling over a problem can exhaust you mentally and emotionally and not allow the right intuitive decision to surface.

2. *Over-procrastination:* perpetually putting off facing a stressful problem can allow some situations to escalate, and force you down the slope towards burnout.

3. *Seeking the ideal easy solution and getting discouraged:* if a stressful problem has arisen, then there is unlikely to be any easy solution because it would have been implemented before it became a problem. Any way of dealing with a problem is going to be difficult to carry out, so do not allow yourself to get immobilised by the inevitable disadvantages of the options open to you. Perhaps it is better to think of 'ways of dealing with a problem' rather than 'solutions'; the latter implies the problem can be solved. This is not usually the case; it can usually only be dealt with, or the situation improved a little.

4. *Passing the buck:* it can be tempting to get into a victim role and blame 'Them' for the stress you are experiencing, and leave it up to 'Them' to sort it out for you. It is important to take responsibility for initiating the process of sorting out your own stresses. It may involve asking for help or delegating but this is rather different to passing the buck.

5. *Getting tied down by 'oughts', 'musts' and 'shoulds':* you might find yourself expressing your options for dealing with a problem in those terms. Instead, consider what *you* think is the best course of action, rather than what you think you might be expected to do.

6. *Underestimating your abilities in either intuitive or rational thinking:* many of us have been put down by arrogant people who think in a different way to us. Apart from the widespread disdain for intuitive thinking in the Western culture as a whole, in nursing there also seems to be contempt for rational thinking. Nurses who are seen as intellectuals are often assumed to be incompetent in the practical field and they have to be more practical than the average nurse to prove themselves. So it is no wonder that thinking is undervalued in nursing.

References and further reading

1. Ornstein R. (1977). *The Psychology of Consciousness*. New York: Harcourt Brace Jovanovich.
2. Stevens J. (1973). *Awareness: exploring, experimenting, experiencing*. London: Bantam.
3. Buzan T. (1974). *Use your Head*. London: BBC Publications.
4. Lakein A. (1973). *How to get Control of your Time and your Life*. Signet.

Where to learn more about creative problem-solving

Some stress courses run by local adult education institutes, universities, polytechnics or private bodies include problem-solving methods, or they may run specific courses on problem-solving, time management or personal planning. Courses on management or decision-making usually include problem-solving strategies which you then apply to your own stresses.

8

Exercise, diet and physical health

Health education and rehabilitation are intrinsic to the nurse's role in caring for others, exercise and diet featuring highly in both. Yet often we do not apply the same caring principles to ourselves. Although the knowledge is there, mental blocks can stop us applying that knowledge to self-care.

This chapter offers some ways of looking at the problem. I have included little in the way of physiological or dietary information since I have assumed that this is common knowledge or easily accessible to readers.

Assessing your existing levels of activity

According to *The Good Health Guide*, to keep physically fit you need: an average of 30 minutes vigorous activity (i.e. which increases your heart rate significantly) a day; to twist and turn the major joints through a full range of movements to keep supple; to be on your feet two hours a day to help circulation and maintain bone structure; and to lift a heavy load (using proper lifting techniques, of course) for at least five seconds a day to maintain muscular strength (1). It may be possible to achieve all these activities without having to make a special time to do them or to become a track-suited keep fit fanatic.

Without changing any of your habits at this stage, assess how active your life-style is by keeping a diary of your activities for at least 4 days (2 work days and 2 off duty days) using the checklist in

Table 8.1. Show the amount of time you spent on each vigorous activity. Review the diary working out your average time spent on vigorous activity per day. Consider the patterns of activity in your life. Make a plan.

Table 8.1   *Required daily activities for keeping fit.*

- **30 mins vigorous activity** which causes the heart to beat fast: brisk walking, running, digging, vigorous housework such as polishing furniture, windows or the car, labouring work, sawing or chopping logs, cycling, climbing stairs, most sports, disco dancing and others.
- **Twisting and turning** all major joints through full range of movement: neck, shoulders, elbows, wrists, upper spine, lower spine and hips, pelvis, knees, ankles.
- **On your feet** for at least 2 hours a day to stimulate the skeletal system to retain healthy bone structure.
- **Lifting** a heavy weight for at least 5 seconds to maintain muscular strength.

Examples of two nurses' activity assessment are as follows:
Mary is a 22-year-old staff nurse. She feels fairly fit although she thinks she ought to do more. She does not see herself as a sporty type but wants to get her figure in trim.

Mary's activity diary

1. Work day
Vigorous activity: walked to and from bus stop 10 minutes, brisk walking between departments and to and from dining room 10 minutes, up stairs to flat 1 minute. Total 21 minutes.
Twisting and turning: upper body and legs, yes; arms stretched back, lower spine, hips and pelvis, no. On feet: most of day!
Lifting: no problem, lifted patients +++.
2. Day off
Vigorous activity: housework — only about 10 minutes of it made me puff. Disco dancing 1½ hours. Total 1 hr 40 mins.
Twisting and turning: yes, whole range while dancing.
On feet: yes, more than 2 hours.
Lifting: nothing heavy.

3. Day off

Vigorous activity: lazy day recovering from party! Total 0!

Twisting and turning: top half of body while doing washing, cooking and pottering around; not pelvis and hips.

On feet: yes, 2 hours just.

Lifting: nothing heavy.

4. Work day

Vigorous activity: to bus stop and back 10 minutes, brisk walking at work 5 mins, up stairs 1 min. Frantic tidy up 10 mins. Total 26 mins.

Twisting and turning: upper body and legs, yes; pelvis and hips, no.

Lifting: yes, quite a lot.

Mary's average for vigorous activity was 39 minutes a day though her disco dancing session put up that average quite a lot. Since she only dances once every few weeks, she needs to consider her usual rate of activity. If we assume that the low score on day 3 was due to her need to recover from the dancing the previous night, we see that the average for the other 2 days is 23.5 minutes. So she probably only needs to increase her level of vigorous activity by about 7 minutes a day when she is not dancing. She manages to do most of the twisting and turning during her work or housework, although the shoulders and hips need a few extra daily exercises to take them through full range of movements. Ensuring that she lifts and is on her feet is no problem in her job. To get her figure more trim, she needs to increase her overall level of fitness and then embark on a further series of exercises for exercising all her muscles, particularly the abdominal muscles about which she is especially concerned.

Mary's plan is as follows:

1. Walk to the bus stop and back when it's not raining — adds 10 minutes per day.

2. Go along to the aerobics class with Evelyn on Thursdays and practise the exercises in between classes.

We will follow up Mary's progress later in the chapter.

Ahmed is a nurse manager and is 44 years old. He used to play football and cycle in his youth but has given both up. He is a calm sort of person who gets a lot done by moving about at a steady rate. Once a week he takes out his aggression on a squash ball, although he is not very good at squash and feels fairly unfit. He would like to be able to sleep every night of the week as well as he does after playing squash.

Ahmed's activity diary

1. Friday
Vigorous activity: precious little, walked about quite a bit but not what you'd call briskly, used lifts, drove to work. Total 0!
Twisting and turning: top half of body while doing cleaning up and washing up.
On feet: over 2 hours.
Lifting: yes, children.
2. Saturday
Vigorous activity: busy day doing housework and ferrying the children around but not much got the heart going except sex! Total about 15 minutes.
Twisting and turning: yes, probably everything except high kicks!
On feet: most of the day.
Lifting: yes, shopping, furniture, children.
3. Sunday
Vigorous activity: did some gardening and walked the dog, but again, took it easy most of the time. Only 10 minutes puffing when I first started digging till I slowed down.
Twisting and turning: most joints except hips again.
On feet: yes, more than 2 hours.
Lifting: yes, children, digging.
4. Monday
Vigorous activity: played squash with Simon — 35 minutes.
Twisting and turning: yes, all except full range of hip movements.
On feet: yes, over 2 hours.
Lifting: yes, children and dog.

Ahmed is making the same dangerous mistake as many people in his age group. Having developed a slowish but well-planned and steady pace for getting through their daily tasks, they have only occasional but intense bursts of vigorous activity, in his case squash and sex. The squash in particular is dangerous: a forty minute game in which competition is likely to spur him on beyond healthy limits may help him feel temporarily emotionally better, but it is putting a strain on his heart. It would be much safer for him to gradually increase the daily time spent on vigorous activities to 30 minutes before resuming his weekly squash game. Probably just being more vigorous in some of his normal activities would be sufficient. He also needs to loosen his hips each day. He manages to get in the necessary time on his feet and the lifting (though he may need to notice whether he does enough lifting when his younger children grow up).

Ahmed's plan:

1. Use the stairs instead of the lift.
2. Take a lunch break more often and walk to the shops.
3. Explain to Simon that I have to cut out our squash games for a while.
4. Try to persuade Sarah or Anne to let me teach them squash, then knock the ball around vigorously on my own for about 5 minutes at each end of the session while she gets changed.
5. Walk the dog more briskly or jog across the park with him (I want to keep to that slow meander back, I need that peace and quiet).
6. Take the family out cycling on Sundays.
7. Swing my legs about each day, if I can get some time on my own so I'm not laughed at!
8. Starting in 3 weeks time, go by bike and train to work sometimes instead of driving.

This sort of assessment helps to highlight the potential for integrating relevant keep-fit activities into daily life and to move your concept of fitness away from athleticism to something more realistic. When there is no necessity to take exercise, it can often take an immense amount of will-power to get going and to sustain an exercise program. So building into your life opportunities to exercise which also contribute towards the personal survival and maintenance tasks can make the effort seem more useful and natural.

The high-tech nurse in a Stone Age body

It is salutary to consider that the ancestors of nurses now living in a high-tech labour-saving environment and eating highly processed foods were gatherers and hunters not so many generations ago. Our bodies have not yet had the time to evolve ways of adapting to the changes in patterns of activity and diet which have taken place in most parts of the world in relatively recent times in contrast to about a million years of gatherer/hunter lifestyles (2). Our anatomy and physiology is still geared to a way of life in which exercise and survival are inextricably linked. The motivation for taking exercise in a Stone Age culture arises from hunger or the prospect of hunger, from danger or fear of danger, from exposure or the prospect of exposure to the weather, and from the desire to celebrate. So all the walking, chasing, running away, fighting, bending, stretching, digging, carrying, building and dancing takes place as an integral part of living with no need to apply will-power and usually with a lot of laughing and singing with other people.

Contrast this to the nurse who tries to force her lonely way through the exercises on her Jane Fonda Workout Record, to the sounds of her own groans and yelps or the taunts and sulks of her family, before she switches on the machines which make the breakfast and gets into another which takes her to work. No wonder she usually gives up. Although she knows intellectually that exercise is good for her, this type of exercise can feel artificial and pointless and can be difficult to sustain.

So we are accepting and acknowledging our Stone Age ancestry by giving ourselves the chance to exercise while:

1. 'Gathering and hunting for food': e.g. gardening, walking to the supermarket or cycling to the job which brings in the money to buy the food.

2. 'Building fire and shelter': DIY in the home and garden, shovelling coal, collecting and sawing wood, housework.
3. 'Dealing with danger': e.g. sports, hobbies or housework which give you the chance to enact the 'fight' response, bashing, kicking, throwing, competing, wringing, shouting, wrestling, chasing and the 'flight' response, running, jumping.
4. 'Celebrating': e.g. dancing, noisy group activities, fooling around, playing for the sake of playing.

If you can build activities covering each category into your life, you are likely to have a greater sense of balance and satisfaction from your attempts to keep fit, than if you have to push yourself to do exercises which do not have any other function.

Dealing with exercise problems

If assessing your existing level of activity exercise does not get you where you want to be in terms of fitness, then you could try applying the problem-solving spiral in Chapter 7.

1. Write the question 'What's stopping me from getting fit?' on a sheet of paper and list as many possible answers as come into your head. Add any from Table 8.2 that are relevant to you personally. Underline the two or three factors which most interfere with your getting fitter and number them in order of importance.
2. Then write the question 'What would be the purpose of my getting fitter?' and brainstorm as many possible answers which could relate to you. Add any from Table 8.3 which also apply to you. Underline two or three which are most important and number them in order of priority.
3. Bearing in mind these goals, brainstorm a list of possible ways of minimising the two or three main blocks you identified.
4. Then choose one of the solutions and make a step-by-step plan, pinpointing the first small step very clearly. Review your progress and adapt your plan if necessary.

If we go back to Mary's situation, we would find that two months after her initial plan, Mary was managing to walk for the extra ten minutes on most days, although she had found it difficult initially to allow enough time when setting off to work. She had not had much success with the aerobics exercises and had virtually given

Table 8.2   *Examples of blocks to getting fit.*

No will-power, always take the easy way, e.g. drive for even short distances, use lift.
Listless during off-duty time.
Embarrassed about body.
Don't want to be teased, mocked or whistled at.
Can't find the time.
Getting started too difficult.
Just another chore to fit in.
Lack of suitable environment.
Lack of suitable equipment.
Results are so long term; get discouraged.
Seems pointless, no end product.
Lonely.
Expense of equipment, classes, facilities.
Hopeless at anything energetic.
Partner/family would resent my doing it.
Likely to make me ache too much and feel awful.
Boring.
Can't bear being with hearty sporty types.
Don't like team or group activities
Don't want to develop big muscles.
Don't see myself as the type; it's just for sporty types.

up. Applying the problem-solving spiral, she pinpointed the following three blocks:

1. Getting discouraged by not being able to keep up with the speed of some of the instructions (even though it's a 'beginners' class!).
2. It's such a performance to get Tuesday evenings off, it's not worth the hassle.
3. I have to wait until my flatmates go out so I can use the living room to practise the exercises between the classes.

Her main aims were:

1. To get my figure trim.
2. Feel more confident about myself.
3. Get a sense of achievement at improving at something.

She decided to start swimming again instead. She enjoyed having a sauna very much, and reckoned that it would not take a lot of

Table 8.3   *Some possible reasons for taking more exercise.*

Lose weight.
Feel more confident about my body shape.
Improve complexion.
More resistant to injury, e.g. when lifting patients.
More agile and graceful.
More stamina, tire less quickly.
Feel more energetic and lively.
More alert.
Think quicker.
Get everyday tasks done quicker.
Sleep better.
Able to eat more without putting on weight.
Save money.
Save time.
Cure backache.
Bend and stretch for things more easily.
Prevent illness.
Have a tangible end product, e.g. growing or building things.
Sense of achievement because of getting better at something.
Win in a competitive sport.
Feel the cold less.
Relax more.
Switch off mentally.
Celebrate being alive.
Improve sex life.
Enjoy company of other people.
Enjoy time on my own.
Get rid of nervous or aggressive energy.
Get some fresh air.
Get out and see some pleasant scenery.
More independent, not having to rely on transport or on stronger people
to do tasks for me.

will-power to get into the swimming pool afterwards. Then she
could keep a mental note of how many lengths she had swum each
time and gradually increase it. Her first step was to find out the
times the sauna and pool were open at the local council sports
centre. This solution set up a different plan without all the blocks
that prevented the aerobics from being a success.

In two months, Ahmed had done better than he had hoped. He
had stuck to his plans about using stairs, walking at lunchtimes,

walking faster with the dog and the limbering-up exercises. He could not persuade either his wife or his eldest daughter to learn squash or go cycling with him on Sundays. However, he had started cycling to work and found that he enjoyed it so much that when he sold his car, he decided not to replace it immediately with another, but to try to spend the summer without one (his wife had a car so they used this at weekends). This had the added advantage of helping to solve some financial problems. He was very pleased with himself, had lost 5 lbs in weight, and was planning to resume his squash in about a month's time.

There are many useful self-help books on the market to help you build up your exercise levels. Fern Lebo's (3) and Michael Carruthers' and Alistair Murray's (4) both give a gentle start, while Kenneth Cooper's (5) and the Royal Canadian Air Force book (6) will get you fighting fit!

Pressures which lead to poor eating habits

Nurses are well aware of the importance of a balanced, varied diet containing all the requisite nutrients and of recent (belated) health education campaigns to encourage the public to decrease the amount of fat, added sugar, salt and chemicals we eat. But knowledge is not enough and many nurses report that they have problems with their own diet. This is not surprising, given the political, institutional, social and internal factors currently affecting nurses as well as everyone else.

In past decades people who were interested in unrefined, uncontaminated food were dismissed as cranks or hippies. However, medical evidence of the dangers of eating any other type of food has been rapidly accumulating. In spite of the evidence, health education campaigns and legislation to safeguard consumers have been delayed because of pressure from the main sector of the food manufacturing industry. So the majority of the food which is available for nurses to buy has had most of the fibre and natural food value removed, and contains high levels of fat and added sugar and salt, a bevy of chemicals which have preservative and cosmetic functions, and residues of pesticides and hormones used in growing vegetables and rearing animals. Millions of pounds are spent in propaganda to promote unhealthy foods and to counteract what little health education can be carried out with comparatively meagre financial resources. Although the organic wholefood industry is expanding, it does not as yet have the resources to advertise widely or the turnover to produce food, particularly 'convenience food', which is cheap enough for most nurses to afford on a regular basis.

Nurses who have to rely on the food prepared by hospital catering services face the same risks as patients. Recent environmental health reports have shown that the standards of hygiene in many hospital kitchens would render the District Health Authority liable to prosecution if they were not exempt from liability because of being Crown property.

The other side of the conflict experienced by nurses is the social pressure to conform to sex-role stereotypes by dieting to achieve some currently fashionable body shape (7). Even the recent 'health' boom has its advertising emphasis on how you look rather than your true health. So another barrage of messages is coming at us. The real health message hardly has a chance to get through to influence the way we care for ourselves.

The external pressures to eat badly add to internal pressures. If refined, high fat food was used as a symbol of love, comfort and reward in the family in which you were brought up, it can be extremely difficult to resist that mental association in adulthood. Likewise, if being made to go hungry was used as a method of punishment or to avoid 'spoiling', then even ordinary between-meals hunger pangs can be unbearable as an adult; the adult becomes reluctant to 'punish' herself by waiting for food.

Another internal pressure which may operate is a physiological one: addiction. The human body has not evolved to cope with repeated doses of the same substances ingested daily, year in year out. There is a physiological stress adaptation response to this continued overdose, the person becomes generally physically under par, especially when other stresses are also being experienced. This low feeling is temporarily relieved by ingesting more of the substance and the body is stimulated for a while, giving a feeling of 'lift'. This soon wears off leaving the person feeling low, so she seeks more of the substance and so the cycle goes on. This phenomenon is well known in relation to alcohol, but less so with regard to other foods. This addiction is a chronic form of food allergy. The most common chronic allergies are to those foods with which we most commonly 'overdose' ourselves: wheat (particulary white flour), cow's milk products, sugar, coffee, tea, eggs and chemical additives. Indeed, it is very difficult to find a prepared food or a recipe which does not contain any of these. Therefore it can be quite common for these foods to crop up, not only every day, but in almost every single meal a Western person eats. For more details, read Richard Mackarness' book (8) or Marshall Mandell and Lynn Waller Scanton's book (9).

Assessing your diet

Keep a diary for at least 4 days (2 working and 2 off duty days) of exactly what you eat and drink and also of your feelings throughout each day, keeping to your usual eating habits. At the end of 4 or more days, look back through the diary and notice any patterns or links between the way you felt and what you ate.

Carol, a health visitor in her late forties, had been struggling with her weight most of her life. She felt her diary did not show her anything she did not already know about her eating patterns, but it did highlight them and help her to consider them a little more objectively.

These patterns were:

	Full of aches early in the morning, sluggish.
1. Same breakfast each morning: muesli, milk.	Feeling satisfied, alert and energetic in the mornings, more sluggish and aching in the afternoons.
2. Similar low calorie lunch each day: cheese and apple/celery/tomato.	Hungry before lunch but no time to notice it when at work. Fairly satisfied by lunch.
3. Starch-free evening meal: meat or fish or cheese-based recipe, green vegetables, fruit.	Ravenous and very irritable by supper so usually eat snacks before supper, supper satisfying for a while. Rather lethargic in evenings.
4. Snacks in late afternoon and late evening on work days, any time at weekend: chocolate, biscuits, peanuts.	Stops hunger, feel guilty.

5. Large three course high calorie, high fat meals when entertaining or going out (once a week at least).

Enjoy these meals a lot, don't really feel guilty at the time. Feel very happy and satisfied afterwards, pretty groggy the next day.

6. Two or three alcoholic drinks, three or four evenings a week.

Companionable, drink with husband or friends. Always lose will-power though and pick at peanuts and snacks. Don't care at the time, do afterwards.

7. Coffee or tea with each meal and extras in between.

Enjoy a cup, often companionable, refreshed.

Looking at the diary, she had no inspiration about ways to deal with the problem since she felt she had tried everything (e.g. eating more slowly, persuading husband to agree to having no fattening things in the home, cuisine minceur when entertaining, low calorie meal replacements, Weight Watchers etc.) but had slid back each time. She still felt quite discouraged. However, the next exercise helped a little more.

Dealing with dietary problems

If you are interested in improving your diet you could apply the problem-solving spiral from Chapter 7.

1. Write the question 'What's stopping me from eating the ideal diet?' At the top of a sheet of paper and in 3 minutes list as quickly as you can as many factors which might possibly have any influence on you. Then look at the examples in Table 8.4 and add any to your list which also apply to you. Underline the 2 or 3 factors which you think have most influence.
2. Next, write the question 'What would I be aiming for if I tried to sort out my diet?' on the top of a sheet of paper and quickly list anything that might possibly be your aim. Add any from Table 8.5 which might also apply to you. Select 2 or 3 aims as your main priorities.
3. Bearing in mind your goals, brainstorm a list of possible ways of minimising the 2 or 3 main contributing factors.

Table 8.4   *Possible factors contributing towards dietary problems.*

Don't really know enough about the 'right' diet to eat.
No time to shop, cook the right foods.
Poor food in staff dining room.
Too worried about other people coping without me so don't have proper meal breaks.
Prefer to work right through and get off early instead of proper meal breaks.
Don't get enough exercise.
Don't like wholefoods, not used to them.
Get very hungry if I cut out forbidden foods, then will-power goes and I eat the wrong things.
Difficult to find a place to buy wholefoods.
Was a fat baby, so now may have too many fat cells.
Problems run in the family.
Eat the leftovers, can't bear to see waste.
Eat too quickly.
Desire to be fat/thin so that I won't have to face anxieties about my sexuality which I'd have to do if I was more attractive.
Desire to be fat/thin to rebel against stereotypes.
Certain foods (the wrong ones) associated with comfort so eat more of them under stress.
Eating the wrong things feels as though I am being nice to myself, e.g. 'why should I deprive myself, I deserve it'.
Addicted to certain foods, can't resist them nor stop once I've started, they give me a 'lift' when I eat them.
Can't bear to feel hungry, especially under stress.

Table 8.5   *Possible reasons for improving diet.*

More energy.
Lose weight (exactly how much?).
Gain weight (exactly how much?).
Feel better about my body shape.
Prevent illness.
Improve complexion.
Less constipated.
Feeling of self-respect.
Think better, more alert.
Be able to wear nicer clothes.
Be able to take more exercise without feeling so tired/embarrassed.

4. Choose one of the solutions and make a step-by-step plan, pin-pointing the first small step very clearly. Review your progress and adapt your plan if necessary.

Carol's three main contributing factors are:

1. Get discouraged when nothing works permanently.
2. Less exercise since moved jobs to this rural patch — have to go round by car whereas I used to be able to walk in built-up area I worked in before.
3. Sweet things, particularly chocolate, hard to resist — can't stop when I've started.

When perusing the list shown in Table 8.4, she reacted quite strongly to the two 'desire to fat/thin' examples. The reaction was along the lines of: 'How ridiculous, who the hell wants to carry around two extra stones of fat like this?' This reaction proved to be significant to her later.

Her main goals are:

1. Lose weight (two stones).
2. Gain feeling of self-respect.
3. Prevent illness — heart disease and diabetes are in the family, I'm lucky not to have got them already.

Her plan:

1. To get more exercise. First step, do an activity assessment, then work out how to get more exercise in daily life, enlist husband's support.
2. To find out more about chronic food allergies and if possible test myself. First step: get books out of Health Visitor Association library. Then work out a test and take it from there.

Two months later, Carol had increased the amount of exercise she took by buying a medium-sized dog who reminded her in no uncertain terms when his walk was due. She and her husband had also started exploring the local countryside by walks on Sundays. She had discovered that she had mild allergies to wheat, cheese and sugar. At the end of the five days 'Stone Age' diet (see the next exercise), she felt very well and was amazed to discover that her aches and lethargy had cleared up. On further testing, she found that wheat and sugar were responsible for her lethargy and bladder irritation, coffee for her irritability and cheese for the joint aches. Possibly because she had another reason for sorting out her diet, she found it less of an effort of will to do so. After six months of keeping off the offending foods (with only the occasional lapse after which the symptoms returned with a vengeance) and eating more starch in the form of potatoes, brown rice and rye bread, she had lost a stone; she lost a further half stone in the following four months without feeling she was denying herself too much. By this time the allergies seemed almost cured, since when she lapsed the symptoms were almost negligible. She reintroduced the avoided foods into her diet again, although this time she ensured that she did not eat them more than about three times a week, and stopped them if any symptoms returned. At this point, however, her weight began to slowly increase again. A conversation with a colleague of hers made her remember the 'considering contributory factors' exercise mentioned earlier. The colleague had been enthusing about a sexuality workshop she had attended and about how helpful it had been in gently helping her to realise and sort out some of her own personal attitudes to sex. Carol remembered her own strong reaction to the 'desire to be fat' factors and wondered if the strength of that reaction indicated they might have hit an important nail on the head, which she was not prepared to face at that time. We leave her now planning to attend a similar workshop to explore the link between her eating habits and attitudes to sex. (See Orbach (7) and Dickson (10).)

One way to find out if you have any chronic food allergies is to put yourself on a 'Stone Age' diet as described in MacKarness (8) and Mandell (9), then to reintroduce the omitted foods one by one to pin-point possible allergies.

For a period of five days, eat a variety of unrefined foods completely omitting any foods which you normally eat often. For instance, if beef is a meat you eat very often, but you seldom eat others, then eat a variety of any other meats during your five days. If chicken eggs were part of your staple diet, eat only duck or goose eggs. If you normally have your daily 'pinta' as the adverts have conditioned us to do, then cut out all cows' milk products and have soya or goats' milk instead. Other staple foods, like wheat and potatoes, must be omitted also if they feature frequently in your usual diet. Try eating brown rice, ricecakes, porridge oats, pure rye bread and oatcakes instead to keep plenty of starch in your diet. If possible, drink only bottled mineral water. You may feel below par for the first few days but if by the time five days are up you are feeling better than before, and some of your chronic stress symptoms and ailments have cleared up, then you definitely have a chronic food allergy (or more than one). Reintroduce each of your common foods one by one at a rate of one a day and notice which of them make your symptoms return. If you then cut the offending foods out of your diet completely for a period of six to nine months, you may well be able to cure yourself of the allergy provided you eat them only occasionally after that period.

Specific health problems

Readjusting exercise and dietary patterns are two out of many possible starting points for dealing with specific stress-related health problems. A nurse who is seeking a solution to her particular problem can become bewildered by the conflicting and often dogmatic approaches of the champions of the many and varied methods. Each person needs to find the most appropriate method for herself so that she can interrupt the 'feeling terrible — not taking care of self — feeling terrible' cycle. Three common examples of stress-related health problems experienced by nurses are given here, along with a range of ways in which they can be tackled.

Low resistance to infection

Nurses are more exposed to infection than the public at large because of the nature of their work. Furthermore, like anybody else, their resistance to infection is reduced by stress. Some nurses have reported that each of the following methods have helped in some way towards improving resistance.

- *Getting enough exercise of the right kind.* This is likely to keep your metabolic rate from becoming sluggish, and thus it stimulates the immune system to work properly.
- *High fibre, low sugar/salt/artificial additives/fat diet, with special attention to adequate vitamin C intake.* While there are conflicting research results on the value of large doses of vitamin C, overall it would seem that a diet rich in vitamin C or with added supplements can increase resistance to infection. Garlic has been claimed to be a useful prophylactic; garlic extracts can be

bought in tablet and capsule form from health food shops and some chemists.

- *Ensuring adequate rest.* Nurses often find that having a heavy cold or influenza every couple of months is the only way they can allow themselves to spend a day or two resting. If this applies to you, perhaps you could plan one day every so often which you set aside for yourself, in which you achieve absolutely nothing except to improve your ability to rest without guilt. Annie, a district enrolled nurse, found that the guilt was the worst problem when she tried this. She called her rest days her GRP (guilt-free rest practice) days: she literally had to practise. Eventually it worked for her.
- *Safe emotional release.* There is some evidence to suggest that emotional repression reduces the effectiveness of the immune system. Nurses who co-counsel regularly report that they feel better and seem to have less infections than before they took up co-counselling.
- *Homeopathic preparations.* Homeopathic tablets for the prevention and treatment of colds and flu are now widely available in health food shops and chemists.

Premenstrual syndrome

This comprises such premenstrual symptoms as fluid retention, sore breasts, nausea, dizziness, depression, tension, irritability, forgetfulness and difficulty in concentrating. These abate with the onset of the menstrual flow.

It has been estimated that about 10% of women suffer severe symptoms of premenstrual syndrome, with about a further 30% suffering moderate symptoms. So it is no surprise that many nurses themselves find this a problem. The following are some options for starting to deal with premenstrual syndrome:

- *Eating a high fibre, low sugar/salt/artificial additives/fat diet, taking particular care to ensure adequate intake of minerals and vitamins,* particularly vitamin B6 (maximum intake 100 mg per day). Cutting out coffee and tea often helps too. The National Association for Pre-Menstrual Syndrome recommends that your diet be high in starch and that you eat little and often to prevent hypoglycaemia (11). This is particularly relevant to nurses, who often skip meal breaks and catch up by eating sugary snacks and a large meal in the evening. As a dietary supplement, evening primrose oil is recommended by the premenstrual syndrome clinic at St Thomas's Hospital, London. Herbal remedies containing motherwort, valerium, pulsetilla, skullcap and gelsemium may also be helpful dietary supplements (12).

- *Exercise.* Keeping a healthy level of fitness is likely to help towards preventing or rectifying the endocrine imbalances which lead to premenstrual syndrome.
- *Ensuring adequate rest.* Exhaustion is bound to exacerbate any physiological imbalance, so ensure that you have total rest days to give yourself the chance to recuperate from busy periods of your life. Some women find that PMS develops or gets worse as they get older. This might be related to not allowing for the slowing down of your ability to recover by giving yourself longer breaks. If you find it hard to give yourself breaks or make the most of rest periods, try practising some of the relaxation and meditation exercises in Chapters 3 and 4.
- *Taking the emotional aspects into account.* Often the emotional outbursts of women with premenstrual syndrome are dismissed as being totally out of touch with reality and just part of the syndrome. In severe cases, this may be true, but there is a danger of ignoring valid emotional signs which are usually repressed but which surface premenstrually. These emotional events, if taken seriously to some extent, may tell you something about your true needs. Then, when the tension has abated, you could set about working out how these needs could be met. For instance, Elaine reported: 'Usually, at least once before my period, I get really ratty with one or other of the family and slam out of the house, telling them to "leave me alone", and I go off for a walk on my own. We all just put it down to PMT, but then I got to thinking that I don't actually get any time to myself alone anymore and I always used to enjoy my own company. So I talked it over with Richard and things are getting a bit better.'

  Talking to fellow premenstrual syndrome sufferers can help you feel less alone, especially if those around you are unsympathetic. Also, finding safe ways of releasing some of the emotional tension that leads to over-reaction may help you to feel better. Co-counselling may be useful in this respect.
- *Medical treatment.* Nurses with severe symptoms will probably find the above self-help suggestions ludicrous: the nature of the symptoms makes it impossible to make changes in lifestyle when

it is all you can do to keep yourself together. Lack of sympathy from GPs and from other women who are luckier than you does not help. You deserve some treatment which will help your metabolism to regain some balance so you can feel well enough to set about making the changes which will enable you to take care of yourself more. Eventually you may be able to reduce or do without the treatment. Dalton recommends progesterone therapy for severe PMS (12). If your GP is not interested in this approach, you can refer yourself to a premenstrual syndrome clinic (details at the end of the chapter).

Difficulty in giving up smoking

Currently there is concern about nurses who smoke. The percentage is as high as in corresponding groups in the general population who are less informed and have less first-hand experience of seeing the effects of smoking on health. This contrasts to the rapid decline, since the evidence became conclusive that smoking is dangerous, in the percentage of doctors who smoke. Nurses continuing to smoke, despite the damage to their health, is probably symptomatic of the difficulty nurses have in caring for themselves, while being expert at caring for other people.

If you still smoke and find difficulty in giving up, some of the following options might be worth considering.

- *Exercise and diet.* Paying attention to the health of your body by improving the exercise and diet patterns might result in your feeling better and developing more respect for your own health.
- *Teaching others.* Deliberately developing your health education role with patients in this respect may be a way of not only helping them, but helping yourself. Teaching others is one way of getting the message home to yourself. It is not hypocritical as long as you are prepared to admit to being a smoker if asked. You can empathise with a patient's difficulty in giving up when you have that same experience.
- *Keeping a diary.* You could assess how important smoking is to you by keeping a diary for four days. List the time, place and importance of the cigarette: you could use the following scale: 3 = desperate for a smoke, 2 = keen, 1 = just fancied one, 0 = didn't realise you were lighting up. This might raise awareness of your feelings about smoking and the extent of the habit. If you decide to try giving up by cutting down on all but

the 'desperate' category, you might be able to reduce the physiological dependency.

- *Substitutes according to your main smoking type.* The Good Health Guide (1) makes the following suggestions for giving up according to what type of smoker you are:

1. *Pleasure and relaxation.* Try breaking the association in your mind between smoking and pleasure, e.g. by smoking three cigarettes very quickly, and substitute other pleasures, e.g. carry around a good book to read when you might smoke or listen to music instead.
2. *Handling.* If it is mainly a comfort habit, try carrying something else to fiddle with, e.g. a pen to doodle, jewellery.
3. *Tension.* Learn mini-relaxation techniques (see Chapter 3); find physical activities to get rid of frustration; ask GP for a short course of tranquillisers while you give up.
4. *Stimulation.* Buck yourself up with some exercise instead; save the money you would have spent and buy yourself a reward.
5. *Craving.* Work out really powerful rewards; make a contract with someone you love; get help for the craving problems.
6. *Habit.* Change the habit chain, e.g. leave your lighter somewhere else; notice the trigger situations when you light up and change those, e.g. drink something else if you smoke with coffee.

- *Attend a self-help group.* Your local health centre, Citizen's Advice Bureau or ASH (address at end of chapter) may know of a local group.

Pitfalls in changing exercise and diet patterns to prevent or cope with stress

1. There is nothing wrong in becoming a little preoccupied with your physical health while changing these patterns, but beware of becoming obsessional or boring. Although stress may be 'not all in the mind', it is also not all in the body. Remember that the mind and body are inextricably linked: the mind/body split, the either/or approach in Western medicine is unnatural and unhealthy. So pay some attention to the emotional factors as well as the physical, and avoid boring your friends with endless details of your exercise programme or diet unless they really want to hear.
2. Overdoing exercise (such as suddenly taking up vigorous exercise without building up the required fitness level gradually) or

dietary restrictions (self-starvation) can be a form of self-punishment and can be very dangerous to your health and that of those close to you. So look out for signs of excess and if you cannot stop the process yourself, seek some extra help. There is no shame in having some special attention such as counselling for a particular problem. After all, you give out a lot of expert care to other people, so you deserve some for yourself when you are going through a bad patch.

3. At the other end of the scale, lack of commitment, perhaps because of expecting instant results, can lead you to give up trying to change your patterns.

4. Warn friends who are going to entertain you, about your exercise programme or diet. Cooking a special meal or a pleasant weekend can be spoilt if the guest unexpectedly picks through and discards most of the food or disappears at the wrong moment to do her jogging. On the other hand, as a hostess it is a good idea to check these factors beforehand, when inviting someone, to save embarrassment.

References and further reading

1. Open University/Health Education Council/Scottish Health Education Unit (1980). *The Good Health Guide*. Harper & Row.
2. Cooke A. *et al*. (1976). The New Synthesis is an Old Story. *New Scientist*, 70.
3. Lebo F. (1979). *The Every Other Day Exercise Book*. Harmondsworth: Penguin.
4. Carruthers M., Murray A. (1980). *Fitness on Forty Minutes a Week*. London: Futura.
5. Cooper K. (1972). *Aerobics*. London: Bantam.
6. Royal Canadian Air Force (1970). *Physical Fitness*. Harmondsworth: Penguin.
7. Orbach S. (1978). *Fat is a Feminist Issue . . . How to Lose Weight Permanently without Dieting*. Feltham, Middlesex: Hamlyn.
8. MacKarness R. (1976). *Not all in the Mind — How Unsuspected Food Allergy Can Affect Your Body and Your Mind*. London: Pan.
9. Mandell M., Scanton L. W. (1979). *Five-Day Allergy Relief System*. London: Arrow.
10. Dickson A. (1985). *The Mirror Within — A New Look at Sexuality*. London: Quartet.

11. National Association for Premenstrual Syndrome (1983). *Understanding PMS*. Guildford
12. Dalton K. (1984). *Once a Month*. London: Fontana.

Where to learn more about physical health

Local adult education institutes and council sports centres offer courses in various aspects of this topic. Some are Health Education Council-sponsored 'Look After Yourself' courses which cover exercise, diet and relaxation. Local libraries, health education offices and Citizen's Advice Bureaux will give details of some local facilities. Various organisations such as the following run courses or self-help groups nationwide or provide information:

Action on Smoking and Health (ASH), 25–27 Mortimer Street, London W1N 7RJ.
Alcoholics Anonymous, 11 Redcliffe Gardens, London SW10 9BG.
Amateur Swimming Association, Harold Fern House, Derby Square, Loughborough, LE11 OA1.
Anorexic Aid, Gravel House, Copthall Vorner, Chalfont St Peter, Bucks.
British Nutrition Foundation, 15 Belgrave Square, London SW1 8PS.
Health Education Council, 78 New Oxford Street, London WC1 1AH.
Keep Fit Association, 70 Brompton Road, London SW3 1EX.
National Association for Premenstrual Syndrome, 25 Market Street, Guildford GU1 4LB. Helpline: 0483-572806, 10 a.m. to 4 p.m.
Open University, (Health Choices' Course) PO Box 76, Milton Keynes, MK7 6AN.
Ramblers Association, 1–4 Crawford Mews, York Street, London W1H 1PT.
Scottish Health Education Council, 21 Lansdowne Crescent, Edinburgh, EH12 5EH.
Slimming Magazine and Clubs, Burnwood House, 16 Caxton Street, London SW1H 6QH.
Sports Council, 70 Brompton Road, London SW3 1EX.

For exploring the link between body-image and sex-role stereotyping or sexuality, contact the following organisations for details of courses (send s.a.e.):

Redwood, 83 Fordwych Road, London NW2 3TL.
Womens Therapy Centre, 6 Manor Gardens, London N7 6LA.

9

Transforming stress

Growing, not just coping

Given the opportunity for exploring self-awareness in relation to stress, nurses can achieve a change of perspective away from the commonly-held belief that dealing with stress is a matter of responding to whatever life has to throw at you. A more positive approach is to look inside and become aware of your resources, to nurture them and use them to make changes in yourself and in the pressures which come at you. As gardening is not just about keeping the weeds down but about making space for and feeding the flowers and vegetables of your choice, dealing with stress is not just about coping but about making space in your life for your potential abilities to grow and develop.

However, growing and developing involves change, and many nurses are frightened of change. With our rapidly changing society and health service, many nurses seek security, first, by reinforcing the common misconception that the human personality is static and, second, by trying to keep their idiosyncratic ways of doing things consistent whether these ways are effective or not. 'Keeping up appearances' brings a false, tenuous stability. The only true stability comes from looking into yourself and discovering the real centre of the self, the part which is intrinsically you, while being willing to learn and change throughout life. The human being, although strongly influenced by upbringing and cultural conditioning, is not the helpless victim of her background. She can take responsibility for her own personal development and take the opportunities open to her and indeed create more opportunities for learning how to develop self-awareness and expand her methods of dealing with stress in a growthful way. If nurses cannot be self-directing in their own development but sit around waiting for someone else to make them do it, how can they enable patients to develop independence and self-determination?

Altruistic egotism

Nursing in Britain now has an international reputation for being behind the times as far as enabling self-determination in patients is concerned. We have been slow to adopt and apply models of nursing which encourage the patients' abilities for self-care and participation in decision-making about individual care and about the system which provides the care. This is mainly because the climate of our nursing culture has been slow to change to allow us our own self-determination. The emotional barriers between us have prevented us from seeking and giving the support which is necessary to not only cope with but initiate cultural and organisational changes for the better, such as those discussed by Jane Salvage (1) in the first book in this series. So spending time and effort in building our own self-awareness and expanding our abilities to deal with stress are not selfish navel-gazing exercises (2). Through looking after ourselves and each other we will discover more resources for looking after our patients, enabling them to care for themselves and enabling ourselves to work alongside them to contribute towards positive changes in the health care system.

References and further reading

1. Salvage J. (1985). *The Politics of Nursing*. London: Heinemann Medical Books.
2. Selye H. (1974). *Stress Without Distress*. Sevenoaks: Hodder & Stoughton.

Feedback about the book

I would find it very helpful if you could reply to some or all of the following questions and send the replies to me: Meg Bond, Dept. of Educational Studies, University of Surrey, Guildford, Surrey GU27 3QS. You could just number your replies according to the number of the question: there is no need to tear the page out or copy it out in full.

1. To what extent did you find the book useful to you personally? (0 = not at all, 5 = very much) 0 1 2 3 4 5
2. If useful to you personally in what way(s) in particular?
3. To what extent did you find the book useful to you in your work? 0 1 2 3 4 5
4. If useful in your work, in what way(s) in particular?
5. What is your work?
6. Which aspect(s) of the book were least helpful?
7. Can I quote you in further editions of the book? Yes/No.

'No's' will be absolutely respected, I promise. You can sign your letter or leave it blank (obviously I need your name and address if you want a reply). I would like to use your reply to help me gauge the degree to which my aims in writing the book have been achieved, and to make the necessary changes in further editions of the book.

Index

activity
  diary, 196, 197, 199
  levels, 196–9
  patterns of, 33, 200–1
addiction
  alcohol, 10
  drugs, 10, 59
  food, 206–7, 209
adrenalin, 24
advice, 12, 138, 139, 148–51, 170, 174
advocacy, 97–8
advocate
  patient's, 97–8
alcohol, 10, 59, 206, 208
Alexander Technique, 40
allergy, 12, 206–7, 210–11, 212
allowing
  as a step in problem-solving, 181
  emotional expression, 65, 159, 164–6
  others to decide for themselves, 100
  and sharing, 28
  stress to increase, 7
  yourself to fantasise, 84–5
  yourself to let go, 28–30
  yourself to relax, 48
anger, 24, 27, 28, 162
  expression of, 29–30
anxiety, xi, 1, 16, 19, 21, 23, 138, 147, 162
  about criticism, 124
  about joint action, 148
  about making requests, 109
  about performance, 119, 151
  about saying 'no', 114
  about trust, 136
apologising, 116–17, 127
assertiveness, 28, 96–133, 151, 174
  and advocacy, 96–8
  body language in, 100–4
  and compliments, 119–22, 131

and cooperation, 117–19
and criticism, 122–8, 131
and making requests, 109–14, 130, 170
nurses' need for, 96–8
pitfalls in, 128–32
rights, 99–100, 107, 109, 132
saying 'no' using, 105, 114–17, 130, 174
and talking, 104–9
where to learn more about, 133
autonomy, 138
awareness
  as emotional skill, 27
  as self-consciousness, 129
  increasing through noticing, 73
  of emotions, 16
  of helping skills, 159

Berne E., 175, 176, 177
biofeedback, 41, 56–7, 63, 69–70, 90–1
blaming, 107, 108, 130, 149, 176
body
  fight and fear responses, 24
  focussing attention on, 41
  language
    aggressive, 101–2
    assertive, 101–4, 129
    awareness of in intuitive thinking, 179
    in listening, 160–2
    in massage, 51
    in questioning, 167
    in saying 'no', 115
    manipulative, 101, 102
    submissive, 101, 102
    while receiving criticism, 127
  massaging one's own, 47–9
brain
  anatomy of, 183
  functioning, 107
  impulses from, 40

brain – *cont.*
  in listening, 142
  left side of, 86, 178–80
  and reception of stimuli, 88
  and relaxation of face and hands, 43
  right side of, 78, 86, 178–80
  waves, 69–70, 88
breathing
  exercises, 11
  hyperventilation in, 63, 91
  in assertiveness, 103
  in massage, 53
  in meditation, 73, 75–6, 77, 78, 79, 80,
    81, 82, 87, 91
  in relaxation, 36, 38, 39, 43, 44, 45, 61,
    62
  in yoga, 54, 55, 56
  shallow while stressed, 5
Buddhism, 69
busy syndrome, 33, 34, 40, 67, 89

caffeinated drinks, 12, 59, 206, 213
cancer, 24
catharsis
  allowing, 165, 166
  as emotional expression, 12
  as emotional skill, 28–31
  following relaxation, 65
  through co-counselling, 173
change
  avoidance of, 24
  making, 30
    political, 91
    potential for, 31
  of habit chain in smoking, 216
  rapid social, 10
  through assertiveness, 129
Chaitow L., 72, 94
CHAT Service, 177
children, 27, 68, 135
choice
  acting from, 31
  as trust-building ground rule, x, 4, 138
  between control and spontaneity, 27–30
  needs, 18, 20, 21, 30
Christianity, 69
Christians, 87
co-counselling, x, 12, 65, 165, 172–3, 177,
  213, 214
communication, 6, 27, 31, 33, 34
  non-verbal, 101–4
  touch as, 48
compliments, 119–22, 131, 175
concentration, 36
  impaired by emotional repression, 24
  impaired by premenstrual syndrome,
    213
  improved through meditation, 77, 79,
    89, 90
  improved through relaxation, 42
  in support groups, 172
  interrupted, 67

confidence, 20
  impact of stress on, 98–100
  improved, 42
  undermining others', 64
confidentiality, 136, 137, 158
  as trust-building ground rule, 138
conversation, 139–44, 159, 160, 170, 174,
  175
coping mechanisms
  imbalance in, 12
  repertoire of, 10, 31, 32
counselling, 33, 65, 89, 158, 159, 162, 165,
  177, 217
creativity, 69
  as emotional expression, 12
  releasing, 78, 85–6
criticism, 23, 164, 175–6
  dealing with, 124–8, 131
    asking for, 128, 131
    listening to, 125–8, 131
    protecting yourself from, 125–8
  destructive, 136
  excessive self-, 64, 75
  giving constructive, 122–4, 131, 151
  language of, 108
  supporting colleagues under, 145–6
  toning down self-, 49, 75
culture
  British, 22, 57, 94, 129
  nursing, 14, 22, 27, 68, 134, 194, 220
  shame, 134
  Stone Age, 201
  uncaring, 160
  Western, 68, 194

decision-making
  impaired by emotional repression, 24
  improved by catharsis, 30
  in assertiveness, 129, 130
  professional, 96–7
  strategies, 172
defence mechanisms, 22–5, 30, 135
denial
  of own emotions, 23
depression, 21, 22, 97, 114, 213
development
  personal, vii, ix, 24, 27, 31, 219–20
  professional, ix, 153
Dickson A., 99, 125, 128, 132, 133, 211,
  217
diet, 205–13
  assessing your, 207–8
  chemicals in, 205–6
  dealing with problems of, 208–12
  diary, 207–8
  excessively restrictive, 216–17
  healthy, 12, 205–7, 212–13
  Stone Age, 210, 211–12
  where to learn more about, 218
disassociation, 23
doctors, 145
  conflict with nurses, 97